Achtung
Spitfire

Fw. Heinrich Rodder at 7,000m

Achtung Spitfire

LUFTWAFFE OVER ENGLAND
EAGLE DAY 14 AUGUST 1940

HUGH TRIVETT

The History Press

Junkers Ju 88A of LG 1, 1940

First published 2010

The History Press
The Mill, Brimscombe Port
Stroud, Gloucestershire, GL5 2QG
www.thehistorypress.co.uk

British Library Cataloguing in Publication Data.
A catalogue record for this book is available from the British Library.

ISBN 978 0 7524 5720 8

Typesetting and origination by The History Press
Printed in Great Britain
Manufacturing managed by Jellyfish Print Solutions Ltd

Contents

Acknowledgements

Since I started writing this over twenty years ago, most of the combatants and many of those involved in the events, whose accounts form the backbone of the text, and even some of my fellow researchers, have unfortunately passed on but I will always be grateful for all their help and advice.

I am particularly indebted to the many RAF ground crews who endured the attacks on the airfields and who took the trouble to write accounts, often in great detail, of those traumatic events, but as they are all named in the relevant chapters I have not listed them here individually. For a similar reason the civilian eyewitnesses are also not listed. However, special mention must be made of the service provided by the Record Copying Department of the National Archives. They often sent detailed answers to my frequent enquiries that I was unable to resolve during my visits to Kew.

Information on the air battles of the summer of 1940 has been exchanged with many similarly interested individuals over the years, but especial thanks are extended to those listed below without whom this book would not have seen the light of day:

Perry Adams, Peter Ayerst, Jim Beedle, Mike Bent, Michael Boddington, Karl Brossler, Annette Collard, Peter Cornwell, Fritz Dietrich, Dieter Dorner, Mary Douglas-Osborn, Heinz Ebeling, Peter Foote, Adolf Galland, Erna Gerke, Walter Gietz, Heinrich Gramling, Clifford Gray, Ralph Havercroft, Anthony Hillman, Otto Hintze, Philippa Hodgkiss, Ian Hutton, Peter Johnson, Gerhard Kemen, Heinz Kochy, Christine Koschemann, Stephen Kramer, Wilhelmine Krause, Kurt Kupsch, Hedwig Liebchen, Walter Meyer, Jacob Neff, Phyllis Orr, John Penny, Erna Puttfarken, Hans Ramstetter, Erhard Reif, Heinrich Rodder, Irmengard Sauer, Ewald Schank, Walter Schaum, Gerhard Schopfel, Kurt Sodemann, Werner Stahl, Geoff Stephens, Ivor Sydenham, Margarete Thiel, Stanford Tuck, Hans Tuffers, Gustav Ullman, John Vasco, Artur Wiesemann, Dave Williams and Allan R. Wright.

To those whom I have inadvertently overlooked I apologise. Also, the original source of some of the featured photographs has been forgotten or mislaid over the years, and again to anyone whom I have not given a credit I apologise. I hope that I'm forgiven.

To avoid any possible confusion, all times in the book have been adjusted to British Summer Time (which ran one hour behind German *Sommerzeit*, in use by the Luftwaffe). Thus, 7.00 hrs shown in official German documents becomes 6.00 hrs in the text, and this expediency has been used throughout.

Hugh Trivett

Introduction

Flying over the rubble-strewn streets of Dunkirk early in the morning of 5 June 1940, Erhard Milch, the chubby Inspector General of the Luftwaffe, observed from the cockpit of his personal aircraft the absolute chaos left by a beaten army in full flight. Over 50,000 abandoned vehicles, trucks, lorries, cars and many heavy guns choked the roads and fields leading to the sea, and hulks of half-submerged British ships could be seen offshore. He couldn't wait to land and inspect the devastation at first hand.

The beaches and sand dunes were littered with the spoils of war – bicycles, shoes, ammunition boxes, weapons, canned food, personal effects and souvenirs – all abandoned by the departing Allies in their mad scramble to board the armada bound for England. Fleeing as fast as they could from the constant bombing and strafing, they didn't really appreciate that, ironically, it was the actions of the Luftwaffe that had enabled them to escape.

Goering had convinced Hitler (despite furious army opposition) that his air fleet alone could carry out the destruction of the British forces in the Dunkirk pocket, and this meant that the advance of the German army was halted for a crucial few days so enabling the Allies to regroup and erect a strong defensive perimeter. But fog blanketed the bomber bases for those three vital days and, when the beaches were finally attacked, the bombs buried deep into the sand inflicting few casualties. Furthermore, the mass of small boats presented poor targets and, with the French fighting a valiant rearguard action, the British army managed to slip away.

Equally significant was the protective 'umbrella' put over the beach by the RAF. The waves of Luftwaffe bombers and fighters were broken up outside the perimeter before they could attack the vast concentration of exhausted men huddled in the sand. Brian Kingcombe of 92 Squadron, then flying daily cover over Dunkirk, commentated, 'the bombers were easy meat; a short burst from behind – the rear gun would tilt up, meaning the gunner was dead; later the rest were dead'. However, this tremendous effort was not without cost. In forty days the RAF had lost over 1,000 planes, of which 509 were fighters, losses they could ill afford for the coming defence of Britain.

As Milch picked his way through all the discarded clutter, accompanied by General Hoffman von Waldau of the Luftwaffe General Staff, the desolation on the beaches was an awesome sight but the dearth of dead bodies worried him. Except for the rearguard that had surrendered to the encircling German army, it appeared that the bulk of the British troops and many French soldiers had got clean way. The Luftwaffe had not wiped out the men trapped in the Dunkirk pocket. He did not share his companion's view that a pile of empty bottles sticking out of the sand represented the gravestones of the British army. They were not beaten yet.

That evening he attended a meeting of the Luftwaffe High Command aboard Goering's armoured train *Asia* and found the Field Marshal congratulating everyone for the annihilation of the British army on the beaches of Dunkirk. But Milch, ever the realist, said that he had only seen a handful of dead soldiers amongst the sand dunes and that the British had returned to England virtually intact.

Taken aback by his view that the war was not yet over, Goering asked Milch what he thought should be the next move. He was forthright in his reply: all available Luftwaffe forces should be moved up to the Channel coast for the immediate invasion of Britain. Paratroopers would have to capture a few vital airfields to enable the Luftwaffe to fly in fighter and Stuka squadrons, and to land the several hundred Ju 52 transport planes that would fly over two or three divisions. It would be a great gamble without the back up of heavy guns and tanks, but he was convinced that for the next few days the British would be incapable of beating off a determined landing.

'I warn you Herr Field Marshal that if you give the English three or four weeks to recoup, it will be too late.' He warned that to leave them in peace for any longer could be a fatal mistake and that the invasion must begin without any delay, but Goering was not convinced. It would be a huge and extremely risky undertaking, and his initial reaction was that it could not be done but, as the talks continued, he slowly began to come around to Milch's point of view. He liked the idea, in that it would be an operation run solely by the Luftwaffe, and over the next few hours the plans for the invasion started to come together.

The next day he presented Hitler with their plans for the invasion and subjugation of Britain. Goering appreciated that the battle would be costly and bloody but, if they proceeded with the utmost speed, they could finally defeat the enemy. Hitler appreciated the initiative of the bold plan put before him but he was against putting it into operation. 'Do nothing!' he told Goering. Britain was on its knees and it would soon come to accept the hopelessness of its position and ask for peace.

Milch, however, did not believe that the British would make peace and was convinced even now that they would be preparing for battle. The only way to force them to sue for peace would be to land on their soil, blockade their ports and destroy what remained of their air force. But this was not to be and, despite his warning, the British actually got not four but almost nine weeks to rebuild their forces before the Luftwaffe launched their first major assaults on RAF airfields. On Eagle Day, 14 August 1940, the attacks began in earnest.

As Milch stood in the Chancellery on that August afternoon waiting to accept the bejewelled baton from Hitler, in recognition of his elevation to field marshall, did his thoughts wander back to that lost opportunity to invade England after the fall of Dunkirk? If so he kept them to himself as Hitler outlined his future intentions. Hitler wanted peace not the destruction of Britain, but the air war was to continue with the destruction of the RAF as a prelude to any invasion.

CHAPTER ONE

Night Operations 13-14 August 1940

As the Whitleys of 4 Group streamed back from attacking the Fiat factory in Turin and the Caproni works in Milan, the Heinkels He 111H of pathfinder group KGr 100 were returning from their first mission over England where they had bombed the Dunlop works east of Birmingham and the Spitfire factory at Castle Bromwich.

The RAF claimed to have inflicted serious damage on to the Italian factories, where fire and explosions were observed, with hits on railway lines, bridges and a marshalling yard. But with only four bombs apiece the destruction caused by the thirty-two Whitley bombers was hardly significant and the only tangible result of this, and subsequent raids, was to annoy Mussolini to such an extent that a detachment of the Italian Air Force was deployed against Britain towards the end of 1940.

This first RAF attack against the industrial heartland of Italy involved a 1,500-mile flight over the Alps, and it was a great morale booster for the moribund Bomber Command. In addition, the casualties were remarkably light because the Italian defences were so poor. In fact only one plane was hit by enemy fire, but the Whitley was such a robust plane that even on just one good engine it still managed to fly back over the Alps. As it crossed the English Channel and came within sight of the shore, the pilot attempted to land the crippled plane on the beach at Lympe, but the badly buckled aileron finally broke off and Whitley P4965 plunged into the sea taking Pilot Officer Ernest 'Pip' Parsons and Sgt Alfred Campion to their deaths. Their bodies were later washed up on the French coast and they are buried at Boulogne's Eastern Cemetery in the Pas-de-Calais.

The other three crew members managed to extradite themselves from the plane as it sank below the waves, and Sgts Chamberlain and Sharpe were lucky to be rescued by a passing fishing boat. Even luckier was Sgt Marshall who was saved by Peggy Prince who paddled out in her frail canoe when she saw the Whitley hit the water. For this brave action she was awarded the British Empire Medal.

But what of the twenty-one Heinkels He 111H of KGr 100, which had set off from Vannes on their first mission to England? Nine were scheduled to attack the Spitfire factory but only five managed to find the target, and the bomb spread was so wide that fighter production was not seriously disrupted. A 'Purple' warning had been received at 22.54 hours and, ten minutes later, five bombers were reported coming in from the south and the searchlights and AA guns went into action as the bombs started to fall. In this first attack nineteen bombs fell on the 60-acre site, with some landing in the fields and on the roads, while a few hit the factory blocks wrecking the buildings and damaging the machinery. The bombs continued to rain down but little further damage was done though eight workers were killed, forty-one were seriously wounded and over 100 suffered minor injuries.

At the Dunlop factory there was even less damage or disruption to output as the bombers again failed to pinpoint their target. A stray bomb did land on the Bromford Tube factory in Birmingham that was producing seamless steel tubes for the War Office, but the plant was not damaged. Though a number of windows were smashed production was not halted. For this elite pathfinder unit this was an inauspicious beginning, and accurate bombing through cloud proved to be a continuing problem.

Approaching the Midlands, powerful beams of light had shot up into the air as the searchlights tried unsuccessfully to cone in on the black-coated planes. A trail of lights and flashes seemed to be tracking their flight path across the night sky. The flak was heavy and though the AA shells were initially bursting away in the distance, they soon closed in on their targets.

Some of the planes were rocked by the nearness of the explosions but they were not knocked off track and they completed their bombing runs without any problems. The He 111s of the 2nd Staffel came in last and, as the flashes of flak faded in the distance and with no sign of any threatening night fighters, they switched to auto-pilot and laid back hoping for an uninterrupted journey home.

They all managed to land safely back at Vannes, returning on a line via Birmingham–Carmarthen–Brest, even though some crews experienced in-flight problems with the auto-pilot and the master compass and, in one unfortunate incident, a signal pistol was fired inside the plane causing burns and blisters to two of the airmen. There were no further reports of any injuries or fatalities but Uffz. Fritz Dorner did not return from the raid. And his aircraft did not reach the target area.

As the He 111H (6N+HK) flown by Feldwebel Kaufmann made its directional turn towards Swindon, before heading north to the Midlands, there was an almighty thunderclap as a shell exploded alongside sending a shock wave shooting along the whole length of the plane, shaking it from end to end. A shower of sparks from the electrics started a fire in the fuselage that the flight mechanic fought frantically to extinguish. The aircraft then started to roll alarmingly from side to side and, out of control, it slid into a shallow dive. Kaufmann fought desperately to right the plane but there was no response from the controls, and he gave the order for the crew to abandon their crippled machine.

Uffz. Freidrich 'Fritz' Dorner

The pilot sat in an all-in-one parachute suit but, because of their in-flight duties, such an outfit was impracticable for the rest of the crew. Instead, over their flying suits they wore a harness into which the parachute had to be manhandled into place. The wireless operator Fritz Dorner was the first to clip on his parachute and, with a quick farewell, he baled out into the darkness.

Yet, as the remainder of the crew struggled with their parachute harnesses the plane remarkably righted itself and, as it levelled off, Kaufmann, with the aid of the flight mechanic, regained control of the shattered machine and, after a quick check, was satisfied it was still flyable. But to continue with the mission, with the plane in such a perilous state, would be foolhardy and he gently pointed the bomber back towards the Channel and home, even though without the radio operator it would be a hazardous return journey. As he nursed the battered bomber back to base he pondered on how he was going to explain the absence of one of his crew to his commanding officer.

As he floated down, Fritz peered into the gloom hoping to catch a glimpse of the white parachutes of the rest of the crew but, no matter how hard he looked, there was no sign of them. So intent was he in scanning the night sky that he didn't realise how fast the ground was rushing up towards him and, by not bracing himself, he landed heavily, badly injuring his left leg. He came down in a grass field near some farm buildings on the outskirts of the small town of Balcombe, but despite the debilitating injury he managed to haul himself towards a farmhouse that he could see in the distance. Knocking on the door he fell into the hall as it opened and, looking up at the startled the farmer, he uttered the words he had rehearsed, 'I have come from the air, can you help me?' The farmer helped him into the house and made him comfortable. The police were soon on the scene and, when the military arrived, he was taken to a nearby hospital. Briefly

'Fritz' Dorner (second left, front row) with fellow POWs at Camp Angler. (Photograph: Friedrich Dorner)

he was interrogated at Cockfosters but they didn't discover that he was a trained instructor in the X-Verfahren blind-bombing system and he was soon packed off to a POW camp. By the summer of 1941 he was languishing in Camp Angler in Canada where he sat out the rest of the war.

Fritz had joined the Luftwaffe on 1 November 1935 and, after qualifying as a radio operator, he became an instructor before joining KGr 100 in February 1939 where he received intensive training at Wurzburg on the operation of the then secret X-Verfahren system. His flying book shows that these in-flight training sessions were undertaken in a variety of aircraft but mainly in the three-engine Junkers Ju 52 and the excellent, all-metal Focke-Wulf Fw 58. Mysteriously his flying book contains no entries for the three months from September to November 1939, even though he flew combat missions in He 111s during the invasion of Poland. During the attack on Norway, though KGr 100 was heavily engaged, it seems that Fritz stayed out of the action. And during the month of April, once the invasion had started, ten long-distance flights of over 600 miles were undertaken in Ju 52s from their forward base at Konisberg on the shores of the Baltic, which they completed without incident.

During the *Blitzkrieg* in the West, Fritz was off flying duties during which time the unit had moved back to Germany for its Heinkel He 111s to be re-fitted with the X-Verfahren blind-bombing system, which had been taken out of the plane for the Norwegian campaign. In addition to the W/T mast, the Heinkel He 111s with this equipment now carried two extra radio masts mounted on top of the fuselage and the three were easily recognisable. Promoted to unteroffizier in 1940, he would now be flying with the 2nd Staffel as Feldwebel Kaufmann's radio operator from the unit's bases at Kothen and Luneburg, where they would make almost thirty familiarisation flights, concentrating on all aspects of night flying and navigation, before KGr 100 was transferred to France in early August that year in preparation for pathfinder operations over Britain. His stamped logbook shows that he was signed off as an instructor on 10 August. Training was now over. The next flights would be for real.

Their new base was near Vannes, a town of some 30,000 inhabitants on the south-west coast of Brittany, a part of France he had never visited before. With its cafes and restaurants and not too unfriendly locals, it was a reasonable posting and being lodged in a hotel in the centre of the town was something of a bonus, but the airfield facilities were pretty basic. There were no concrete runways and very little maintenance space with only one small hangar and a few wooden buildings, and the planes were therefore kept out in the open where most of the servicing had to be undertaken. Canvas covers were flung over the engines to protect them from the salty sea air but, at best, this was a stop-gap solution because exposing aircraft to the corrosive Atlantic winds was a bad idea.

On 10 August, out of their total operational strength of thirty-nine Heinkel He 111s, only nineteen were serviceable, though this had more to do with the supply of parts than the weather. By 13 August extensive repairs must have been urgently carried out to get the planes up and running because twenty-one were ready for action for the unit's first major attack on Britain that very night.

Taken by coach to the airfield, Fritz and the rest of the crew were in good spirits when they climbed aboard their plane. As they carried out their pre-flight checks they watched in excited silence as the other aircraft fired up their engines ready for take-off. As the exhausts glowed red it was a colourful and powerful

Helmut Meyer's three master Heinkel He 111 of KG 26 shows that it was equipped with the X-Verfahren system. The aircraft was badly damaged prior to the attack on Poland when one of the bombs waiting to be loaded blew up. (Photograph: Helmut Meyer via Geoff Stephens)

ROYAL CANADIAN MOUNTED POLICE

otograph No 88

DESCRIPTION FORM

Angler, Ont. July 15th. 1941.19.

1. Name and Aliases   P/W No. 51138 DORNER, Fritz UFFZ

2. Wanted for

3. Nationality or Race   German

4. Colour   White   5. Age   26 yrs

6. Height   5 ft 8 ½   7. Weight   158 lbs

8. Complexion   Fair   9. Hair, how worn   Brown to right

10. Hair on face   None   11. Eyes   Blue

12. Nose   Long, Straight   13. Mouth   medium, straight

14. Chin   Round   15. Teeth   Good

16. Build   Well built   17. Scars, marks   Blemishe bac
                                        right hand

18. Physical peculiarities   Protruding ears

19. Voice, accent, speech   soft

20. Languages spoken   German, Little English

21. Dress   Air force

22. Appearance, carriage   erect

23. Gait   24. Manner

25. Education   26. Occupation   Soldier

27. Criminal occupation and record

28. Habits

29. Photograph, if obtainable, date taken   July 15th. 1941

30. Remarks

31. Warrant issued

32. If located and :

If description telegr

Royal Canadian Mountain Police
POW record sheet

sight as the seven *Ketten* (chain) of three aircraft lined up and took off in staggered intervals, with their aircraft one of the last to take-off.

For Fritz this would be his first and last *feindflug* or battle flight over Britain, and his plane would be the only one that failed to reach its destination and scatter its bombs over the intended targets. Fritz had no way of knowing, but with their mission abandoned the bombs were probably jettisoned over the Channel – it would have been folly to make a forced landing with a full bomb load. As he fell badly he was just grateful to be alive and, as he shook himself down and limped towards the farmhouse, he started to feel a bit more hopeful and the initial feeling of gloom disappeared with every step. He thought he would not be incarcerated in a POW camp for too long as Britain must soon come to its senses and either surrender or sue for peace. Either way his time as a POW would be short.

The Red Cross would notify his family that he was alive and well and, with luck, he could be home by Christmas though there might be some delay as the 'Tommies' were known to be stubborn. Little did he know that he was going to spend the next seven years behind wire, mostly in the snowy wastes of Canada.

He finally made it back home to Thalmassig in 1947, and died in the nearby town of Greding on 9 October 2002, leaving behind a son Friedrich, also known as Fritz, to carry on the family name.

CHAPTER TWO

Messerschmitts over Manston

Early on the morning of 14 August 1940, Hauptmann Walter Rubensdorffer, Commander of Erprobungsgruppe 210, dispatched all serviceable aircraft from their home airfield at Denain to Calais-Mark, the forward base from which all their operations against England were now being launched. The only mission listed for that day was a lightning, low-level attack against Ramsgate and Manston aerodromes.

The 2nd and 3rd Staffels, equipped with Messerschmitt Me 110 *Zerstorers*, set off first for the short 25-minute flight at about 7.00 hours with the Me 109s of 1st Staffel – under the command of Oberleutnant Otto Hintze – taking-off slightly later, landing at Calais-Mark at 07.45 hours. The planes were then refuelled and made ready for action but, for some reason, Hintze's pilots would not be thrown into the fray and remained inactive all day before flying back to Denain at 18.20 hours.

An experimental unit, Erprobungsgruppe 210 had only been formed some six weeks earlier, primarily to evaluate the dive-bombing capabilities of the Luftwaffe's front-line fighters, the Me 109 and the Me 110. But such was the calibre of the crews and the enthusiasm generated by their energetic Swiss-born leader that it quickly became operational. By the middle of July it was already attacking shipping in the Thames Estuary and engaging with the RAF.

During the following weeks they continued to harry convoys in the Channel, sink ships in Dover harbour, and dive-bomb and badly damage the escorting naval destroyers. They certainly played their part in reducing the traffic in the Channel to a trickle but, despite this success, by the middle of August – except for an aborted attack on the Boulton Paul factory in Norwich – they had still not been given a target on the English mainland.

Then, on 12 August, they received orders to destroy four radar stations on the south coast and precision attacks were carried out against Dover, Rye, Pevensey and Dunkirk, but despite accurate dive-bombing they did not succeed in putting any of them permanently out of action. Although three of the targets initially went off air, by early afternoon they were all back in operation, albeit with

Rubensdorffer in a jovial mood with the airmen of Erpro Gr 210. (Photograph: Otto Hintze)

Officers of Erpro Gr 210. Obltn. Otto Hintze third from right. (Photograph: Otto Hintze)

Dornier Do 17s of KG 2 heading across the Channel. (Photograph: C. Goss)

reduced capacity. Perhaps the attacks should have been pressed home and the radar stations completely destroyed, but this was no longer the concern of Erpro Gr 210 as they had other orders. By midday they had landed back at Calais and rearmed, refuelled, and were ready to make up for this unsatisfactory perform-ance by launching a devastating assault on RAF Manston with fourteen Me 110s of 1st & 2nd Staffels.

Almost by accident they had joined up with some eighteen Dornier Do 17s of KG 2 and the ensuing double bombardment appeared to have reduced the airfield to rubble. The Dornier's intended target was an inland airfield near Canterbury but, as Manston came into view, it seems that Oberst Johannes Fink, in the lead aircraft, couldn't resist the opportunity to test his finely honed bomb-aiming skills. Having spent many a long hour glued over the new bombsight in simulator practice, Manston presented a quick and easy target and he swung the formation to starboard.

Flying in over Pegwell Bay, the Dorniers bombed in a dense pattern while almost simultaneously the *Zerstorers* had come in fast unleashing their 500kg bombs with almost pinpoint accuracy. They caught the RAF on the hop and were back across the Channel almost before the RAF fighters were airborne.

In less than five minutes 150 high-explosive bombs had been dropped right on target and, seeing the huge pall of black smoke spiralling skywards, the Germans reported that Manston had been completely destroyed. The war reporter Kurt Rasche, flying with KG 2, was stunned by the view from the air, and hurriedly took some photographs of the devastation and subsequently filed a comprehensive report that he was sure would be featured in one of the Luftwaffe war magazines.

And now the Heinkels of III/KG 55, under the command of Major Hans Schemmel, also made an appearance over Manston and, unhindered by fighters, leisurely dropped their bombs onto the airfield below. Three of their planes had strayed off course and bombed Ramsgate by mistake and some of the bombs had drifted off target, cratering the surrounding countryside and blocking the approach roads, but most fell on Manston adding to the already chaotic condi-tions on the ground.

But their presence had not gone unnoticed and out of the sun a swarm of Hurricanes came at them, all guns blazing. Lt Hans Tuffers saw them too late to take evasive action and his Heinkel shuddered as a stream of bullets blew the cowling off his left engine and set it on fire. Pouring smoke and oil, the engine coughed, spluttered and died. The plane rapidly lost height and speed and, Tuffers and his flight mechanic worked desperately to adjust the trim to keep it flying but it continued to sink lower and lower. When, over the in flight radio, he heard someone shout out, 'Let him go', he thought all was lost.

Their strenuous efforts to stabilise the machine were having very little effect when, miraculously, the Heinkel steadied itself and levelled out. There was now some response from the controls but, as Tuffers coaxed the crippled machine south, he spotted a Hurricane coming around for a second attack.

Kurt Rasche – in flying helmet – with a Dornier Do.17Z of I/KG 2. (Photograph: K. Rasche)

Suddenly a Me 110 appeared overhead and pointed out a clear exit path away from the menacing Hurricanes. It stayed with them flying in a defensive circle around their damaged plane until they were safely out over the Channel. Then, with a wave of the hand, the pilot wished them goodbye and sped away.

They now had every chance to make it home and, by shutting down the fuel to the wrecked motor, the fire was brought under control and eventually extinguished. Flying on the one good engine they limped back across the Channel to their base at Villacoublay but their ordeal was far from over. Approaching the airfield, Tuffers lowered the landing gear, only to be confronted with a big wheel-disk bearing the letter 'R' that showed that his right wheel was missing. Ignoring the warning to retract the undercarriage and make a crash-landing he continued with his approach and yelled to his crew to take up crash positions.

He was coming in a bit on the fast side but that extra bit of speed enabled him to keep the right wing up, and the plane touched down perfectly on the left front and rear wheels. A great piece of flying but as the plane ran on and slowed, the right wing dropped and the damaged landing gear ploughed into the ground gouging out a deep furrow. Tuffers tried to keep it in a straight line but it slewed around sixty degrees before coming sharply to a halt. Tuffers had a small gash above the right eye but his observer was badly wounded, though he made a full recovery.

It was a lucky escape but Tuffers had an even luckier escape on 15 September 1940 when his Heinkel 111P was shot down into the Channel. Attacked by seven Spitfires during a reconnaissance sortie to photograph the damage inflicted by

KG 55 on Portland harbour, both engines were shot away and the plane glided down from 4,000m to splash into the sea. Most of the crew were wounded and died in the sinking plane but Tuffers and his observer Uffz. Heinz Rothen were rescued after floating in the cold sea for over 2 hours. Wounded in the arm, Tuffers was operated on at Cherbourg-Marine Hospital but was back in action within ten days to take part in the missions flown by the group against London, Liverpool and Bristol.

Then, as the last days of the Battle of Britain were being fought, he was shot down, for the third and last time, on 15 November, during a night attack on the Victoria docks in London. Hit by AA fire at high altitude the plane fell like a stone and he ordered the crew to bale out. Tuffers escaped through the top hatch but his head smashed against the radio antenna and he lost conscious. He woke at daybreak in the middle of a freshly cut cornfield to the sound of aircraft engines overhead, having no recollection of drifting through the air in the darkness or of hitting the ground.

Crawling along the ground on all fours he reached a small farm cottage where a 'nice old couple' helped him into the house and served him tea. His whole body hurt and he had a thumping headache but as he sat there it slowly dawned on him that they had no idea he was an enemy airman, even though the owner was in the Home Guard. His all-in-one canvas flying suit hid his Luftwaffe insignia and, to save his hosts any further embarrassment, he dropped a couple of hints as to his identity, finally in frustration blurting out 'I am a German pilot shot down over London last night.' They didn't seem to believe him so to press home the point he said, 'I think you should call the police.' At this the wife, without saying a word, left the room to return later with a police-

Lt Hans-Adalbert Tuffers at the controls of Heinkel 111P (G1+AT) with Obfw. Martin Reiser

Dornier Do 17 of KG 2 unloading a bomb over an RAF airfield. (Photograph: C. Goss)

man who called an ambulance to take him to Hornchurch Hospital. There he was treated for injuries to his head, legs and spine. Making a full recovery after further treatment at Woolwich Hospital he spent the next six and a half years in captivity, most of it in a POW camp in Canada. A holder of the Iron Cross 1st and 2nd Class, he had also been awarded the Deutsche Cross in Gold. After the war he was in government service and died aged seventy in Koblenz, all thanks to his guardian angel.

As the Me 110s of Erpro Gr 210 sped away from Manston the elated crews could hardly imagine that they would have to make a follow-up attack in two days' time to try and finish the job. From the air the station appeared to be an utter ruin with hangars and buildings ablaze, aircraft destroyed, and the ground chewed up and badly cratered. They had seen their bombs explode amongst a group of fighters and were sure they had taken out a squadron of Spitfires before they could take-off. All but one of the Spitfires made it into the air and climbed out of harm's way, though too late to engage the enemy.

As Manston only had grass runways it was proving difficult to put out of commission and, with the holes quickly filled in, it was soon made operational. To put the station out of action, once and for all, the hangars and buildings would have to be reduced to rubble and a return visit was inevitable. The date was fixed for 14 August.

Having emerged almost unscathed from the midday raid on Manston two days before, the entire 2nd Gruppe of KG 2 would in the late afternoon again set out, but this time their target was the RAF Station at Lympne, some 3 miles inland from Hythe, which had already been attacked earlier that morning at around 08.15 hours by the Do 17s of the 1st & 2nd Staffels of KG 2 when considerable damage was done to the airfield and buildings. Over 140 bombs had been released over the target, badly damaging three hangars, hitting the Pay Office and destroying some of the accommodation blocks. The place was a complete mess and a clean up was hurriedly organised because the airfield was scheduled to be inspected later in the day by Air Chief Marshall Sir Edgar Ludlow-Hewitt.

As they homed in on their target, Fink was in the lead aircraft and kept the Dorniers in a tight formation, but he wasn't satisfied with the first untidy bombing run and the formation was taken in a big loop around the coast. As the bombers started to turn they came under determined, if sporadic, attacks by Spitfires that were faced with an amazing sight as a barrage of wire, grenades and even toilet paper was thrown in their direction. Stunned by these actions, the fighters immediately broke away only to be caught in the accurate crossfire from the Dorniers well-drilled gunners. In the ensuing mêlée one pilot baled out from his flaming fighter, probably Hurricane Pilot Officer Alan Geoffrey Page who landed in the sea suffering appalling burns to his face and hands.

Despite their efforts, the fighters failed to break up the formation and the second pass was right on target with the bombs dropping in a perfect line, hitting the hangars and buildings and ripping up the grass runways. A few of the Dorniers, whether intentionally or not, had released their bombs a little early and they landed on RAF Hawkinge just as it was being hit by Erpro Gr 210.

Though they didn't lose any planes in this prolonged air battle, the Dorniers took some heavy hits with bullets shredding the cabin of the lead aircraft tearing up Finks' map table but somehow failing to hit bone or flesh. Ofw. Hans Wolff's aircraft of the 6th Staffel was hit eight times shredding the tail plane and fuselage, and two of Burkner's crew were badly wounded but the bombers had much the better of the combat and they pressed home the attack on RAF Hawkinge.

The damage was as devastating as that caused by their earlier combined attack on Manston, with one hangar completely gutted, another wrecked, stores and workshops set on fire and large craters all over the place, but the airfield was not finished. The casualties were light with only five dead – three servicemen and two civilians – and six badly wounded, though many others had superficial wounds caused by splinters and flying glass.

Me 110 of Erpro Gr 210 being 'bombed up'. (Photograph: J.Vasco)

Leutnant 'Grock' of Erpro Gr 210 waiting to scramble. The dog, believed to be a Scottish terrier, sitting in the deckchair 'waiting to scramble' is Leutnant Karl-Heinz Koch's dog Grock, named after a popular German comedian of the 1930s. (Photograph: Otto Hintze)

Two Spitfires were wrecked by the blasts and a few more were rocked by flying debris, but they were all repairable. Almost thirty large bomb craters pitted the aerodrome but, despite this devastation, the morale of the airmen and civilian contractors wasn't broken. Within two days the airfield was up and running, albeit on reduced capacity.

Erpro Gr 210, unlike the hits taken by KG 2, had dodged the defenders' bullets during the attack on Hawkinge and, after making an uneventful journey home, arrived back at base completely unscathed. Within twenty-four hours the crew were fit and ready for action but their only battle flight on 13 August was aborted owing to the foul weather over the Channel. The next raid pencilled in for the next day was once again to be a lighting attack against Manston and, for some reason, the nearby airfield at Ramsgate.

Both Manston and Ramsgate, being less than 40 miles away, were prime targets but with heavy cloud hanging over most of the Channel it seemed the intended mission would have to be abandoned. As the morning of 14 August wore on, the weather conditions improved slightly but the crews were still expecting to be stood down when the attack order was received.

For whatever reason Rubensdorffer had decided that a successful raid could still be mounted. Possibly he thought the RAF fighters would be so occupied in their dogfight over Dover with the experienced pilots of JG 26 that little resistance could be expected. Standing down his Me 109s he used only the Me 110s on this mission, and sent 2nd Staffel to attack Manston at 12.00 hours followed slightly later by the eight aircraft of the 1st Staffel to attack Ramsgate.

Top cover was provided by the Me 109s of Jagdeschwader 52 should the RAF make an unexpected appearance. Feldwebel Ludwig Bielmaier of 5/JG 52 noted in his flying book that he was airborne from 11.32-12.32 hours operating over Ramsgate.

At a range of just over 30 miles they engaged Spitfires and Oberfeldwebel Hans Potthast was shot down into the Channel. Hoping against hope that his friend was not dead, Bielmaier entered in his log that Potthast was missing. But Potthast had not baled out and had gone straight down into the sea with his plane. His body was never recovered.

During this escort mission two pilots from the 4th Staffel of JG 52 also failed to return. The body of Ofw. Heinz Weiss was later washed ashore near Broadstairs and buried in Margate Cemetery but no trace was ever found of Ofw. Gunter Ruttinger. It is something of a mystery which RAF squadron shot down these three airmen as in his log Bielmaier entered that they had encountered Spitfires, but no Spitfire squadrons were covering Manston when the Me 110s of Erpro Gr 210 came into attack.

The Spitfires of 65 Squadron had been detailed to patrol the airfield but, probably itching for a fight, they had left their watch and flown south when they saw the barrage balloons over Dover being shot at and set on fire, and 'A' Flight dived to attack the raiders. 'B' Flight broke away from a possible attack against an enemy formation because they turned out to be friendly fighters, possibly the Hurricanes of 151 Squadron that had been ordered to intercept Raid 29 that was approaching Manston. 'B' Fight then heard over the radio that Manston was being bombed but arrived back too late to intercept the *Zerostorers*, though it is possible that they did engage with the Me 109s of JG 52 with the Hurricanes that had now become entangled in a fierce dogfight over Manston.

The nine Hurricanes of Red, Yellow and Green Sections of 151 Squadron had encountered about fifteen Me 109s some way out to sea, to the west of Margate, flying 3,000ft above them and though outnumbered Squadron Leader John 'Pete' Gordon led them into the attack. In the ensuing mêlée he latched on to the tail of one that went into a steep dive to shake him off, coming down to 2,000ft, but he gradually closed, firing a ten-second burst at 900ft.

The enemy plane started to smoke under the impact of 1,600 rounds but Gordon broke away and, when he turned towards him again, saw an aircraft going into the sea with the pilot floating down by parachute. This was his only victory claim during the Battle of Britain as he was shot down, wounded in the head and leg, and badly burned only four days later. He was killed in 1942 when he failed to return to return from a sweep over France.

Out of the corner of his eye Sub Lt Harry Beggs saw Gordon's kill go down in smoke as he lined up a Me 109 in his sights. Closing in from 900ft he fired a deflection burst until he overshot the target and then fired again as it went into a dive. Following it down he once again closed to within 900ft, and continued to fire until it splashed into the sea, sending up a huge plume of spray. On loan from the Fleet Air Arm he would be shot down and severely wounded the next day. Although he recovered from his wounds he didn't survive the war and was killed when his ship was sunk in 1942.

Pilots of 5th Staffel of JG 52. Left to right: Herbert Hoffman, Hans Pottharst, Leo Zaunbrecher, Ludwig Bielmeir. (Photograph: G. Bielmeir)

Pilots of 5th Staffel of JG 52 with Me 109 displaying the unit insignia: Left to right: Beilmeir, Zaunbrecher, Potthast, Hoffman, Greiner and Jug (Jung?). (Photograph: G. Beilmeir)

Clearing up the damage to No.2 Gun Post at RAF Manston after the attack on 12 August 1940. Tom Beggs is second from right. (Photograph: Tom Beggs)

The Canadian Pilot Officer James Johnson was firing away at another enemy fighter and was sure it was severely damaged, but he lost sight of it as he was forced to brake away when he came under attack. This was his only victory claim as he would be shot down into the Channel and killed the following day. His body was recovered from the sea. But 151 Squadron did not get it all its own way during this confrontation because Sgt George Atkinson, who had led Green Section into the fight after abandoning convoy escort, was attacked and his Hurricane was shot to pieces.

Hit by a cannon shell and raked by bullets the plane almost broke up and, though slightly wounded, he somehow managed to bale out safely. Bobbing about in the sea he was lucky enough to be picked up by a boat and then transferred to the Margate lifeboat. But his wounds were not serious and, after three weeks in hospital, he was able to return to the squadron. He almost survived the war but was killed in a flying accident in March 1945.

The airmen of Erpro Gr 210 hadn't witnessed this fighter skirmish and thought their speedy approach across the Channel had outwitted the RAF. The skies seemed empty of Spitfires and Hurricanes and, as they climbed through the ten-tenths cloud barrier to 10,000ft a trouble-free attack on Manston aerodrome was in prospect. Ramsgate, situated about 2 miles north of the town centre, was a small commercial airport that, in common with other civilian airfields, closed at the outbreak of war. It had no real military significance and was a strange choice for a Luftwaffe attack. Possibly it had been photographed when some dispersed planes had been parked there and subsequently incorrectly listed by Luftwaffe Intelligence as an operational fighter base.

Manston, on the other hand, about 2 miles west of Ramsgate, was an important RAF station at the heart of 'Hellfire Corner'. Standing guard over the Thames Estuary, being ideally placed to defend London, it was constantly manned by single and twin-engine fighter squadrons. The single-seaters arrived at dawn after their first patrol and flew back to their home bases after the dusk patrol. But Manston was also extremely exposed and vulnerable to swift, low-level attacks because it was just 3 miles from the coast. Even heavy bombers could attack it before any radar warning was received. The aerodrome was in a perilous location and an easy Luftwaffe target.

The raid on 12 August had badly cratered the airfield, damaged two hangers in East Camp and almost levelled the workshops where a civilian worker was killed. During the attack a couple of Blenheims of 600 Squadron had been badly hit (one subsequently being written off) and three Spitfires taxing for take-off suffered superficial damage. There were holes everywhere but within twenty-four hours the aerodrome was almost fully operational.

By lunchtime on 14 August the ground crews were filling in the last of the remaining craters that pitted the airfield, and looking forward to a well-earned tea break when, once again, they heard the drone of approaching enemy planes. Should they down tools and run for cover or wait for the air-raid siren? Some dived for the nearest slit trench but most rushed for the comparative safety of the air-raid shelters. But hiding in the bunkers was out of the question because

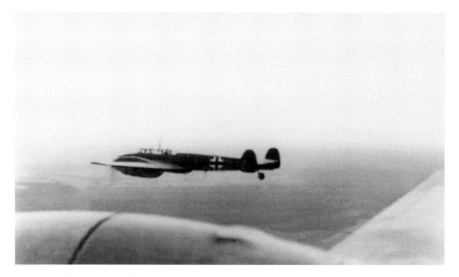

Me 110s of Erpro Gr 210 heading for the Channel

Station Warrant Officer Jackson would have malingerers out in double-quick time as soon as the all-clear was sounded. The civilian workers, though, were not so easily moved.

Banking away from the formation, the 1st Staffel commenced their descent to Ramsgate airfield only to find their flight path blocked by barrage balloons over the harbour. Breaking off the bombing run they turned and climbed fast to join the Me 110s of 2nd Staffel in a concerted all-out attack on Manston.

Out over the Channel two of the Me 110s of 1st Staffel developed engine trouble and, with their instruments showing serious problems and with oil pressure dropping, were forced to turn for home. Both managed a tricky but safe, wheels-down landing at Calais-Mark.

The remaining aircraft, under the command of Oberleutnant Willhelm Rossinger, lined up in pairs and, in a shallow dive, at over 350mph, commenced their attack from 10,000ft. The raiders were almost on top of Manston before it sounded the red alert and, as the wailing sirens blared out a warning of an immediate attack, everyone rushed for cover.

Used as a low-level dive-bomber, the twin-engine Me 110 was an impressive aircraft. Carrying two 500kg bombs it could deliver them almost as accurately as a Ju 87 Stuka, but it had the added advantage of being able to defend itself once the bombs had been released. In the hands of the experienced pilots of Erpro Gr 210 it was a deadly instrument and, as they rapidly closed in on Manston, they carefully selected their targets. The rear gunners, alert for fighters, primed their MG 15 machine-guns and checked that the 75-round magazines were correctly positioned for easy replacement.

Manston was equipped with a motley but nevertheless pretty formidable arsenal. In addition to the 40mm Bofors guns and three armoured cars mounted with twin machine-guns, manned by the Royal Artillery, there were four gun posts housing 20mm Hispano cannons and Lewis machine-guns manned by the station airmen. All this was backed up by the improvised defences rigged up by 600 Squadron, creating a very decent *ad hoc* defence.

Probably because of the poor weather conditions no single-seat fighter squadrons had arrived at Manston, but some of the twin-engine Blenheims of 600 Squadron were parked out in the open like sitting ducks. The warning had come too late to get them airborne and they were left to their fate as the raiders roared in over East Camp.

When not flying, Sgt 'Tom' Townshend, an air-gunner with the night fighters of 600 Squadron, was often called on to man the field telephone sited on top of the firing butts in front of the East Camp hangars. From this vantage point he could report the movement of all aircraft and was in direct telephone contact with Sector Control at Kenley.

Protected by sandbags piled up to provide a small, defensive square, he was accompanied by an armourer who was responsible for manning the four fixed .303 Browning machine-guns mounted on a specially constructed tripod. Fired from a standing position, the guns were operated using tracers for sighting but the sandbags only gave limited protection up to waist height. It was a dangerous place to be when the airfield was under attack.

On August 12 the armourer completely lost his nerve when a fragmentation bomb exploded next to the firing butts and he cowered down in the corner without firing a shot. Townshend also hit the deck and remained glued to the floor throughout the bombardment. Ashamed of his almost cowardly behaviour

The Ground Defence Team of No.1 Gun Post. The barrel of the 20mm cannon can be seen poking out from behind the sandbags. (Photograph: Tom Beggs)

Sgt. Thomas William Townshend. His photograph was taken after he had gone over to Bomber Command in 1941

he vowed that next time he would take over the firing duties. He'd show the enemy that he could fight.

At 12.00 hours the amber alert turned to red, and Tom could hear a faint drone of aircraft engines but nothing appeared on the horizon. Orders to keep a sharp look out for enemy planes, swinging along the coast, were continually being transmitted by Sector Control but no positive sightings were received. Suddenly a warning flashed along the line that fifteen-plus enemy planes had crossed the coast between Margate and Ramsgate and were speeding towards Manston.

'Can't you see them? They must be on top of you!'

They were and, through the haze, he could make out two long lines of twin-engine fighters coming in fast with all four .303s cocked. He fixed his sights on the leader. Steeled by Tom's resolve the armourer also stood his ground. As the sound of the enemy engines grew to a crescendo those manning the gun emplacements held their positions and hurriedly checked that their weapons and equipment were in full operating order. The ammunition boxes were opened and the shells and ammo hastily stacked within easy reach.

At No.1 Gun Post Tom Beggs had already methodically placed the bullet holders of his twin Lewis machine-gun around the inside ledge of the gun post. The gun posts originally had a single Lewis gun but another was fitted next to it to double the firepower. Though a good idea it had one major drawback because the empty shells from one gun hit the finger holding the trigger of the other. The shells were red hot and, on the first test firing, they cut and burnt his fingers so badly that they had to be bandaged up. A gold ring given him by his girlfriend – later his wife – had to be removed and put on his other hand but it was a very loose fitting and was knocked off during a game of football. Lost in the grass it was never found and could be lying there still.

Now the Manston-bound aircraft would have to face more than the puny, shambolic defence offered on 12 August when hardly a shot was fired. Some of the machine-gunners had already felt the wrath of Flying Officer Charles Pritchard, after that day's poor performance, and they had no intention of experiencing another tongue-lashing. This time they intended to make a determined defence and concentrate all their firepower on the leading plane, hoping to break up the attacking formation in mid-air.

The Royal Artillery manned the three armoured cars but, short of trained Lewis gunners, one airman from the RAF Ground Defence team was seconded to each car. Ken Cox was one of the unfortunates who had to endure the soldier's jibes about 'Brylcream Boys'.

Prior to any attack they had been ordered to take up their positions on the corner of the Ramsgate–Canterbury road to pick up parachutists or shot down German aircrew. But because the sirens were late to scream out a warning they found themselves next to the workshops on the Birchington Road, directly in front of the incoming dive-bombers as they came in over East Camp. In the second armoured car Ken had barely managed to touch the trigger of his Lewis gun, letting off just half a dozen rounds when he saw two bombs heading straight for him. He instinctively let go of the gun and crouched down in the corner, shouting at the driver to put his foot down, but it was too late.

The bombs blew the workshops to pieces sending up a shower of bricks, glass and debris that covered the road, halting the lead car in its tracks. They tried to

Tom Beggs manning the Lewis machine-gun at No.1 Gun Post. (Photograph: Tom Beggs)

Armoured car crew at Manston. Ken Cox is second from the left, front row. (Photograph: Ken Cox)

Left to right: Unknown (possibly F. Ebner), Richard Meyer and Heinrich Brinkmann. (Photograph: John Vasco)

reverse but the remains of the workshops were strewn across their path. With their exit blocked there was no alternative but to stand and fight.

Through the enveloping dust all three guns opened up in unison in the general direction of the attackers. With a bit of luck they might get in a telling shot and they emptied their magazines into the sky.

Keeping perfect formation the raiders swept by Tom Townshend in two parallel lines sending their bombs crashing down on the airfield, blowing the roof off one of the hangars that went up in a huge ball of smoke and demolished the workshops. One hangar was completely ablaze and three of the Blenheims were burning fiercely. Great clouds of dust and smoke were billowing across the airfield but, somehow, Tom managed to keep the lead aircraft in his sights. The raiders were so low he thought he could take one out with a cricket ball and the raking salvo from his four Brownings proved absolutely lethal.

As the tracers leapt skywards he watched, almost in disbelief, as the hail of fire tore a row of holes in the port wing, shattering the aileron. The Messerschmitt rocked alarmingly and the bullets smashed into the fuselage and ripped pieces off the cockpit, sending the plane slamming straight into the emergency landing ground. The pilot, Leutnant Heinrich Brinkman, and his gunner, Unteroffizier Richard Mayer, were completely incinerated as their Me 110D (S9+NK) exploded on impact and burst into flames. Small fires broke out amongst the scattered wreckage and the sickly smell of burning flesh spread over the airfield.

In No.1 Gun Post, Tom Beggs had also opened up with his twin Lewis gun emptying a complete magazine at the leading plane. It shuddered in mid-air and he was sure he had struck home but, at that moment, a great ball of smoke blew across the gun post, momentarily obscuring his view.

Then, with a flash of flame, the raider ploughed into the ground within 150ft of him and he was almost deafened as it blew up on impact. The explosion sent bits of wreckage in all directions with small pieces landing inside the gun post. Later some airmen sheltering in a nearby slit trench told him they had seen his tracers bring down the Me 110. At such a distance, and using only one magazine, he wasn't convinced he could have done such a telling amount of damage but he accepted their praise without any argument. It felt good to be the hero of the hour, even though he knew it wasn't really deserved.

Tom Beggs had to remain on duty at the gun post until after five o'clock when the relief took over and only then did he, and his gunnery mate Doug Cotterel, have a chance to examine the wreckage. Mostly it was a mangled mess but they did manage to rescue the paddle from the aircraft's rubber dinghy as a souvenir. There was a .303 bullet hole in it proving that at least one of the machine-gunners had scored a hit.

Tom and Doug were back at the gun post that evening because they had also drawn the all-night shift. At least it was a warm night to be out of doors, their billets having been reduced to rubble and, for the time being, meals were being cooked al fresco on a small Primus stove.

Tom Beggs pointing to a bullet hole on
the dinghy paddle of Me 110 (SK+NK).
(Photograph: Tom Beggs)

Next to No.1 Gun Post, encircled by a high wall of sandbags, was one of the
four 20mm Hispano cannons that were positioned around the airfield. Manned
by Tom Beggs' pals Harry Skitt and Bill Brown, it was an easy gun to fire providing that the correct procedure was followed and Bill had got this down to a fine
art. With his left hand on a bar, and his fingers over a lever to operate the Bowden
Cable that fired the gun when squeezed like the hand brake on a bicycle, Bill
found that the Hispano could be rapidly fired but changing the sixty-round magazine was a different matter. His armourer, Harry Skitt, should have quickly faded
under the weight of the 56lb magazines but with that extra burst of energy that
only combat can give, he was making light work of it.

When the Nazi planes came in almost all the gunners opened fire simultaneously but the swirling blast and dust from the exploding bombs, and their own
cordite fumes and smoke, played havoc with their eyes making it almost impossible to see. They were practically firing blind but through the gaps in the heavy
haze they could just make out the formation as it swept overhead and concentrated all their firepower on the leading plane.

The Bofors gunners were also putting up a fearful barrage but the dive-
bombers seemed to have a charmed life as they sailed through the hail of fire.
Then, as Bill Brown banged away a huge, orange flash shot across the sky as one
of the raiders blew up in mid-air and broke in two. He saw a parachute unfold
but lost sight of it in the swirling smoke.

In a Me 110D (S9+MK), the pilot Unterofficer Hans Steding held the plane
steady despite the intense AA fire, and he released two 500kg bombs right on top

of the East Camp hangars. As he eased back on the controls he put the aircraft on full power to send it speeding away from the murderous flak.

Climbing quickly to 1,000ft through the huge clouds of smoke rising from Manston, he turned to speak to his rear gunner Gefreiter Ewald Schank but, before he could say anything, a massive explosion racked the machine, tearing it completely in half. The front section, with its engines screaming wide open, hurtled earthward taking Steding to his death. Turning over it plunged straight down smashing into the ground, partly burying itself in the red gravel. Steding's body was compacted beyond all recognition.

As the mangled tail section rolled over, the canopy flew off and shattered pieces of fuselage whirled around the remains of the cockpit ricocheting off Schank's head as he was catapulted from his seat. Half-conscious, he was nevertheless aware that his foot was trapped in the wreckage of the smashed compartment. Hanging upside down he desperately struggled to pull himself free. Suddenly he was in the air and instinctively he pulled the ripcord of his parachute as he momentarily passed out again.

Coming in on the second wave, Lt Erich Beudel briefly lost sight of the chief as they dived through the clouds. Suddenly the aerodrome loomed into view. Bombs had been dropped between the buildings and, slightly to the left, columns of smoke were spinning skywards. Then he dropped his 1,000kg bomb load to add to the mounting destruction.

The AA guns were putting up a terrific barrage and an exploding shell rocked his plane. Flying through the flak made his hair stand on end but, in less than five minutes, the immediate danger was over and he sent the aircraft back at full power into the safety of the clouds.

Manston was in a chaotic condition as the blasts from the fragmentation bombs shattered the buildings and left huge, deep craters in the grass runways almost big enough to swallow a Spitfire. The barracks and the workshops had been blown to pieces and three of the parked Blenheims were burning hulks. Two hangars were ablaze and another a complete wreck but, amazingly, there were no fatalities. Everyone had made it to the safety of the shelters in double quick time.

Schank's parachute opened just enough to save his life but he landed heavily and again passed out. A blast of hot air filled the parachute and dragged him across the concrete towards a fearsome fire raging amongst a mass of strewn wreckage. Coming to he managed to pull the harness release buckle and the parachute flew away leaving him inches from the inferno.

He struggled to his feet but then fell over backwards in a crumpled heap. With blood gushing from a head wound, a sprained ankle and just one boot, he couldn't keep his balance. He had landed near the crashed tail section of his plane close to the separated front end with its engines rammed firmly into the ground. Painfully he crawled towards the shattered wreck to see if there was any hope for his comrade but there was no sign of a body. Somehow he hauled himself to his feet and, as the bombs exploded all around him, he stood alone and helpless in the middle of the devastation.

Unteroffizier Hans Steding   Gefreiter Ewald Schank. (Photograph: Schank)

His watch had stopped but his heart was beating fast. There was no one in sight but then suddenly out of the swirling smoke he saw three men in blue uniforms running towards him. They grabbed him and half-carried him to the nearest slit trench and safety.

As they dragged him along he tried to explain that the pilot was still in the plane but they didn't seem to understand and he again passed out with the pain. When he regained consciousness he became aware that he was in some sort of hospital and surrounded by men in brown uniforms, some wearing steel helmets and carrying guns.

One of the soldiers started to speak to him German. Again he asked about his comrade. Rather bluntly he was told that he was probably dead but as they continued to interrogate him the questions didn't really register. In a daze he replied, 'Ich bin glücklich, sehr glücklich' which in the confusion some misunderstood. Thinking he had said 'The big lick, soon the big lick', they had visions of an even greater raid. How many more attacks could Manston take? The aerodrome was proving too vulnerable to lightning low-level attacks and before the month was out it had been all but abandoned.

Meanwhile the German chief had given the order 'Collect above the clouds' and, circulating slowly, the remaining Me 110s of Erprobungsgruppe 210 reformed and headed back for Calais-Mark but all was not well, as several of the *Zerstorers* had suffered minor hits.

The aircraft of Oberleutant Werner Weymann was losing oil an alarming rate and he was forced to shut down one engine. Flying on reduced power over the

Channel seemed never ending and, even with Lt Beudel flying escort, he was relieved when he finally crossed the French coast. It would be a precarious landing but, keeping the wings straight and level, he set the plane down safely.

He jumped from the machine elated at the landing and the success of their mission. He didn't know that three of his comrades had died in the raid and another was lying seriously wounded in an enemy hospital.

The crashed Messerschmitts were lying about 300ft apart on either side of the public road that ran through the centre of Manston aerodrome. As the dust began to settle Ken Cox was drawn to the mangled wrecks as much out of genuine interest as of morbid curiosity. Alive or dead he hadn't seen the enemy at close quarters. Looking inside the shattered forward section of Me 110D (S9+MK) he could make out the mutilated remains of Hans Steding and he immediately turned away.

The wreckage of the other dive-bomber was spread all over the emergency landing ground. The main section was a burnt out shell and the RAF fire crew was still extinguishing some small fires amongst the scattered pieces of fuselage. One was using a small hand extinguisher and, as Ken stood talking to him, he kicked over a roundish, smouldering lump. It was a blackened, eyeless face. He stared at the dismembered head in horror.

★★★★

Sgt Tom Townshend was in full flying kit, ready for the first night patrol of 14 August when he wandered over towards the breakdown crane that was about to lift the remains of the Me 110D (S9+MK) out of the hard red shale.

The squadron doctor, attending the recovery of the mangled bodies, knew that Tom would soon be flying and asked what he was doing gazing at such a gory mess. He replied that sooner or later he had to harden himself to war. Now was the time to find out how he might end up one day. The doctor understood and ordered the winch to commence the lift.

As the wreckage was hanging in mid-air the doctor went to work with his orderlies and cut the pilot's bloody remains from the harness. What little there was of the mutilated corpse was laid out on a blanket and covered over.

They searched through the pockets of the shredded flying suit and found a bloodstained diary with Steding's name in it. This would be passed to the intelligence services and crash investigators to form part of their report. The initial reports of both incidents were fairly brief but the full A.I.1 (K) Report No.255/1940 read as follows:

Place, date and time: Manston Aerodrome, Kent.   14.8.40   12.10 hours
Type and marks: Me 110   S9+MK   Shield, yellow. Bomb-sight over
                                   map of England and N. Ireland in red.
                                   S. Ireland only outlined.
Unit: 2 / KG 210
Identity disc: 5385

Shattered remains of Me 110D (S9+NK) spread over the emergency landing ground

Feldpostnummer: L 25082

Ausweiss: ------

Start and Mission: Started from Benain at 11.30 hours. Refuelled at
                               St Omer to attack Manston aerodrome.
                               Two x 250kg bombs were dropped.

This Staffel has been at Benain aerodrome since 10.7.40.

The present operation consisted of about 3 aircraft from 1st Staffel and 4 from the 2nd Staffel with 7 Me 109s as escort. This attack is reported as being carried out by diving.

Just after dropping the bombs the aircraft sustained a direct hit from the Bofors AA gun which exploded the aircraft in the air and wounded the W/T who baled out.

Immediately after pulling the ripcord of his parachute he went unconscious and came to in the sick ward of Manston aerodrome.

The aircraft is badly smashed but it appears to be in essential a standard Me 110 with two bombs racks underneath the front of the fuselage similar to those of a Ju 88. No bombsight has been found but there is a mark on the pilots' windscreen, which presumably serves as a sight.

Crew: Pilot Unteroffizier Hans Steding dead.
         Gefreiter Ewald Schank wounded.

A further Me 110 crashed at Manston marked S9+NK. This is a complete write off and is burnt out.

★★★★

Remains of Me 110D (S9+MK) compacted into the hard core in front of the hangers

Basically the report is correct except that no Me 109s took part in the raid on Manston. Only the third Staffel of Erpro Gr 210 was equipped with Me 109s and, according to the surviving Luftwaffe records, this Staffel was grounded for the day. The fighters of JG 52 that provided top cover did not follow the dive-bombers down and strafe the aerodrome with machine-gun fire.

However, the fourteen planes reportedly involved in the attack does roughly tally with the total number involved. Two complete Staffels, of nine planes each, would give a possible total of eighteen aircraft available for combat. Deduct from this the one or two that were usually not operational, and the two that returned home, and it is likely that fourteen or fifteen Me 110Ds took part in the raid. Bearing in mind that the Luftwaffe recorded that twenty-eight bombs were delivered on target, and that there were two bombs per plane, this backs up the number of fourteen.

However, the airfield described as 'Benain' is possibly a typographical error and should have read 'Denain', the name commonly used by British Intelligence when referring to Erpro Gr 210's base at Lille. Similarly St Omer was often confused with Calais-Mark.

Schank believes he was kept in the hospital wing of Manston aerodrome for ten days, but this seems unlikely because they only had one casualty room and did not have the facilities for long-term care. He was probably moved to a nearby hospital when unconscious and kept under close guard. From there he was taken to a hospital in London and then to a POW camp near Manchester. Later, like most German airmen, he was transported to Canada. In 1947 he was released from captivity, but his home in the east of the country had been overrun by

The remains of No.4 Gun Post after the attack of 24 August 1940 (Photos: Tom Beggs)

Bill Brown manning a 20mm cannon at RAF Manston. (Photograph: Ken Cox)

the Russians and he remained in West Germany. The bodies of his three dead comrades were originally buried at Minster Cemetery in Wingham, Kent. In the 1960s they were re-interred in the German War Cemetery at Cannock Chase, near Stafford.

Manston's Record Book described the raid rather laconically, although for some reason the date entered for the raid is given as 15 August, not the 14th. The entry ran:

> The station was again attacked by nine Me 110s. They were heavily engaged by ground defences and two e.a. [enemy aircraft] were destroyed - one by a RA post (Bofors) and one by RAF post (Hispano). Two hangars on the east camp were partially wrecked and damage was caused to a Bellman and Bessoneau hangar. One large crater made in the aerodrome.

Equally brief, 600 Squadron's Operational Record Book merely stated:

> More bombing, which destroyed one of our hangars, and three aircraft, certain damage was done to the aerodrome. The only casualty was the Commanding Officer who received a black eye from a stone that rocketed off the Adjutant's steel helmet.

But the devastating attacks of 12 and 14 August 1940 had taken their toll culminating in the virtual abandonment of the airfield after it was bombed and burnt out on the 24th. It did not to become fully operational again until the Battle of Britain was over.

CHAPTER THREE

Dogfight over Dover

As the Spitfires of 'A' Flight of 65 Squadron flew south to intercept the balloon shooters over Dover, they didn't realise that they would be flying into a hornet's nest of whirling and wheeling machines locked in a mighty air battle. A fight to the death was in progress as squadrons of Spitfires and Hurricanes were set upon by the Me 109s of JG 26 and some Me 110s of ZG 26 that were protecting almost eighty Ju 87 dive-bombers that were intent on attacking the Goodwin lightship off the coast of Folkestone.

Whether this was the dive-bombers' original target seems doubtful, and it seems likely that they were diverted away from an attack on the nearby RAF aerodrome at Hawkinge by the ferocity of the defending fighters. Of course the presence of so many Stukas could possibly have been just a feint to draw the RAF into the air in an uneven aerial contest. And if this was the case, the ruse certainly succeeded as twelve Hurricanes of 32 Squadron and twelve Spitfires of 610 Squadron were ordered up at 12.20 hours to intercept Raid 34 that was approaching Hawkinge. The twenty-four planes patrolled over Dover/Folkestone at 15,000ft awaiting the arrival of the raiders. They were expecting some heavy enemy fighters but not all three Gruppen of Jagdgeschwader 26. All of the serviceable Me 109s of this first-rate fighter wing were in the air guarding the dive-bombers and, after the previous days inactivity, when only the II Gruppe claimed victories, they were itching for a fight, especially the pilots of Adolf Galland's III Gruppe.

The I Gruppe under the command of Hptmn Kurt Fischer was to fly as close escort to the dive-bombers and to stay glued to them once they had crossed the coast, heading across the Channel. Their combat role was to provide the last impenetrable shield against the fighters they expected the RAF would throw at them when alerted by the radar at Dover that a large enemy formation was approaching the Kent airfields. And to get at the Ju 87s they would have to first fight their way past Hptmn Ebbighausen's II Gruppe that were flying in loose support some way off the main formation. Weaving in and out but never far enough away to be drawn into a decoy skirmish, they would be an effective first barrier against the RAF fighters.

The three Staffelkapitans of III Gruppe discussing tactics in August 1940. Left to right: Hptmn Gerhard Schopfel, Obltn. Georg Beyer and Obltn. Kuno Wendt

The main danger would be from the pilots of Galland's III Gruppe who would be operating ahead and above the Stukas, ready to swoop down on any attacking fighters. Such was the calibre of these pilots that they already accounted for over eighty Allied planes and, in addition to Galland and his wingman Joachim Muncheberg, there were three other aces, Hans Ebeling, Gerhard Schoepfel and 'Micky' Sprick, who were anxious to add to their total. They were a formidable bunch.

Rather than leading the Geschwader into battle their commander Major Gotthardt Handrick preferred to direct operations from the rear and, covered by his wingman Obltn. Walter Horten, had taken up his usual safe place above and behind the formation to observe the tactics and outcome of any aerial combat. A winner of the modern pentathlon in the 1936 Berlin Olympics and a veteran of the Spanish Civil War, he was now coming to the end of his combat days and would be transferred out of JG 26 on 21 August 1940 to take up a staff post in Romania.

Handrick was a well-respected officer but his continual failure to come to grips with the enemy was a cause of some considerable irritation to Horton who, though a technical officer, was eager to test himself against the RAF. Being tail cover to a virtual non-combatant was not his style but, within a week, he would have his wish and be right in the middle of the action flying as Galland's wingman. He'd be taken off flying duties when all technical officers were grounded at the end of September, but in just over one month he then accompanied Galland on over forty missions to become an ace who'd down seven enemy planes.

Obltn. H. Ebeling and mechanics of 8th Staffel/JG 26 prior to take off on 14 August 1940. Messerschmitt Bf.109, Nr.14, can be seen in the background. (Photograph: Ebeling)

The RAF formation was heavily outnumbered by over two to one despite an additional six Spitfires from 65 Squadron, and this disparity was evident in the air battle. The formation also linked up with twelve Hurricanes of 615 Squadron that were already in the air, having taken off earlier at 11.50 hours when ordered to intercept Raid 28 over Dover. A formidable force of over forty RAF fighters awaited the incoming raiders.

The Hurricanes of 615 Squadron were the first to come into contact with the Me 110s and Ju 87s when Red Section, flying at 12,000ft, was attacked from astern by a pack of Me 110s. Flying Officer Richard Gayner recalled that a lone Me 110 swooped down out of the clouds firing its canon. Luckily most of the shots hit the armour plate but he took a piece of shrapnel in his side, and as a cannon shell blew a hole in the port wing a string of bullets raked the fuselage. Gayner knew he should have turned hard on the Me 110 and tried to shoot it down but, with blood weeping from his wound, he broke away and lost himself in the clouds. The Hurricane was a complete mess but it was still flyable and, as the adrenaline cut in, he somehow overcame the pain barrier and managed to make it back to Kenley where he made a wheels-down, though somewhat bumpy, landing. Red 2 and Red 3 also came under fire but both declined to fight and fled before they were hit.

The rest of the squadron had not yet come under attack and Blue and Green Sections lined up behind nine Stukas, flying in three Vics. They had spotted the Germans dive-bombing from 3,000ft, attacking the Goodwin lightship off Folkestone. Pilot Officer Keith Lofts, flying as Blue 2, opened up on the second section as they kept a tight formation, firing back at him as they skidded away. He was not able to arrest their attack but once they had released their bombs he

Major Gotthardt Handrick
(centre) the Geschwader
commander of JG 26.
Right: Hptmn Wilde,
Operations Officer. Left:
Oblt. Rothenberg, Adjutant

Obltn. Kurt Gramling and
Uffz Frans Scwatzki sitting
astride their Junkers Ju 87.
(Photograph: H. Gramling)

dived onto the tail of the No.3 and fired a 6-second burst at it from dead astern. It shuddered under the hail of bullets, swung round to the left and seemed to momentarily stop in mid-air before crashing into the sea. The kill was confirmed by Flt Lt James Sanders flying as Blue 1.

This dive-bomber was probably the Junkers Ju 87 of the 10/LG 1 flown by Obltn. Kurt Gramling that failed to return from a mission over Folkestone but his body, like that of Uffz. Frans Scwatzki his radio operator and gunner, was not recovered from the sea. He was just twenty-four years old having been born in Osterburken on 29 December 1915, leaving behind his grieving parents and a younger brother Heinrich who survived the war. Scwatzki was born on 6 December 1914 in Goldop/Ostpr, which was annexed by Poland after the war but no surviving relatives could be traced.

It is possible that Gramling's aircraft was also attacked by Pilot Officer Stanley Norris of 610 Squadron who reported that he had attacked a Ju 87 flying at the rear of a large formation, and which was seen to go down in smoke and flames, turning over on its back, but he lost sight of it when he hit a small bank of clouds. He then saw another mixed formation of Me 110s and Ju 87s and he closed and fired at a Stuka on the edge of the formation that went down burning fiercely in a pall of smoke. He also gave a short burst at another from close range that he thought he had damaged, before it swerved out of harm's way.

Who shot Gramling down into the sea will remain something of a mystery as, in addition to Lofts and Norris, a probable claim was submitted by Pilot Officer

Obltn. Kurt Gramling and Uffz. Frans Scwatzki. (Photograph: H. Gramling)

Obltn. Kurt Gramling sitting astride a bomb. (Photograph: H. Gramling)

Left to right: Obltn. G. Beyer, Obltn. G. Sprick (Staffelkapitan of 8th Staffel from 8 August 1940). Obltn. J. Muncheberg & Obltn. G. Schopfel. (Photograph: Schopfel)

Brian Rees, also of 610 Squadron, who picked off a Ju 87 as it dived down to attack. This plane was flying on the left side of the Vic and he delivered a long burst at it from 300 yards before closing in to 600ft. It went into a spin and seemed out of control but there was no sign of smoke as it disappeared into a patch of low cloud. And Lofts, after he had finished off one dive-bomber, turned on the No.2 as it pulled up out of a dive but this one put up a bit of a fight with the rear gunner blasting back at him but, just as he ran out of ammunition, the gunner ceased to return fire and may well have been wounded, if not dead.

The proliferation of claims is to be expected in the heat of battle but the Luftwaffe actually lost only one Ju 87 in the dogfight over Dover and, although others suffered superficial hits, only one was badly damaged with its wounded rear gunner Uffz. August Muller being rushed to hospital on landing back at Calais. He recovered from his wounds caused by that brief, intensive exchange of fire when he engaged Lofts in combat.

It was only because the Spitfires of 610 Squadron, and to some extent the Hurricanes of 32 Squadron, had taken the initial brunt of the Me 109s protecting the Ju 87s, that the Hurricanes of 615 Squadron were able to get in amongst the enemy and break up the formation. But Galland's III Gruppe was quick to spot the danger and his fighters bore down unnoticed on the Hurricanes as Flying

Officer Eyre and Sgt Porter – flying Green 1 and Green 2 – fired at the third section of the Ju 87s after they had released their bombs and were pulling out of the dive. Eyre let loose a five-second burst at the leader but had to throttle back to evade the cross-fire and, as he fired from dead astern, pieces of metal were seen to fly off the Stuka before it was lost in the clouds. Porter also had a pop at it and bits of the plane flew into the air under the impact of two long bursts, but it wasn't on fire or blowing smoke as it dived out of harm's way. He also fired a short burst, without result, at the No.2 before it too sought the safety of the clouds.

As the RAF fighters broke away they didn't realise how close they had come to disaster, because before Galland was upon them another Hurricane hoved up into his sights. This was attacking the last Stuka and Galland fired from long range to try and force it to break off its attack. As the bullets splattered into its tail fin the Hurricane finally gave up the attack on the Ju 87 and dived for cover into the wispy clouds. But it couldn't shake off its pursuer, who had guessed correctly that it would pull up through the clouds and, making a right curve to within 600ft, Galland fired a salvo of lead at the Hurricane. A three-second burst from Galland's guns sent a stream of bullets ripping through the flimsy fuselage and crashing into the cockpit. With the pilot dead or fatally wounded the plane was seen to go down, spiralling out of control, in a sheet of flames. The burning aircraft disappeared into the low streaky clouds but Galland didn't see it splash into the sea because he had to take evasive action as a hail bullets whistled past his canopy.

A Hurricane had latched onto his tail but the pilot must have forgotten to check his rear-view mirror as he was almost immediately blown out of the sky by a cannon shell from the Me 109 of Obltn. Joachim Muncheberg who, as Galland's wingman, was covering his rear. On his return to base Galland was informed that the burning hulk had not recovered from its dive, and the doomed Hurricane was chalked up as his nineteenth victim.

As the air battle continued to rage, Flt Lt James Sanders of 615 Squadron, flying as Blue 1, watched in awe as, one by one, three planes dived into the sea not realising that two of them were probably the Hurricanes from his squadron dispatched by Galland and Muncheberg. In the confusion he was not aware that two pilots had been lost until after the planes landed back at Kenley at 13.30 hours after first landing at Hawkinge where one of the Hurricanes, flown by Pilot Officer Everett Rogers, crashed on landing. During the debriefing he learned that Pilot Officers Peter Collard and Cecil Montgomery had failed to return, and there was no report that they had landed at another RAF station or emergency landing field. They must have gone down in the sea and, even if they had survived, the cold water meant that their chances of being picked up alive were extremely remote unless they were fortunate enough to land near a passing ship. Sanders and his fellow pilots did not hold out much hope.

Both bodies were later washed up the other side of the Channel and today they lie buried in the war graves plot in the far left-hand corner of the Communal Cemetery at Oye-Plage, a small town on the coast 8 miles east of Calais. Collard lies in Row 1, Grave 10 with Montgomery in Row 1, Grave 19.

Pilot Officer Cecil Robert Montgomery of 615 Squadron. (Photos: Mrs P. Orr)

Montgomery was born into a farming family on 12 February 1914 in Tullykenneye, County Fermanagh, Northern Ireland, and educated at the Royal School in Enniskillen. A keen rugby player he played at every opportunity and managed to break his collar bone in his first game in the RAF. A lover of speed, he owned a powerful Norton motorbike in his teens and, fascinated by flying, spent many hours making and flying model aeroplanes with his brother Hugh.

His first job was with the Northern Insurance Company in Belfast, from where he moved first to Glasgow and then to the General Accident Company in London. In 1938 he was in the process of moving to India where the company was opening a new office when this venture was cancelled at the eleventh hour because of the unsettled political situation. Bitterly disappointed, he decided to try his luck with the RAF and was accepted for a short-service commission in April 1939, and underwent a course of preliminary training at the Civil Flying School at Cambridge.

Posted to 615 Squadron in France in May 1940, Montgomery was back in England within a few weeks, flying into RAF Tangmere before the unit took up residence at RAF Kenley on 21 May 1940. His sister Phyllis had taken up a nursing post in Windsor, and writing to her the following day he said he had never expected to be back in England so soon but he wasn't sorry as France was now a most unpleasant place with the Germans making far too much progress. And since Kenley was only twenty minutes by train from London he'd try and get an afternoon off to see her, but he suspected that things were going hot up, in which case this might not be so easy.

Except for the occasional recce aircraft at great height there was no sign of the enemy, and he was able to put in some extra flying time in Hurricanes, even swooping down to less than 400ft over her hospital. On one scary occasion he even had to make a forced landing in a Gladiator in a rough field when the engine cut out.

When as duty pilot he had the office to himself, he was able to make some social telephone calls and write a long letter to his sister explaining that as the squadron was on home defence they sometimes had to go for several days without being allowed to leave the aerodrome. Nine pilots must always be available within a half-hour call and at least three of them must be able to get away within five minutes, but as this might be sensitive information he told her to keep it to herself.

Phyllis was only eighteen years old and was very proud to be called for at the nurses' home by a tall, handsome RAF officer sporting his wings when they managed to get a day off together. She was the envy of the other nurses who asked to be introduced to her brother and his fellow officers, and though there was eight years between them they became very close in these final months.

In one of his last letters he gave a long account of being in the parade when the king visited the station, and having to borrow the equipment required for such an occasion. But with new gloves in short supply he had to wear his old well-worn ones with holes in the fingers hoping that no one would notice. He might have got away with it but after the Royal Salute the king spoke to some of the men personally, including 'Monty'. The king asked how long he had been in the RAF, if he was keeping fit and how many enemy aircraft had he shot down. Mortified, he had to admit that so far he had not shot any down. The king passed no comment and, moving along the line, appeared not to notice the worn-out gloves. But 'Monte' was sure he had.

His last letter to Phyllis was dated 8 August, less than one week before he was killed in action, arranging to meet her the following day as she was usually able to get Friday nights off. The letter made no mention of the war and was full of girlfriend and family matters, and referred to his request that his mother send on his slippers before his brother Hugh wore them out. Such footwear was already in short supply.

After spending the afternoon and evening together they said goodbye at the station. There would be a few more hurried telephone calls but the fighting had now really started to hot up and he wasn't able to get up to London in the day. When Phyllis heard that he was missing in combat she held on to the hope that he had landed in France, or had been rescued from the sea by the Germans and was now a POW. When the bad news finally came through she couldn't forget that last farewell.

Flying Officer Peter Collard lived with his wife Annette in a little bungalow on the edge of RAF Kenley, and when they flew back in the squadron dipped their wings to let her know that they were all back safely. On 14 August there was no such salute and Annette feared the worst. She knew that at least one of them was missing.

Flying Officer Peter Collard (centre). (Photograph: Mrs A. Collard)

Peter was born on 26 December 1915 in the Queensgate Nursing Home in London, the son of an old established Kent family. One of three brothers, his father was a stockbroker and had been a captain in the First World War. Peter spent his early years in Egypt but his father died during the General Strike of 1926 when Peter was only eleven years old, but growing up an orphan was tempered by the presence of his elder brothers. One would become a regular RAF officer and later the adjutant of 615 Squadron at Kenley who probably influenced Peter to join the Auxiliary Air Force in 1937.

Just prior to the outbreak of war he was called up to full-time service and, after a quick course on Hurricanes, was posted to 615 Squadron that was still flying out-of-date Gladiators. In the middle of November 1939, as part of the Air Component alongside the Advanced Air Striking Force, he flew with the squadron to France where, in April 1940, it was finally being equipped with Hurricanes just in time to try and halt the German advance. The squadron was heavily mauled during the ensuing air battles over the Low Countries and northern France, though Peter did have the satisfaction of damaging two enemy planes, a Me 109 and an Hs 126, without receiving any concerted return fire.

However, he came within a hair's breadth of death when flying a Miles Master to Vitry to check whether any of the Hurricanes left behind had been restored to flying condition. In fact they were all burnt out, and flying back with the bad news he was set upon by a Messerschmitt that, half-heartedly, shot at him in passing. A bullet pierced the canopy, missing him by inches, and though scared he was relieved that the Messerschmitt did not press home its attack.

Before the war Peter had worked in a non-flying executive capacity with the original British Airways organisation and, being an active sportsman, played most competitive games though he was also a man of letters enjoying a love of poetry, especially Keats. An idealist and a romantic, he was also very good looking, kind and full of fun. By midsummer in 1940 Annette was heavily pregnant with a son he'd never see.

For a few months she clung on to the hope that Peter was still alive but, when she finally heard that his body had been washed ashore in France, she was absolutely devastated. Annette never remarried and named their son Peter, who later presented her with four grandchildren, three boys and one girl.

As the Hurricane 615 Squadron were going down under the guns of JG 26, the Spitfires of 610 Squadron tried to divert the attack onto themselves by attempting to break through the massed fighter screen surrounding the incoming Stukas. Patrolling at 15,000ft above the clouds, 'A' Flight of 610 Squadron sighted a large formation of fifty or more Ju 87s approaching Folkestone but, before they could get amongst them, they too became embroiled in a ferocious air battle as they mixed it with the escorting Me 109s and Me 110s.

Norris and Rees had both broken through the defensive cordon and managed to fire a phalanx of almost 4,000 rounds at the first formation of dive-bombers, but the fighters of JG 26 were soon upon them forcing them to break off the attack having run out of ammunition and petrol. Seeing that they were in trouble, Sgts Ronald Hamlyn and Horatio Chandler dived down to protect them and were joined by Sgt Douglas Corfe, who was also flying alone having lost sight of

Pilots of 610 Squadron at RAF Hawkinge in 1940. Left to right, men to the left: Unknown, H. Chandler, J. Ellis, N. Ramsay, F. Gardiner, W. Warner, R. Hamlyn. Men to the right: Unknown, D. Wilson. Men sitting: E.B.B. Smith, C. Parsons, C. (Joe) Pegge, D. Corfe.

Pilots of 610 Squadron during the Battle of Britain. Left to right: Sgt R. Hamlyn, Sgt N. Ramsay, Flg Of. C. Pegge, Sgt D. Corfe, Sgt A. Baker

his Blue Leader and Blue 2. Climbing through the clouds, Corfe emerged about 3,000ft from fifteen Me 109s flying in a defensive circle and, seeing he was alone, three of them peeled off from the formation and headed straight at him.

He immediately went into a steep right-hand turn through 360 degrees and lined up one of the attackers who was now dead ahead. Closing to within 900ft he jabbed at the firing button firing a sequence of one-second bursts that set the enemy's engine ablaze and tore a huge piece off the starboard wing. Pouring smoke it turned on its back and, in a flash of flame, vanished into the clouds. In pursuit Corfe again became lost in a bank of clouds but, as he burst back into the sunlight, he was right on top of another Me 109 that took the brunt of a salvo of shots from less than 450ft.

At that range the bullets must have punched home. There was a sputter from its exhausts, suggesting a hit in the engine, and it went into a controlled shallow dive. With two bandits on his tail, Corfe gave up the chase and once again dived into the clouds before heading back to base, low on fuel.

Sgts Hamlyn and Chandler, flying Yellow 1 and 2, were also busy. Hamlyn was trying to beat off the attentions of four Me 109s that seemed intent on downing his Spitfire. But by twisting and banking in a sharp circle he was able to shake them off, and firing a quick burst at one he saw it start to smoke but had to break away as he again came under attack. Once again he shook them off but by now he was over land about 5–10 miles west of Dover when he saw an Me 109 going down in flames and exploding on impact as it smashed into the ground.

Chandler attempted to get on the tail of an Me 109 but it outmanoeuvred him and, in a game of cat and mouse, they dodged one another's bullets for nearly fifteen minutes. Then tired of the game or running low on fuel, the German pilot tried to out-climb the Spitfire but sensing the move Chandler easily caught up and opened fire. The Messerschmitt rolled over and went straight down trailing smoke and Chandler followed it down continuing to fire until it splashed into the sea. He then turned for home and after about six minutes made landfall three miles west of Dungeness.

'B' Fight of 610 Squadron had spotted a bunch of Me 109s shooting down the barrage balloons anchored over Dover and Sgt P. Else flying as Green Leader, and Sgts B. Gardner and N. Ramsay flying as Green 2 and 3, headed to intercept but they were bounced from above by Me 109s, Me 110s and what looked like He 113s. The balloon shooters turned out to be decoys to lure the Spitfires into an uneven combat with Me 109s waiting in the wings, but they hadn't reckoned with the experienced pilots of Green Section who were not afraid to fight.

As a Spitfire burst out of the cloudbank pursued by two Me 109s they were caught from behind by Else, but the rear wingman must have caught sight of him in his rear mirror because he banked away before he took any hits. Else then fired a seven-second burst of explosive rounds at the lead Me 109 that was glued to the tail of the Spitfire and it shuddered under the impact as the bullets struck home. Billowing petrol smoke it passed from view as it flew into a heavy black cloud and Else with his ammunition almost extinguished headed back to base.

A very fast enemy aircraft, with a black fuselage and yellow wing tips, that Gardner identified as a Heinkel 113 came at him head on with all guns blazing sending flashes of light shooting past the cockpit. Taking immediate evasive action he somehow managed to get behind his attacker and, chasing it out to sea, fired one long burst that set it alight. He watched the smoke pour out as it plunged into the sea. Bravely he then launched an attack on ten enemy planes but, in this uneven contest, his Spitfire was raked by gunfire with round after round hammering into the armour plate at the back of his seat.

Some of the tracers splattered into the cockpit shattering his left arm and, though in terrible pain, he was still able to fly the busted machine and took it down through the heavy overcast sky. Seeing he was over land he checked out a flat-looking field and made a forced landing outside the small country village of Wye about 5 miles from the coast. The emergency services were quickly on the scene and he was taken to Ashford Hospital for treatment. Making a full recovery he was soon back in the air but was killed in the summer of 1941.

Unable to keep up, Ramsay had lost touch with Green Leader and Green 2 but, as he searched around, he found himself below and behind a Me 110. Closing up astern to within 450ft he let loose a three- or four-second burst sending over 1,000 rounds at the twin-engine fighter. With oil and smoke pouring from its engines it started to climb to the left but Ramsey was determined that it wouldn't get away and, as he positioned himself for another attack, one of the crew was seen to jump out. There was no sign of a parachute and as he fired again the

Jones, Robert Reid
MacPherson, Webb.
(Photograph: R.
MacPherson)

Robert Reid
MacPherson
standing far right

Unknown, Robert
Reid MacPherson

damaged machine seemed to drop out of the sky, turning on its back and going down trailing smoke. Ramsey didn't continue with his attack but the Me 110 seemed out of control as it disappeared into the thick murk. Suddenly he was alone in the sky and, realising he was too near the French coast, he turned and ran for home.

Detailed to patrol over Manston aerodrome, the pilots of 65 Squadron had reluctantly resisted the invitation to fight the ten or twelve Me 109s they had spotted at 10,000ft. As they patrolled further south towards Dover they could see in the distance some barrage balloons going down in flames, and 'A' Flight peeled off to intercept the enemy aircraft but they were intercepted by a large formation of Me 109s that had swooped down to protect the balloon shooters. As they became embroiled in a fierce dogfight, Flt Lt Charles Olive was the first to score and four other pilots working in pairs shot down two other planes.

Flying Officers John Nicholas and Jeffrey Quill shared one, and Flying Officer Robert MacPherson and Sgt Michael Keymer got another. MacPherson and Keymer, flying as Red 2 and 3, were chasing a Me 109 when it was suddenly blown out of the sky by another Spitfire that had shot across their bows and blasted it beam on. As the plane went down in flames the enemy pilot baled out and was last seen swinging safely on his parachute.

Me 109s were now all over the sky and Keymer though he had hit one before it took evasive action and climbed steeply away. Then he followed Red 2 as he got on the tail of another Me 109 that was flying in a tight circle. Keymer attacked it head on firing two short bursts from about 150ft as they passed one another with at least one bullet striking the starboard engine cowling. He felt a sharp shudder and thought his Spitfire had taken a hit but he returned to the attack and saw that Red 2 was still sticking to the enemy's tail and, as he also positioned himself to fire at the Me 109, it dived steeply away into a bank of cloud. Keymer followed it down and, emerging from the clouds, he saw a patch of greenish oil on the surface of the water where a stricken plane had plunged into the sea.

Meanwhile, Pilot Officer Lawrence Pyman found himself in a perilous predicament. Having become detached from the rest of the group, and flying alone, he was set upon by several Me 109s that came at him one by one. Choosing not to flee, he shot one down in flames and damaged another before his Spitfire was raked from end to end by return fire. Luckily he was unharmed but at least six shells had been pumped into the wing and fuselage, severing the controls and putting his wireless out of action. But somehow it was still flyable and he was able to make it back to Manston where he made a forced landing further damaging the tip of the wing.

'B' Flight of 65 Squadron had not become involved in this action as the enemy planes that they had swooped down to attack actually turned out to be Hurricanes and, just in time, they broke away without anyone firing a shot. The Hurricanes of 610 Squadron had a lucky escape.

Then 'B' Flight heard over the radio that Manston was being bombed and they hurried to intercept the bombers but arrived too late to prevent Manston being

Unknown, Obltn. Gustav Sprick, Obltn. Klaus Mietusch and Obltn. Heinz Ebeling. All holders of the Knights Cross

savagely mauled. With a huge pall of smoke and dust hanging over Manston they were ordered to return to RAF Rochford where eleven Spitfires landed safely. Pyman flew back later in another aircraft.

Meanwhile the twelve Hurricanes of 32 Squadron that had left Biggin Hill to intercept Raid 34 were patrolling over Hawkinge when they encountered the full force of the Me 109s of the II Gruppe of JG 26, under the command of Hauptman Karl Ebbighausen. Already an ace, he now added to his total but was killed two days later when he was shot down into the Channel, probably by a Spitfire of 266 Squadron.

Some of the Me 109s had black crosses on yellow roundels on the wing tips but others carried dark camouflage similar to a Hurricane that made identification difficult in the heat of battle. However a flying boat was easily recognisable, and Pilot Officer John Proctor chased one out to sea but was set upon by a lone Me 109 although he did manage a shot at it in return. And Sgt Higgins who had gone to his aid was now busy fighting off the aggressive attention of two of the Me 109s that sported yellow roundels, but this brief engagement was at best a draw as neither side scored any positive hits.

By sheer weight of numbers the Hurricanes of 32 Squadron would be over-whelmed with three pilots having to make forced landings after being badly beaten up against only one victory, though this was a positive kill with the Me 109 crashing on land.

Pilot Officer Rupert Smythe leading Yellow Section had sighted nine Me 109s circling above and, ready to attack at about 16,000ft, he informed the squadron leader of their position and led his six Hurricanes into the fray. No sooner had they come into firing range than another group of Me 109s seemingly came out of nowhere and latched on to their rear, forcing the section to break up in confusion. Two of the enemy fighters were still in front of Smythe. He gave chase and caught them up just behind Dover and, closing in from 300ft down to 50ft, fired two bursts of three–four seconds at the one fixed in his sights. The weight of shells made it break up with shards of the frame flying in all directions. The pilot should have been killed but, as the Me 109 turned on its back and went down vertically, he was seen to bale out and, tumbling through the air, was pulled up sharply as his parachute billowed open.

Smythe now came under attack and with his glycol tank taking a hit he decided not to hang around and headed straight for the nearest cloud. The enemy lost him and he was able to make it to nearby Hawkinge aerodrome just as his engine started to catch fire.

Two other pilots of 32 Squadron were also in trouble with the 'Admiral' – Pilot Officer Anthony Barton, who had been in the navy – having to make a forced landing in his Hurricane at RAF Hawkinge, after coming off worst in a tussle with a couple of Me 109s. But though the fuselage was badly shot-up he managed to bring it down safely. The Hurricane of Pilot Officer Boleslaw Wlasnowoski – affectionately known as 'Vodka' – was in an equally dire condition after he had shunned the danger of too many Germans and taken too many hits. As his engine started to cough and splutter he took the plane quickly down to almost tree-top level looking for a landing place and force-landed in a level, fallow field near Dover. Though both planes were peppered with holes they were repaired to flying condition, but neither pilot saw out the war. The brave Wlasnowoski was shot down and killed over Portsmouth on 1 November 1940, and Barton died when his Spitfire collided with that of Sgt Charles Hamilton on the runway at RAF Llandow on 4 April 1943.

As the 1st Staffel of JG 26 took off from its base at Audembert, near Wissant, to provide fighter protection for a mass of Stukas heading for targets in the Dover area, Feldwebel Gerhard Kemen was one of the last to take to the air. Flying as wingman to Lt Eberhard Henrici, they circled at about 10,000ft awaiting the arrival of the dive-bombers and then, with everyone in position, set out in a tight formation with their unit bringing up the rear. Sited at the far end of the formation, Henrici and Kemen were in reality covering the escorting fighters and when they saw four or five Hurricanes approaching fast they headed straight at them to break up their attack.

Taken by surprise, the Hurricanes briefly scattered and Kemen came up behind one and opened fire but at that moment his plane was shattered by a volley from the guns of Smythe who had opened up at point blank range. Bullets whistled through the cramped cockpit and a stray one hit him in the back opening up a gaping hole just below the shoulder blade and, as blood gushed from the wound, he momentarily passed out with the pain. He was only unconscious for a few seconds and coming to his only thought was to bale out but his hands were cov-

Unterofficier Gerhard Kemen (on left) of
I / JG 26 with an unknown airman. This
photograph was taken a few days before
being posted to France in 1940

ered in oil and it was a struggle to operate the emergency canopy release. With
the aircraft spinning out of control he almost passed out again but somehow his
sticky hands managed to unbuckle the shoulder harness from the seat and with a
whoosh he shot straight out of the inverted plane.

Tumbling through the air he passed out again but he came to his senses just
long enough to pull the parachute release. He had a brief moment of panic just
before the parachute opened but he passed out again and remembers nothing
further as he slowly drifted to earth. No memory of hitting the ground, or of
being picked up by farm labourers and carried on a hurdle to a road before being
transported to a hospital in nearby Dover.

The first thing that confronted him after waking from a life-saving operation
was the sight of stern-faced 'English' soldiers guarding his bed. How they thought
he could escape in his weak condition was puzzling but they said little and did
not hinder the hospital staff when they changed his dressing and cleaned the
wounds. He was grateful for the treatment he received, which he thought was
unusually caring given that he was the enemy. He wondered if other POWs also
receive such sympathetic care.

After about two weeks he was taken to the Royal Herbert Hospital in
Woolwich where he spent many more weeks with other wounded Germans
who were also recuperating from their injuries. It was early winter before the
hospital authorities thought he was sufficiently well to be sent to a POW camp
and, after spending Christmas 1940 in the camp at Oldham, he learned that he
was going to be shipped to Canada. Despite protesting that he was in no fit state

for such a journey, in January 1941 he (with another 1,100 detainees) was herded aboard a transport ship, bound for the POW camp Espaniola near the American border For him the war was definitely over. Well not quite.

Well over two years later he was still suffering the after effects of his injuries and, in June 1943, after being examined by an International Medical Commission he was deemed unfit for further military service and listed for repatriation to German via Sweden. This was to be the first exchange of wounded German and British soldiers, and he was overjoyed to be selected as one of the first *heinke-hrer* (home-goers). The exchange was conducted on a one-for-one basis and was overseen by the Red Cross in October 1943.

After spending just four weeks on home leave he was sent to the Luftwaffe hospital in Braunschweig where, for the next four to five months he received intensive medical treatment that eventually enabled him to recommence military duties, though he was not quite fit enough for flying. In about the middle of 1944 he then took part in a three-month technical officer course, after which he was posted to a fighter squadron that was being reformed at Perleberg/Ludwigslust near the north coast of Germany, to the east of the Hamburg, where he was actively involved in technical support.

In March and April 1945 the unit was equipped with Me 109Gs and was capable of carrying out strafing attacks against the Russian trucks and forward units that gingerly weaved their way through the rubble-strewn, pitted roads. Each plane was also equipped with a single 250 or 500kg bomb, and they were launched as attack after attack was carried out to try and stem the tide of the advanced tank units that were now closing relentlessly on Berlin.

Shortage of fuel and the loss of experienced pilots were seriously curtailing their operations, and anyone who could fly a plane was press ganged into service and, for the first time in almost five years, Kemen was once again in the air and flying against the enemy. To fly over Berlin against the swarms of Russian planes and concentrated ground fire was almost suicidal but Kemen had no hesitation in

Unterofficier Gerhard Kemen – centre back – in convalescence hospital after being repatriated back to Germany in 1943

Left: Kemen with his brothers in 1943 after repatriation. Both were later killed in Russia. Right: With his brother and his future wife Doris in between them. Other girl unknown

reporting for duty.

The Me 109G-10 he was to fly was not too different from the 109E that he had baled out of back in 1940. However it was much faster, being capable of 425mph, and had a 'Galland' hood, but after familiarising himself with the controls and receiving some rudimentary instructions he was confident he could handle the aircraft. And anyway it was good to be flying again, no matter what the danger.

Flying over the front to attack the tank formations congregating on the outskirts of Berlin, he saw flames and dust shooting up into the air from the burning buildings and exploding shells from the Russian guns. The dark pall of smoke that hung over the city was a navigational beacon that could be seen for miles.

Kemen was only able to fly some five combat missions before the severe shortage of serviceable aircraft curtailed the unit's operations but, during one of these sorties over Berlin, he was to claim his one and only victory of the war. A Russian reconnaissance plane – probably a Po-2 – that was acting as a spotter for the Russian howitzers was sighted over the battlefield and promptly shot down in flames.

Down to its last reserves of fuel and with only a few serviceable planes remaining, the unit moved on 2 May 1945 from Ludwigslust to the relative safety of the Schleswig-Holstein area of northern Germany. Kemen and another pilot requisitioned a two-seater Arado 96 for the flight up to Flensburg on the Danish border where the remnants of other Luftwaffe units were gathering, with the remaining airmen of the still formable JG 26 who flew their last combat patrol on 4 May 1945, only minutes before the Germany forces in the north east surrendered.

On 6 May 1945 Flensburg airfield was turned over to the RAF and the Luftwaffe personnel and other servicemen were marched into a temporary POW camp set up by the British where, briefly, Kemen was allowed to keep his pistol. However, his time in the camp was short because, by the end of July 1945, he was discharged and on his way to Austria to be reunited with his wife and eight-

Officers of JG 26 in Bowmanville POW Camp in Canada. Left to right: (standing): Lt W. Fronhofer, Obltn. H. Brucks, Obltn. H-W Regenauer, Hptmn G. Beyer, Obltn. E. Axthelm (JG 27), Obltn. H. Ebeling, Obltn. H. Christennecke. Sitting: Obltn. H. Krug, Hpm. R. Pringel, Obltn. W. Bartels

month-old son. By Christmas they would be back home in Cologne where he continued to live and prosper. But his wartime injuries continued to plague him for the rest of his life and he was forever haunted by the memory of his three brothers who did not survive the war, having fallen on the Russian Front.

The victory claims of both the Luftwaffe and the RAF during the hour-long air battle over Dover are difficult to verify with any great accuracy, but the sinking of the Goodwin Lightship and the almost leisurely shooting down of eight barrage balloons suggests that the Luftwaffe had considerable freedom of action during that midday conflict. Eleven pilots of JG 26 made victory claims and, in addition to the claims submitted by Galland and Muncheberg, the claims made by five other pilots from the III Gruppe would push the pilots under Galland's command to the top of the victory list.

Of the five other successful pilots, Obltn. George Beyer and Lt Josef Burschgens would, within a few weeks, be shot down and taken prisoner and Lt Gerhard Muller-Duhe would be dead within four days. Fw. Konrad Carl recovered from being wounded on the last day of September but is believed to have been killed in action in 1941. Only the leader of the 9th Staffel Oblt, Gerhard Schopfel, with a total of forty-three victories, saw out the war's end with the Luftwaffe.

Of the four remaining claims, one was registered by Obltn. Franz Horning the Staffel Kapitan of the 1st Staffel who claimed to have shot down a Spitfire at 12.20 hours during combat over Dover when he was flying close support to the Stukas. It's possible that this was in fact the Hurricane flown by Rupert Smythe that was attacked from behind and seriously damaged after he had shot down Kemen, but this cannot be established with any great certainty. This was Horning's one and only victory with JG 26 as, on 18 August 1940, he was transferred out of the unit.

Hptmn Karl Ebbinghausen, the leader of the II Gruppe and Lt Hans Krug of the 4th Staffel, both claimed to have destroyed a Spitfire during this engagement as well as Fw. Wilhelm Muller of the 3rd Staffel who, on this day, would become an ace with five victories and eventually reach a total of ten kills before being shot down over the Thames Estuary at the beginning of November. His body was never recovered. And just two days later on 16 August, Ebbinghausen was leading the II Gruppe in a sweep over the same area at roughly the same time when they were bounced by a squadron of Spitfires. He was never seen again.

Krug was a bit more fortunate when, on 7 September, he was forced to land his Me 109E-4 after its cooling system had been shattered during combat over the Weald of Kent. He had been escorting bombers back from the first great daylight raid on London when he was attacked and his damaged plane came down near a farm at Puckley, about 5 miles west of Ashford in Kent. Shipped to Canada with the other POWs, he broke out of the camp at Bowmanville and made it to New York after first dining out in a restaurant in Detroit. With money provided by German sympathisers, he travelled all the way down to San Antonio only to be captured while waiting to cross the border to neutral Mexico.

During this midday air battle two RAF pilots were killed and two wounded and ten aircraft – possibly eleven – were lost or damaged. Two were lost in the sea, one was a complete write-off but the remaining seven were repaired to flying

Uffz. Karl Flebbe of 8/JG 3. Ofw. Erich Labusga of 6/JG 3

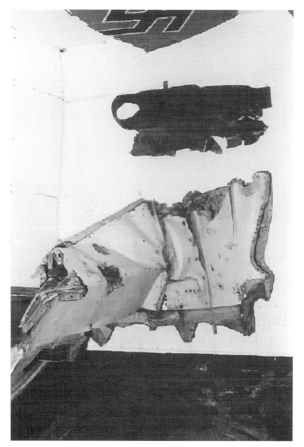

Some of the remains of
Gerhard Kemen's Me 109.
Photograph taken at Chilham
Castle about 1975

Major Adolph Galland debriefs pilots of the III Gruppe on 14 August 1940 From second left:
unknown, G. Schopfel, G. Beyer, G. Muller-Duhe, J. Burschgens, A. Galland, H. Christinnecke,
G. Sprick, J. Muncheberg, then three unknown staff officers. (Photograph: H. Ebeling)

condition, even if some were later downgraded to the training units. The actual RAF losses correspond somewhat uncannily with the eleven victory claims made by JG 26, even though the German pilots claimed to have shot down eight Spitfires and only three Hurricanes. However, the RAF claims however do not tally up.

During this conflict the Luftwaffe only lost one fighter, with one Ju 87 dive-bomber down and another badly damaged, and suffered a slightly mangled twin-engine fighter but the RAF claimed to have shot down seven Me 109s, six Stukas, one Me 110 and a He 113 that was shot down into the sea. The latter 'propaganda plane', more commonly known as an He 100, would never be seen in the skies over Britain.

In addition several enemy planes were listed as probable kills, with two Me 109s and two Stukas possibly shot down, and they also claimed to have damaged at least six others during the mêlée. In all it was a fruitful, if somewhat over-optimistic, day for the RAF while, in addition to the two losses suffered by JG 26 and LG 1, two other fighters were also lost by the Luftwaffe. It seems that some of the Me 109s of JG 3 had strayed into edges of the fray and, in their brief engagement with the RAF, they suffered two casualties.

While on patrol over Dover and Folkestone, Uffz. Karl Flebbe, flying as the third man in a *Kette* led by the Staffelkapitan of the 8th Staffel Oberleutnant Stange, was surprised by the sudden appearance of thirteen Spitfires, and they quickly turned about and fled back across the water towards France and safety. But Flebbe, flying at the rear of the trio, was overhauled before he could reach the coast and, under a ferocious attack from behind, his aircraft was shredded taking hit after hit that completely disabled it, plunging him into the sea.

Though wounded Flebbe managed to parachute down into the cold water but because of the severity of his wounds, he died – possibly drowned – before he was picked up by a German rescue boat. His body was brought ashore and he was buried with full military honours in the German cemetery in Calais on 16 August 1940.

Born in Bantorff Kreis, near Hanover, he was just twenty-five years old and he left behind grieving parents, a younger brother Heinrich and younger sister Anna. In 1962 his body was disinterred and today he lies buried in the German military cemetery in Bourdon/Somme.

Also around midday, the 6th Staffel of JG 3 was on a free chase over the Channel operating as far as the coast of southern England, but they did not seem to have made contact with the British. But on landing back at base Ofw. Erich Labusga was missing though no one had seen his plane go down. His disappearance is shrouded in mystery and it is possible that when the unit was returning to Calais his plane was caught from behind and shot down by a lone RAF fighter. But it's equally possible, and more likely, that when flying low over the Channel his aircraft suffered sudden engine failure and spun into the sea before he could extradite himself from the cockpit and take to his parachute. His body was never recovered or washed ashore, and he has no known grave except the sea.

Erich was born on 19 August 1911 in Hohenwestedt and, just five days short of his twenty-ninth birthday, was somewhat old for a frontline fighter pilot. It may well have been that he was shortly to have been stood down from combat duties but death came first. We will never know.

After landing back at Caffiers the pilots of JG 26 added up the cost of the day's action and Galland was especially pleased with the performance of his III Gruppe. They had largely prevented the RAF fighters from getting amongst the Ju 87 dive-bombers and had suffered no casualties. They had downed at least seven enemy aircraft and, if they could continue to tempt the RAF into fighter-to-fighter con-frontations, he was confident that the German Air Force would soon be masters of the skies of southern England. The Spitfire was a tricky adversary but the Hurricane was proving no match for the Messerschmitt Bf 109E. They would continue to pro-vide good cover for the bomber formations so long as they were allowed freedom of movement and weren't tied to their coat tails. That the three-fighter Gruppen of JG 26 was needed to cover one Stuka Gruppe preceded Goring's directive of 15 August 1940, but Galland believed that such a tactic was a waste of their limited fighter resources and merely gave the initiative to the enemy.

Fighter Command had learned a lot from this engagement and now carefully looked after its fighters to avoid such bloody encounters as much as possible. It would only commit its fighters in such numbers in seemingly uneven combat when confronted by the sight of massed bomber formations ranging over Britain. And even then the Spitfires would concentrate on the fighters with the Hurricanes concentrating on the bombers, a tactic that worked well especially when Goring ordered his fighters to be chained to the bombers, seriously reduc-ing their effectiveness.

When in September the massed daylight raids were finally launched on London in an attempt to force the RAF to do battle, the Luftwaffe had been so drained of fighters and experienced pilots it proved too late for them dominate the war in the air. If such attacks had been launched in early August, the fighter arm of the RAF could have been so overwhelmed that the outcome of the Battle of Britain may well have been a lot different.

A.I.1. (K) Report No.259/1940
Place, Date & Time: Coldred (N. of Dover)   14.8.40   12.45 hrs
Type & Marks: Me.109 > + 8   Badge: Black German Eagle
Unit: 1 / JG 26
Identity Disc: Fliegerschule Gorlitz
Feldpostnummer: L.35464 – Munster
Ausweis: Red, issued at Furth on 14.5.40
Start & Mission: From near Calais, escorting bombers attacking aerodromes.
The engine No. of this aircraft was 1371, delivered 4.4.40.
The pilot is badly injured and is not expected to recover.
It appears that he came down on the tail of a Hurricane which looped above him,

The 'Running Man' emblem of 8th Staffel/JG 26   Flying Officer Peter Collard of 615,
                                                   killed in action 14 August 1940

Ofw. Josef Gardner in Me 109 displaying the Running Man emblem of 8/JG 26

Lt Gerhard Müller-Dühe of 7th Staffel/ JG 26 next to the Spitfire of Pilot Officer R. Roberts of 64 Squadron shot down on 15 August 1940. Müller-Dühe was shot down and killed on 18 August 1940 when his Bf 109 crashed at Chilham, Kent

Hptm Karl Ebbinghausen, Kr of II Gruppe of JG 26. He was killed in action on 16 August 1940

got on his tail and shot him down.

The pilot has recently been carrying out 3 sorties daily with every 4th day off.

The pilot is 20 years old, has been nearly three years in the GAF. The first year was spent in ordinary infantry training and the next one and three-quarter years at the Fliegerschule Gorlitz, after which he joined his operational unit.

Morale: Fair

Crew: Pilot ------- Uffz. Gerhard Kemen wounded

CHAPTER FOUR

KG 55 enters the Fray

Although the main bomber assault on Britain during the afternoon of 14 August 1940 was being orchestrated by *IV Fliegerkorps* using aircraft from LG 1 and KG 27, for some reason the III Gruppe of KG 55 of the *V Fliegerkorps*, based at Villacoublay south-west of Paris, also decided to enter the fray, sending out a token force of eleven Heinkel 111s against targets in the south-west of England. Setting out in two waves, with six aircraft taking-off at 15.30 hours and five aircraft at 16.45 hours, the last one was away at 16.50 hours heading for Netheravon.

Except for a *Kette* of three aircraft that set off on a long and hazardous journey to attack the Rolls-Royce engine factory at Crewe, the raiders were briefed to concentrate their efforts against the airfields clustered around Oxford, with a *Kette* designated to take out Bicester aerodrome and two lone raiders told to make nuisance attacks on the airfields at Abingdon and Brize Norton. The remaining three aircraft of the Stabsket1e would make rather shorter flights to bomb the hangars at Upavon and Netheravon, with one making a rather roundabout detour to attack the Fleet Air Arm training base at Worthy Down. The latter was an odd target at this stage of the air war but then none of the targets selected by KG 55 were being used by Fighter Command, and any destruction caused to these airfields would have had little, if any, effect on the RAF's plans for the air defence of Britain.

This odd choice of targets seem to have been made at the last minute without any great forethought or reconnaissance or intelligence flights being carried out, though *IV Fliegerkorps* did send out a stream of aircraft to report on the weather conditions over Britain. Ranging as far north as Liverpool, the planes were primarily to report on weather conditions prevailing over the Bristol Channel and along the English coast on a line running through Plymouth to Portsmouth, but they were also to reconnoitre shipping in the Bristol Channel and to observe any movement at the aerodromes of Warmwell, Yeovil, Boscombe Down, Andover and Netheravon. Did KG 55 make use of theses reports? It seems odd that they would not, and with the weather reports showing large banks of cloud hanging over most of the south west they could have decided to launch small bombing and reconnaissance missions that would also double as intelligence flights.

It is also possible that Oberst Alois Stoeckl, the Geschwader Kommodore of KG 55, wanted to check out for himself the problems of flying over England in daylight though it was a risky business for such a senior officer. He had been actively involved with the intelligence services since his time in Spain during the civil war when he was a liaison officer with the *Legion Condor* – the air arm of the German forces in Spain – and an intelligence-gathering flight, though dangerous, was probably irresistible.

Born in Bavaria on 22 August 1895, Stoeckl was just eight days short of his forty-fifth birthday on 14 August 1940, and was one of the oldest airmen to take an active part in the Battle of Britain, having served in the Great War with distinction in the air battles against the British in the Middle East. In 1917-18 he was in Turkey flying as an observer and believed he had once come up against the plane of 'Lawrence of Arabia'.

He married his wife Gertrud in 1922 and they had one child, a daughter Erna Maria. On 9 November 1923 he was involved in the failed Beer Hall Putsch in Munich when, as an adjutant reichschule in the para-military Bayrische Landespolizei, he was caught up in a street battle with Hitler's acolytes. However, this does not seem to have stopped his progress up the ladder because in 1928 he was a member of the military delegation in Amsterdam.

From 1935-38 he was stationed in Berlin at the Reichkreigsministerium in the Luftwaffe section of the office for counter-intelligence under Admiral Wilhelm Canaris. During 1936, at the beginning of the Spanish Civil War, he visited the country three times with Canaris for secret talks with Generalissimo Francisco Franco, the head of the Nationalist Army.

These initial discussions concerned the provision of air transport for Franco's troops, and a small force of cargo planes and a few outdated fighters were despatched to aid his battle against the largely communist Republican forces. This *ad hoc* air force would quickly evolve into the *Legion Condor* that became a significant factor in Franco's victory, and the Civil War was an invaluable 'testing ground' for the fledgling Luftwaffe.

During the next few years further covert visits were undertaken, even to the republican centre of Madrid before he left his desk job in Berlin at the same time as Canaris was promoted. And in 1938 he was back in an active role with the Luftwaffe when he took charge of the III Gruppe of KG 51 'Edelweiss'.

During his time with the Intelligence Service, he held the rank of major but was presumably promoted to the rank of Oberstleutnant when he was appointed Gruppen Kommandeur of III/KG 51. Certainly he had risen in rank to that of Oberst by the time he took over as Geschwaderkommodore of KG 55 in March 1940, prior to being awarded the Knights Cross on 14 July 1940.

Why he decided to lead such a small formation into battle on that August afternoon is something of a mystery. After spending three days on leave in Berlin, Oberstleutnant Hans Korte took over control of KG 55, on returning to Villacoublay, as the new Kommodore, and was aghast to hear from Major Ernest Kuhl, the units Operations Officer, that Stoeckl had flown to Bournemouth in broad daylight on 'a

A *Kette* (three aircraft) of Heinkel He.111Ps of KG.55 heading for England. (Photograph: Hans Tuffers)

clear and lovely day' for a jaunt to have a look around. He couldn't understand how Stoeckl could have been so completely and utterly negligent.

But on board Stoeckl's Heinkel He 111P (G1+AA) there was also another very senior officer, Oberst i.G. Walter Frank, the Chief of Staff of the *V Fliegerkorps*, who might well have had something to do with this dangerous adventure. His role in the aircraft was said to be that of air gunner but it's doubtful whether he took this duty seriously. Only a few days earlier he had pressurised Stoeckl to find him a place on a night flight to England, and Lt Hans Tuffers of the 8th Staffel was amazed to receive a phone call from Stoeckl ordering him to take Frank on a bombing raid to Liverpool.

He had been taken on as an air gunner but insisted on sitting in the observer's seat throughout the journey. Being a big, tall man like Stoeckl, his presence in the cramped front section during the bombing run made it very difficult for them to release the bombs over the target. Tuffers was angry, biting his lip, but he knew better than to question the actions of such a high-ranking officer, especially a fifty-year-old ex-army officer who didn't even hold a pilots licence. Any criticism could easily spell trouble for an aspiring airman. But on hearing of the demise of G1+AA and its crew, Tuffers was one of the few pilots not to be surprised that Frank had hitched a ride aboard the aircraft.

For his personal pilot, Stoeckl had chosen the Geschwader's navigation officer Obltn. Bruno Brossler, an experienced twenty-nine year old who had distinguished himself during the Polish Campaign and in the attacks on allied positions during the *Blitzkreig* of May and June 1940, when they had also pummelled the British Expeditionary Force and its allies on the beaches at Dunkirk.

Major Alois Stoeckl (left) with Admiral Canaris in Spain in 1936. (Photograph: Erna Maria
Puttfarken)

Both Stoeckl and Frank, like most of the older officers coming from the army,
only held an observer's licence though it seems that Stoekl did obtain a pilot's
licence sometime in 1936 when he was back in Berlin. He no doubt took over
the duties of an observer or bomb-aimer on board the aircraft with Frank's role,
once again, downgraded to that of air gunner. But he was no gunner and spent
nearly all his time in the forward section of the plane standing behind the pilot
and observer taking photographs through the glazed nose-cone with his state-of-
the-art Leica camera. Stoeckl, similarly equipped, was also clicking away at every
opportunity.

At least Brossler was able to retain the services of two of his usual crew who
had been with him virtually since the start of hostilities in 1939 and as Feldwebel
Heinz Grimstein, the radio operator, took up his seat beneath the ring mounted
dorsal MG 15 machine-gun and the flight mechanic Feldwebel Jonny Thiel
dropped down into his position manning the gun in the 'bola' slung beneath the
Heinkel, he started up the engines.

Roaring down the runway they were quickly airborne as they had taken on
board only half the normal bomb load for what in reality was little more than a
scouting mission, but they reckoned that the two 250kg 'Flambos' (oil bombs)
and four 50kg bombs would be enough to let them have some fun and shake up
an unsuspecting airfield.

The target map and photograph of Upavon aerodrome, showing the hangars
to be bombed, was passed around for everyone to study with a photograph of
their secondary target Netheravon. After assembling over Paris, the small forma-

Oberst Alois Stoeckl –
Geschwaderkommodore of KG 55.
(Photograph: Erna Puttfarken)

Oberleutnant Bruno Brossler. (Photograph:
Karl-Eugen Brossler)

tion split up over the Channel but the Stabskette stayed close together and, after crossing the coast, Villacoublay received a signal from them at 17.30 hours as they headed inland.

Neither Upavon nor Netheravon were the home of active fighter squadrons. The latter hosted both RAF and Fleet Air Arm training units and had Harvards and Hawker biplanes but no local defence flight and presented no real danger to the raiders, while Upavon, sitting on a slight hill surrounded by open countryside, was an easily recognisable target.

The airfields were less than 5 miles apart and, with both being used for pilot training, there was often a certain amount of interaction between the two but they didn't expect to be the focus of a joint Luftwaffe raid. Though a simultaneous attack should probably have been expected there was in reality very little they could offer in the way of defence.

However the fighter aerodrome of Middle Wallop was only 15 miles away and, having just been attacked by the Ju 88 dive-bombers of LG 1, the Spitfires of 609 Squadron and the Blenheims of 604 Squadron were already up and flying in a defensive circle over their home base. They were now joined in the air by the Spitfires of 234 Squadron that had flown in from St Eval to swap duties with the Hurricanes of 238 Squadron. Two full Spitfire squadrons were therefore patrolling Boscombe Down and Salisbury Plain, covering Middle Wallop aerodrome and the nearby RAF stations from Luftwaffe attack.

If Stoeckl had liaised with the other units of Luftflotte 2 he would have been aware of the danger that awaited them, and he would certainly have known that

Fw. Jonny Thiel (left) and Fw. Heinz Grimstein alongside Heinkel 111P (G1+AA). (Photograph: M. Thiel)

the Ju 88s of LG 1 had already passed this way and alerted the RAF, and that the Heinkels of KG 27 would also be occupying the same air space. Though such a large scattering of aircraft was confusing the defenders, the Stabskette was heading perilously close to this defensive ring and would be lucky not to be caught by the RAF fighter planes that were already on their toes having been woken up by the earlier inbound *Schnellbombers* of LG 1. Though they didn't know it, not every thing was working against them. As well as the safety of a heavy band of cloud from 10,000–15,000ft, with ten-tenths cloud at 12,000ft there were a couple of things in their favour that might just see them safely through.

Owing to a technical problem the radio was out of action and, with no co-ordination possible, the pilots of 234 Squadron had lost contact with one another and were forced to forage on their own. By concentrating their return fire the gunners in the three bombers of the Stabskette could well see off any lone fighter attacking them from the rear. They did not know it but luck was also with them because 609 Squadron, having spent so long in the air, would shortly have to land and refuel. There was hope for a clear passage towards their target.

But as they relentlessly closed on their target one of the motors of Stoeckl's aircraft started to splutter and misfire and he ordered Brossler to abort the mission and head back to base. Banking around in a wide arc Brossler pointed the Heinkel south for home, accompanied by the other two aircraft of the Stabskette.

'Where was everybody?' Sgt Mike Boddington thought as he patrolled the empty sky above Middle Wallop? Where was the rest of 234 Squadron? Flying as Blue 2 where was Blue 1? He was completely alone in a sky that should have been full of Spitfires and perhaps he had flown too far west of the defensive patrol

Mike Boddington (right) enjoying a drink in a bar in Beirut later in the war. (Photograph: M.A. Boddington)

line. He was on the point of wheeling back around when at about 17,000ft he sighted below him an enemy bomber, which he incorrectly recognised as Ju 88, speeding just above the tops of the clouds at about 15,000ft.

Turning to attack from out of the sun, he closed in to open fire but in doing so he was spotted by the rear gunner in the top turret who opened up from about 1,200ft with a quick burst from his MG 15 machine-gun. There was a short lull and then another quick burst as the gunner hurriedly changed the magazine. Ignoring the return fire, Boddington closed to within a suicidal distance of 150ft and let rip with a continuous burst of 15 seconds expending all 2,640 rounds in one do or die blast. From such a short range the sheer volume of bullets shattered the bomber and, as the first volley hit home, the enemy gun fell silent.

The broadside blew ugly gaping holes in the fuselage and with the hydraulics shot away first one undercarriage leg came down and then the second wheel dropped, and as the ferocious fusillade continued large chunks of metal were seen to fly off in all directions from every section of the bomber. Bullets were ricocheting off it at all angles and, in a last, desperate attempt to shake off its persistent attacker, the damaged bomber went into a sharp steep dive and, with thick grey smoke billowing from a fire that had broken out in the fuselage, it headed for the oblivion of the clouds where it was lost from sight. Boddington plunged his Spitfire into the clouds determined not to lose the bandit and, as it emerged from the murk, he followed it down from a relatively safe distance of 60ft. The rear gunner might have some life in him yet.

The Spitfires of 609 Squadron hadn't been idle either. Only minutes earlier Flying Officer John Dundas had tangled with a box formation of enemy aircraft

Flying Officer John Dundas, second from left. (Photograph: Chris Goss)

that he had wrongly identified as Dornier Do 17s and had set about the nearest one, firing off a couple of quick shots. He must have struck home as it broke away and dived into the clouds. He attempted to follow it down but lost it in the heavy cloud barrier at 10,000ft.

Flying back up into the clear blue sky he literally stumbled upon a lone Heinkel 111P, which he also wrongly identified as a Ju 88, that was heading south about 3 miles west of their base. He could see that it was already badly shot-up and, from somewhere, a few shots whistled past him. His aircraft wobbled slightly but his instruments held up and he didn't seem to have been hit. Pressing home his attack he saw its undercarriage come down and, closing from dead astern, he fired off the rest of his ammunition into the starboard engine which ignited with a puff of black smoke. Dundas followed it down oblivious of the other Spitfire also tracking its progress. Keeping it in sight he saw it crash and break up in the Royal Naval munitions dump about 5 miles south-west of Middle Wallop aerodrome.

On returning to base he learnt that Flt Lt James McArthur has also witnessed the crash but, as it had already been damaged before his attack, Dundas only claimed a share of the kill. And that wobble could have been serious. His Spitfire had taken a couple hits in the airscrew and there were several bullet holes in the main spar. The Spitfire was fresh off the production line and had only been received by the squadron the previous day, and they could ill afford the loss of R6961. Repaired at the station, it continued to fly for most of the war, albeit mostly with Operational Training Units.

Though Mike Boddington wrote in his combat report that he had bagged a Ju 88 during the afternoon of 14 August 1940, this recognition error would soon be rectified and in his logbook he entered that he had destroyed a Heinkel

Heinkels 111P (G1+GT) and (G1+FT) part of a *Kette* flying over England. (Photograph: H. Tuffers)

He 111. This was accepted by all those involved as he received from the employees of Melville, Dundas and Whitson Ltd, RNA Depot, West Dean, Wiltshire, a beautifully engraved silver cigarette box bearing his inscribed signature in the left-hand corner and worded:

A MEMENTO OF YOUR FIRST HUN
A NICE, FAT, BOMB LADEN HEINKEL
WHICH YOU SHOT DOWN AT WEST DEAN
ON THE AFTERNOON OF AUGUST 14th 1940.

Michael Christopher Bindloss Boddington, commonly known as 'Bodd' or 'Scruffy', was awarded the DFM and, after being commissioned in October 1940, he helped to set up 118 Fighter Squadron that was being formed at RAF Filton in 1941. Subsequently awarded the DFC, he rose to the rank of squadron leader and saw out the war after tours in North Africa and Italy. He left the RAF in 1946 and retired to his home in Ambleside, in the Lake District, passing away in 1977.

But what of the the three Heinkels of the Stabskette? For some inexplicable reason they had drifted apart as they commenced their turn for home, and Stoeckl's bomber on the edge of the small formation was the one to come under a continuous and ferocious attack. The first attacker was Boddington, and then Dundas, because what they had thought was a Junkers Ju 88 was in fact Heinkel 111P (G1+AA) with two senior Luftwaffe commanders, Stoeckl and Frank. Their loss would be a serious blow to the moral and operational capability of KG 55 and *V Fliegerkorps* and later result in a direct order from Goering forbidding such senior officers from flying together on combat missions.

As he flew out of the clouds, Brossler could see that except for a low ridge there was not a lot of open countryside below and lining up the dying bomber on a large meadow that ran alongside the road he prepared to make a crash-landing. Though shot three times in the stomach and losing blood he still managed to make a controlled descent and, as it sped low over the crest of Dean Hill, the roar of engines caused Mr and Mrs Parsons to fling themselves to the ground in utter panic. Out for a stroll on mild summer's evening the last thing they expected was a German plane making a crash-landing. They had a good vantage point on the hill and, after pulling their faces out of the earth, they watched as the Heinkel half-spun around and crashed in the long field on the south side of the road between Head's Farm and East Dean church, breaking itself in two.

Winnie Reynolds who ran the local post office at West Dean had just closed up shop for the day and was talking with a few friends on the doorstep when she was startled by the rattle of machine-gun fire overhead. High in the sky she could just make out that two fighters had singled out a bomber and, like crows harrying a buzzard, were forcing it lower in the air with each attack. As it came down low it seemed to Winnie that it was attempting to make a landing on the road that ran alongside the new RNA Depot at East Dean and, as it hit the ground, she joined the rush of villagers that were heading in the direction of the crash. A German national, she had escaped interment having been married to an Englishman. Though her fluent German might have been of use had any airmen survived, no one sought her out and she tactfully realised it was not a good time to remind the locals of her German credentials.

As the plane had swept in over Dean Hill with its engines crackling and coughing, an airman was seen to bale out but his parachute failed to open and he was killed on striking the hillside near the road that ran over the hill, close to the ammunition dump. The crumpled body with its legs and arm joints distorted like a badly battered rag doll was Oberst Walter Frank. The carmine-red collar patches on his uniform indicated that he was someone of importance. The corpse was covered in a blanket before being brought down from the hill and laid out on the grass, after which the military took it away to inspect the contents of the pockets.

Whether Brossler was actually trying to land the Heinkel on a road seems doubtful, but with its undercarriage dangling down many observers believed this was the case. There was a double alert at the time and some of the civilian workforce who were building the Royal Naval Depot had taken cover behind a stack of old railway sleepers. As they heard the rat-tat-tat of machine-gun fire overhead they saw a twin-engine plane, which they took to be a German bomber, being harassed by two fighters, and as it sunk lower and lower in the air, and its undercarriage came down, they thought it was attempting to land on the service road inside the depot. Barely clearing the trees, it flew between two buildings and appeared to be heading straight for the loading shed where some of their fellow workers had taken shelter before dashing out in a complete panic.

It seems that Brossler, even in his hideously shot-up state, had picked out the long green meadow for the forced landing. But a collision was waiting to happen.

Colonel William Ashley Nicholls, DSO.
(Photograph: Mrs D. Watkins)

Mr MacLeod, a civil engineer employed by the main building contractors Melville, Dundas & Whitson, was stunned to see out of the side window of his car a huge flying machine heading straight at him and instinctively he opened the door and rolled out onto the grass verge. It was a wise move because the Heinkel smashed through a fence and coming straight at him clipped the top of the car ripping off the roof like a giant tin opener. MacLeod dazed and dirty and covered in chalk dust cursed the loss of his beloved Volkswagen but, looking around at the surrounding devastation, was more than a little relieved to have survived this unexpected ordeal.

Bouncing off the top of the car, the Heinkel hit the ground hard and as it bounced again it lost an engine and bust a wing before slewing around as it skidded across the meadow and ploughed into a huge pile of chalk, which had recently been dug out of a deep trench, sending up a shower of dirt and dust. As it came sharply to rest a wheel broke off that bounced high in the air and ended up in the vegetable garden of East Dean Manor, the home of Colonel William Nicholls and his family located on the other side of the Romsey road. The Heinkel had flipped over and snapped in two just behind the wings, and the bombs were visible still in their racks. One wing had split open exposing the fuel tanks but as the angry villagers, some armed with pitchforks, raced to the scene they were unaware of the danger from the unexploded bombs and the extremely volatile aviation fuel. The still smouldering Heinkel could explode at any minute; even a slight leak from the ruptured tanks could spell disaster.

Colonel Nicholls, an officer in the Home Guard, his wife Hilda Evelyn and 'Nanny' their housekeeper were among the first on the scene. The women were younger and fitter and rushed across the road and up to the meadow where they quickly and quietly took control of the situation. Nicholls followed with a loaded shotgun to make sure that the villagers did not get out of hand and rough up any surviving German airmen.

Feelings were running high as a result of the bombing of Southampton and Portsmouth, and striding purposely forward with the shotgun under his arm he hoped that the villagers would think twice about seeking retribution. A veteran of the First World War, where he had served with distinction in the Royal Artillery and been awarded the DSO, he felt honour bound to ensure that any POWs be treated in a fair and civilised manner.

Much to his disappointment, their twelve-year-old son William – who later won the DFC in Korea – was told to stay behind in the manor house but he did manage to keep an eye on the coming and goings from a bedroom window and the front garden. Spent ammunition had rained down over West and East Dean, and it was eagerly sort after by the village children as souvenirs to be traded in class when the new term started in September.

However, the adults were after more tangible relics and, although Colonel Nicholls kept a watchful eye, some artefacts still managed to go walkabout including the maps and aerial photographs. From his vantage point William kept note of those responsible for the looting and, although he kept this information to himself, most of the pilfered artefacts were recovered by the police. Still, he managed to get a good look at one of the German maps that seemed to pinpoint the manor house. And even though the wreckage was put under guard during the days that followed, there was occasionally a relaxation in the surveillance and William managed to poke about inside the wreckage resisting the temptation to liberate some of the cockpit instruments.

In the moments following the crash, though, his father galvanised the villagers and nearby workmen into an *ad hoc* work party and they picked their way through the scattered wreckage into the shattered nose-cone to search for any possible survivors. Three of the crew – all horribly wounded and barely alive – were brought out and laid gently on the grass.

One was in such a terrible state that it seemed that every bone in his body was broken and that he'd die at any moment. This was probably Stoeckl because he was wearing two – some thought three – Iron Crosses. Brossler had also been badly mangled in the crash and there was no hope for him. Oozing blood from his many wounds, he died in the ambulance on the way to hospital. And Jonny Thiel who had a bullet wound to his head with his right hand shot to pieces, had passed out prior to the impact and was revived by the colonel who poured his last drop of brandy down his throat. As he came to he made a move to surrender his pistol but the colonel, thinking this was an act of aggression, put his foot on his arm to stop him. The colonel then asked him with his smattering of German, learnt in the First World War, if there were any bombs on board to which Thiel, either confused or misunderstanding, said with apparent honesty that they had all been unloaded over Middle Wallop.

Left: Mrs Hilda Evelyn 'Evie' Nicholls. Right: William Nicholls – a scout member in 1939.
(Photographs: Mrs Denise Watkins)

Mrs Nicholls then treated the injured airmen as best she could but the wounds were way beyond her training, and she tried to make them comfortable with the blankets and pillows brought over from the Manor House. Then one of the work-men thought he heard a sound from inside the plane and they scrambled through the wreckage to the upper gun position and brought out a fourth crew member, who was in a pitiful condition covered in blood and grime but still conscious though barely coherent. Shot full of holes and with his face in a mess, Heinz Grimstein should have been dead but he defiantly clung onto life.

Peter Johnson, a bright, good-looking young medical student, was spending the summer holidays at home in Romsey and, unusually for him, was idling the day away doing nothing in particular. Normally he'd spend the morning picking fruit in the orchard or gathering up some vegetables before playing tennis in the afternoon if he was not wanted at the Hospital Supply Depot run by his mother, a trainee nurse. So when the call was received that a German bomber, full of wounded airmen, had been brought down at East Dean, Peter scrambled aboard the ambulance and squeezed between his mother and the driver.

As they approached the entrance to the Naval Depot they were waved in by the sentry and Peter could sense the angry mood of the villagers who were mill-ing around the wreckage and gawping at the horribly injured airmen. It was whispered to him that the Germans had continued to spray the ground with machine-gun fire right up to the moment that their plane had crash-landed, and that some of the villagers would have gladly pitch-forked the crew if they had

Peter Johnson as an officer in the RAMC
later in the war. (Photograph: Dr P.
Johnson)

had the chance. But the authorities were now well in charge of the situation and,
clearing a path through the crowd, they helped load the wounded fliers into the
back of the clean, worn out ambulance.

During the long, bumpy drive to Romsey Hospital his mother tried to make
the airman who was moaning loudly a bit more comfortable and in doing so
discovered a Luger pistol in his clothing. Peter eyed it as a souvenir and so did the
driver but being a stickler for protocol she handed it to the police at the hospital.

The operating room had already been prepared and the surgeon and anaesthet-
ist were cleaning themselves, awaiting the aairman. The Matron, Miss Jackson,
took the Theatre, with Peter Johnson their eager assistant. As was the fashion at
the time, the wounds were debrided but what followed is best left to the harrowing entry in Peter's diary for 14 August.

14 AUGUST, 1940
WEDNESDAY

Up as usual this morning and did a number of odd jobs. There were several warn-
ings today, and at the all-clear at 6.30, about, the mobile unit was called out to
Dean Hill. I went to Rankin's. A large bomber had been brought down. 3 dead, 2
wounded. I have never seen such a mess, bits were scattered yards around. The fuselage was upside down. How anyone survived can't imagine, the corpses were very
unreal, since they had such a lot of thick clothes on, they looked like dummies, with
extra joints for they had many fractures. An enormous crowd there, military, police,

ARPs and civilians. Eventually they were taken to Romsey and I to help undress – clothes had to be cut off them. Purvis [the surgeon] arrived and we took them into the theatre. Bullet wounds all over the place, in abdomen wall, but no penetration, and many others. Also penetrating main wound just in front of ear. Had to do side compression, the other chap has all his wrist joints exposed and the end of his radius ulna completely smashed. Tendons were sutured and the whole bandaged. Also a Potts fracture which could not be dealt with. About a dozen holes including a huge face gash. I put a drip on the latter, much to my great delight, and then came back to bed at 1.45. Very tired but couldn't sleep at first. All so ghastly.

Once the lifesaving operations had been carried out, the patched-up airmen were wheeled into a private ward away from the other patients where a solitary local policeman, sitting between them, was the only one responsible for their safety. In fact they were so badly wounded that the military dispensed with the normal two armed men, though the policeman did carry his Webley pistol.

Purvis had merely carried out a running repair on the perforated gut of Grimstein to stabilise his condition and, the following day, he was sent for further treatment to the Royal Hants Hospital. Thiel with his right hand shot to pieces, remained at Romsey for a few more days and was forever thankful for the kindness shown to him by a sympathetic nurse and for the cigarettes she lit for him. He never knew her name but would always remember her when recounting his days in captivity.

Feldw Jonny Thiel (centre) in the POW Camp at Oldham. (Photograph: Frau M. Thiel)

Reading/Common Room in the POW camp at Oldham. (Photograph: Frau M.Thiel)

Both received further intensive medical care during the following weeks and their injuries were so serious that they spent their first Christmas in England not in a POW camp but in a comfortable bed in a British hospital. Nor could they be included amongst the POWs, mostly airmen and sailors, who assembled at the docks in Glasgow on a cold January morning in 1941 to be ferried to the *Duchess of York,* anchored out in the bay, and a long journey to Canada. Instead they were eventually discharged, after many months of treatment, and ended up in the POW camp for enlisted men at Oldham on the outskirts of Manchester. They almost became the longest-serving men in the camp that, to their surprise, was not as spartan as they'd expected, having decent facilities and accommodation. There was initially no overcrowding, though that changed with the arrival of the captured soldiers of the Afrika Korps before they, too, were shipped to Canada.

Grimstein and Thiel thought they were lucky to remain behind in England, though the menu was routinely dull, unlike the more adventurous and more ample food served up in the Canadian camps where every Christmas the POWs had Turkey and all the trimmings.

In the early part of 1943 a rumour spread around their camp that a Swiss Medical Commission would soon be arriving to assess the number of badly injured POWs who could be considered for exchange on a one-to-one basis with similarly incapacitated allied servicemen held in camps in Germany. Only those considered so physically infirm, or mentally deranged, that they would not be able to carry out further military activities could hope to be considered.

The medical tests were thorough and winkled out most of those who exaggerated the extent of their injuries but some, no doubt, did successfully hoodwink the authorities. However it was immediately clear to all that Thiel and Grimstein

Hospital ship 'Meteor' that ferried the exchanged POWs to Germany. (Photograph: Frau M. Thiel)

Jonny Thiel and wife Margarete at home, Christmas 1944. (Photograph: Frau M. Thiel)

Ofw. Heinz Grimstein with some old comrades at Deblin, spring 1944

Grave marker of Oberst Frank with that of Stoeckl in the background

were still severely incapacitated and both were repatriated to Germany with the first batch of prisoners in October 1943.

Aboard the hospital ship *Meteor* they sailed for Germany and their families, but after being briefly reunited in time for Christmas they were subject to a further thorough examination and extensive medical care. Thiel would then spend some months at the Luftwaffe hospital in Quedlinberg before being retrained as ground support and posted to Bayern in the south of Germany. When the war ended he was captured and interned by the Americans but he didn't spend too long in captivity as, by the middle of July 1945, he was back home with his family in Giessen.

After being discharged from hospital and declared fit for duty, Grimstein was lucky enough to be posted to an air force base near his home town of Giessen. And by the late spring of 1944 he was able to obtain leave to travel to the headquarters of the Geschwader of KG 55 that was then based in Deblin-Irena to the south of Warsaw to meet up with some old comrades. However, except for some of the ground crews who remembered him and made him feel welcome, there were only a few airmen from his time with the unit who were still around to listen to his tale of combat and captivity. Four years of war and Stalingrad had taken its toll of KG 55.

At the end of the war, Grimstein surrendered to the Americans but he was soon discharged and back home with his family in Giessen where, for over ten years, they were near neighbours of Jonny Thiel and his wife and children. Jonny became a local government employee while Heinz joined the local police force and they remained firm friends until Heinz died aged sixty-three in June 1976.

The original grave marker of Obltn. Bruno Brossler in the foreground with those of Obersts Frank and Stoeckl in the group behind

Jonny survived for another twelve years and passed away when he was seventy-four at the family home in May 1988.

The bodies of Oberst Alois Stoeckl, Oberst Walter Frank and Obltn. Bruno Brossler were interred with full military honours on 19 August in Romsey Cemetery by a burial party, under the command of Squadron Leader C.F. Ashley in graves 35, 97 and 130. Each of their graves was marked by a simple white wooden cross that was erected for all the recovered bodies of the men of the German Air Force and only showed the name, rank and date of death, though but the inscription on Frank's marker was incorrect.

His name is shown as Oberst G. Frank whereas his full name was Walter Hermann Oskar Frank and the reason for this error is uncertain but it was rectified when his body was disinterred and reburied in the German War Grave cemetery at Cannock Chase. Their headstones can now be found in Block 2, Row 2, in Graves 30, 32 and 35.

But what of the wreck of the Heinkel? It remained *in situ* for some days until it was thoroughly examined by the RAF and Fairy Aviation, and a few days later it was dismantled by a Nuffield salvage gang that had arrived from Oxford. During this operation one of the workmen suffered a severe back injury when part of a wing fell on him and again the redoubtable Mrs Nicholls was on hand to render first aid. It was believed that he made a full recovery after being laid up at Oxford Hospital.

Following an invitation from the RAF, Frau Erna Puttfarken, who was the daughter of Oberst Stoeckl, attended the official function held at Duxford on 16 September 1990 to commemorate the 50th Anniversary of the Battle of Britain.

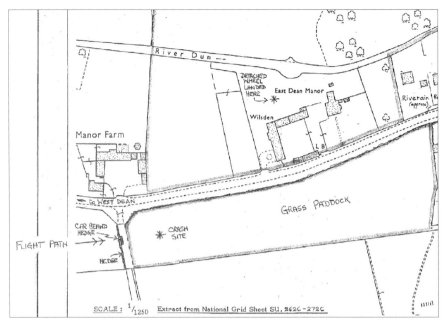

Map of the crash site of Heinkel He 111 (1G + AA) of KG 55

Villacoublay, the Headquarters of KG 55, previously the home of the famous jazz singer Josephine Baker. (Photograph: H. Tuffers)

Mrs Hilda Evelyn 'Evie' Nicholls. (Photograph: Mrs D. Watkins)

While in England she took the opportunity to make a first visit to her father's grave. Her visit to the German War Grave cemetery at Cannock Chase was all the more poignant as there is no gravestone for her late husband, Major Dietrich Puttfarken, who failed to return from an intruder mission over England on the night of 22–23 April 1944. His body was never recovered.

The initial intelligence or K report on the crash of G1 +AA was rather brief in that it only reported the date, time and location of the crash, its intended targets and the ranks and state of the crew, though it did mention that it was loaded with several 'special long delay bombs'.

A later report, though wrongly dating the crash at Denehill [sic] as happening on '15.8.40', did flesh out this basic information because it also stated the aircraft had Daimler Benz engines and carried the crest of a red lion on a sloping pike. The standard armour plate for this type of aircraft had apparently been fitted and ten 50kg bombs were found in the crash. But the authorities obviously thought that a crashed aircraft carrying such important senior Luftwaffe officers warranted a rather more detailed scrutiny, and a further report read:

A.I.1.(K) Report No.269/1940
    Further report on He.111 (G1 + AA) brought down at Eastdene 14.8.40.
    It will be remembered that this aircraft had two Obersts on board.
    One was the Geschwader of KG 55 and the other had the red collar patches of a 'Wehrmachts Beamter'. This man nevertheless had the same Disc No. as the Kommodore showing he was a permanent member of the Staff.

Jonny Thiel on his return
to Germany with his wife,
a neighbour and children.
(Photograph: Frau M. Thiel)

The aircraft was Works No.2898 delivered 9.1.40.

The effects from this aircraft have now been received. The two wounded are still in hospital.

The aircraft had in it a target map No.GB.10232a of Upavon aerodrome. The actual target to be bombed was the hangars which were marked in red pencil; the attack was to have been delivered from the South West.

In the aircraft there were also two aerial photographs about 12" square.

One was of Upavon – this was marked:

114 Z 10V

2.6.40

Under the title 'Upavon' were the letters E. B1.33 and in the right hand corner the same number as that on the target map. On this photograph the aerodrome boundaries were outlined in red ink and ink figures marked in various places. This corresponded to a slip of paper also in the aircraft. This slip of paper was taken at 17.50 hrs on June 20th by Oberleutnant Dressel of 4(F)/122. The key to the number is:

1 = hangars   2 = barracks   3 = aircraft

The aircraft marked are standing in front of the hangars.

The other photograph was marked: F.6v. 4.8.40

    Netheravon GB.10150

The aerodrome was outlined in red, and at various points over the aerodrome figures were written in representing hangars, etc. There are also about 30 aircraft to be seen on the aerodrome mostly grouped together in front of the hangars. To the south of the aerodrome were what appeared to be six bomb craters; these had been ringed.

On the back of this photograph was a rubber stamp which showed the photograph had been taken at 19.25 hrs on 4.8.40 by an aircraft from 4(F)/14. The scale was 1:17000.

The photographs and target map have been sent to A.I.3(b) together with a few ordinary maps from the aircraft.

And what happened to the rest of the mission? After losing their leader the two remaining Heinkels of the Stabskette of KG 55, having aborted their mission, returned to Villacoublay without releasing their bombs on any meaningful target, merely dumping them over Portland docks at 17.10 hours, reporting that they had destroyed a warehouse. But spread over a wide area the bombs caused considerable disruption and damage to the naval base where the jetty was hit, and gas and water mains and telephone cables were ripped out of the ground. The fleeing two had struck lucky but they never knew it.

In fact at 15.53 hours, just as the first wave was approaching the English coast, one of the Heinkels peeled off and dropped a stick of bombs over Hastings wrecking houses in Bexleigh Avenue, West St Leonards, killing a man and woman. The reason for is a mystery as this town had no military significance, unless of course you count the local gasworks, power station and railway. However, like other coastal towns, it provided easy target practice for the Luftwaffe and made good propaganda when they reported that they had attacked 'the harbour works of Hastings'.

Owing to poor weather conditions, only Netheravon airfield of the intended targets was thought to have been hit but, even here, the effect of the bombing was not observed because of heavy cloud over the target. This attack was carried out almost one hour later at 18.05 hours so, presumably, one aircraft of the small formation did press home its attack. Only six SC 250kg and forty-four SD 50kg bombs were dropped over Britain by KG 55 – the probable bomb load of three aircraft – without any tangible results and the mission was a complete failure. In fact, with the loss of their Geschwader Kommodore it was a complete and utter disaster.

CHAPTER FIVE

Flying into History

In late June 1940, after the fall of France, the III Gruppe of the long-range bomber unit Kampfgeschwader 'Boelcke' (KG 27), equipped with Heinkel 111s, transferred from their temporary forward base at Lille, from where they had bombed the crumbling French positions and had carried out a few night sorties over southern England, to a landing strip at Avord, south of Orleans. From here they launched sporadic attacks against shipping out in the Atlantic and their night bombers ranged with impunity against the ports dotted along the South Wales coast. Swansea, Cardiff and Pembroke were the main targets of their nocturnal visits. But the crews were not happy with their living quarters at Avord. They had been billeted in cramped conditions in very small, basic houses and they were glad to be transferred at the end of July to Rennes in Brittany where they were put up in comfortable hotels in the centre of the city.

The 9th Staffel had taken up residence in the Hotel Paris, the 8th Staffel were delighted to be quartered right in the heart of the city at the Hotel Brest while 7th Staffel were similarly based in and around the main square. Most were lucky enough to be lodged in single rooms and, as their meals times were the same as for the officers, they enjoyed excellent food. As one airman later said, 'We lived like gods in France! War also had its good side.'

Besides building camouflaged revetments on the airfield, and checking over and servicing the planes, the airmen still had plenty of free time to visit the many small, surprisingly still well-stocked shops in the town and visited the most popular bistros and bars for a smoke, some idol banter and few drinks. Sitting outside in the warm sunshine they enjoyed watching the pretty French girls even though they realised that there was little hope of any immediate fraternisation. The civilian population were very cold and reserved.

The occasional days of boredom at Avord and Rennes were often broken up by the return of comrades who had been shot down and imprisoned, and who were now dribbling back to the unit having been freed after the French had capitulated. The return of Johann Oekenpohler and his crew was half-expected as they had suffered the indignity of being shot down once before but, when Fritz Bernt arrived clutching a wind-up gramophone, there was a huge round of

A burnt-out Gladiator at Lille with a Heinkel 111P of KG 27 in the background. (Photograph: Heinz Kochy)

applause. He had been shot down behind enemy lines on 18 May 1940 and had evaded capture for some days before being caught. Now freed from captivity, he was heartily welcomed back.

Fritz Dietrich, another returnee, regaled everyone within earshot of his adventures after his aircraft had crash-landed behind enemy lines on 19 May 1940 and he had been captured by the French. He and his pilot, Fw. Englebert Heiner, had first been taken to Paris for interrogation and then sent on a long journey to a camp in the south of France near Toulouse, far away from the rapidly advancing German army. They then heard that POWs were being transported to Canada, but a sea voyage was not on the agenda, they decided to try and escape. They simply dived into the water when bathing in a river and swam away. The guards didn't seem to notice and did not give chase.

They disguised the POW markings on their clothes and initially headed for nearby neutral Spain before turning north. Picking up a couple of other escapees on the way, they then began an eventful nine-day trek posing as Dutch refugees who had lost their papers. Primarily living off the land they bluffed their way past a gendarme and a refugee centre and passed the almost deserted city of Limoges to cross the bridge over the River Vienne at Confolens. Then, in the morning light, they caught sight of a tank in the distance that, to their great relief, turned out to be German. They had made it safely through enemy territory to their own lines.

After meeting up with the all-conquering German forces they were fed and clothed and, after a quick debriefing, flown to Rennes to rejoin their comrades

Fritz Bernt (right)
on his return
to KG 27 after
his release from
captivity

of KG 27. They had been away from their unit for over ten weeks, during which time their families didn't know if they were alive or dead, so despite the eagerly awaited onslaught against Britain they were allowed a few days' leave in Germany. They were therefore away from the Geschwader when it launched its first major daylight attack on 14 August 1940, but more than made up for this absence in the days and nights to come. During the course of the war they flew many dangerous missions together, including flying supplies to the besieged Germany army at Stalingrad, after which Heiner was awarded the Knights Cross. Transferred back to Germany to take part in the home defence, they flew Ju 88G-6 night fighters with IV/NJG until their luck finally ran out in the early morning of 19 March 1945.

Ordered up to intercept a large force of Lancasters that were attacking Hanau, they were blown out of the air by one the Mosquitoes protecting the bombers. As the burning aircraft disintegrated, Dietrich was thrown clear and though severely wounded managed to open his parachute. He landed about 65ft away from the smouldering, mangled wreck that took Heiner to his death. He was subsequently buried near Berchtesgaden but it wasn't until 1989 that Dietrich was able to pay his respects to the man with whom he had flown with from the outbreak of hostilities until almost the end of the war. Standing at the graveside with Heiner's wife it was an emotive final farewell.

On their return to Rennes, they could not believe the disaster that had engulfed the III Gruppe in the late afternoon and evening of 14 August 1940, following their first daylight foray over Britain. With five aircraft lost or missing, another written off in a crash-landing to be cannibalised later for spares, a further three so badly shot-up that they were taken off strength and six more suffering minor damage, the core of the unit had been shattered. After just one day in combat with the RAF fighters, the unit had been knocked out of the Battle over Britain.

They would not return again in such numbers until the winter blitz of 1940–41 but, during these nocturnal visits, they would again suffer significant losses before

Engelbert Heiner (centre) and Fritz Dietrich (second right) in Poland in 1939. (Photograph: Fritz Dietrich)

Englebert Heiner at the controls of a Heinkel 111P of 9/KG 27. (Photograph: Fritz Dietrich)

the unit transferred east for the attack on the Soviet Union. Yet when Heiner and Dietrich had set off on leave they had left behind an experienced and confident battle group eager for action that should have been able to take anything the RAF could throw at it. What happened?

On 12 August 1940, all twenty-seven serviceable Heinkel He 111Ps of the III Gruppe took off from Rennes and, joining up with a large force of Ju 88s, headed for the south coast of England. As they neared they were greeted by a heavy barrage of AA fire and over the radio there came the garbled sound of English voices that they took to be enemy fighters closing in on their formation. The gunners scoured the horizon for any approaching fighters and cocked their MG 15 machine-guns ready for action. But just before crossing the coast they were ordered to return to France, which wasn't completely unexpected as many of the aircraft were not bombed up and those that were had been had smoke-trailing cement bombs. They were unloaded somewhere in Normandy where the outline of ships had been laid out on the ground to simulate an attack on shipping. It wasn't the best of practice but their journey to the English coast, in addition to being a training exercise, was also a ploy to draw the fighters away from the armada of aircraft heading for Portsmouth docks. But this ruse had not fooled the RAF and the Ju 88 dive-bombers of KG 51 were quite badly mauled by the defending fighters.

Returning safely to base without even seeing, let alone engaging, the enemy, the airman of the III Gruppe still felt that something ominous was in the air. As far as they were aware the order for the all-out attack on Britain had not been issued, but everyone knew they would soon be doing battle with the RAF and that the nuisance raids would soon cease. The information trickling down from Luftwaffe High Command made it clear that the 'easy' life would one day come to an end.

On 13 August there was a slight lull and, as most personnel were allocated general duties, Uffz. Heinz Kochy was able to stay in his room in the morning at the Hotel Brest to write a letter home and pack his brand new suitcase with some of the goods he had bought in the town. A suit, shoes, postage stamps, a doll and some odds and ends were neatly packed away before the suitcase was slid under his bed for safe keeping. He still had an uneasy feeling about what was going to happen in the coming days, and had written his name and home address in bold letters on a label attached to the suitcase, just in case. Once before, when he was apprehensive at the start of a mission, he had begged his close friend Bruno Gripp to contact his parents should he fail to return and made him promise that he'd send his belongings on to them. And that's what he asked him to do again before he took off to do battle over Britain by day.

On the morning of 14 August 1940, having breakfasted early, all the crews that were on standby were transported the short distance to the airfield to make their pre-flight preparations. On arrival they could see that the ground crews had been up even earlier as all available aircraft were ready, loaded with 50kg and 250kg bombs, and primed for take-off. Rumours were circulating that they were to

Uffz. Heinz Kochy after returning from combat over France; note the bullet hole in the fuselage. (Photograph: H. Kochy)

be part of a mass raid against the aerodromes defending London, and were to be escorted across the Channel by the Messershmitt 109s of JG 53 that were based nearby. Everyone was just that little bit edgier than in previous days and a nervous atmosphere spread throughout the base. This was going to be their first daylight sortie over Britain. At last they were going to seek out the 'flying lions' in their lairs. The Tommies were in for a big surprise.

All the flying personnel had gathered near the command post eagerly awaiting the battle roster but, owing to the unfavourable weather reports, the take-off was delayed time and again. As the hours slowly ticked by they were allowed to take an early lunch after which most thought that they would be stood-down as any element of surprise had long passed. Then suddenly there was a hive of action and all the combat crews were ordered to form up in a loose square to be addressed by their Gruppe Kommandeur, Major Freiherr Manfred Speck von Sternburg. Having considered and accepted the reports of his Staffelkapitane he explained in concise and clear terms the military situation and made known the mission orders. The Gruppe was not now going to be part of a large air armada. Instead, in small groups, on a broad front, they would be attacking airfields and military targets scattered across the south-west of England and docks and ports clustered around the Bristol Channel. In his short, sharp speech he urged his men to do their duty whatever was thrown at them and to remember that this would be

The airmen of 8th Staffel of the III Gruppe of KG 27

the day they flew into history. There was no need for fighter cover as the latest reconnaissance reports showed that the RAF had suffered such huge losses in the air and on the ground during the last few weeks that they were short of fighters.

As the Luftwaffe High Command had been claiming the daily destruction of thirty to thirty-five British fighters since the end of July, this loss of combat strength by the RAF seemed creditable to Feldwebel Walter Gietz, a veteran of the Polish campaign and the Spanish Civil War where he had flown with the Legion Condor. But some of the other old hands were not so sure. The enemy must have reserves ready and waiting to defend their island home. A flight over Britain by daylight was not going to be a cakewalk.

Major Ulbricht, the Gruppen Kommandeur of the I Gruppe of KG 27 based inland at Tours, no doubt made a similar call to arms before sending his airmen out in eighteen Heinkel He 111s against aerodromes in the vicinity of Andover and those further west dotted around Bath, Chippenham and Cirencester. Setting off in three waves between three and five o'clock in the afternoon most of the airfields targeted were maintenance units, presumably in an attempt to disrupt the supply of replacement aircraft and they did not expect to meet RAF fighters in any numbers. Of their targets, only Boscombe Down housed a fighter squadron and then only because twenty Hurricanes of 249 Squadron had flown in around midday, but there were still the operational fighter squadrons at Middle Wallop standing in their way.

The first bombers away were five He 111s of the 3rd Staffel with the Staffelkapitan taking the lead in his aircraft coded 1G + DL with 1G + BL and 1G + HL tucking in closely behind, but the latter aircraft suffered an engine malfunction and fell further and further behind. Finally forced to return home it left the other two flying northwards towards their designated objectives, Little Rissington and Minchinhampton (Aston Down), leaving the two bombers picking up the rear to attack airfields in the Andover area.

The second wave, of seven He 111s, from the 2nd Staffel, had set off to destroy Hullavington and Upavon, with everybody's favourite target Netheravon being personally sought out by a small force led by Major Ulbricht in 1G + BK. This formation managed to fly unchallenged through the fighter screen over Middle Wallop to dump its bomb load on the airfield in the mistaken belief that it was bombing Netheravon. This was one of the four devastating attacks that Middle Wallop had to endure on the afternoon of 14 August in what was probably its blackest day of the war.

The last bombers into the air were the six machines of the 1st Staffel, under the leadership of Hauptman Reinhard in 1G + HH with orders to attack Netheravon and Boscombe Down. But owing to bad weather and concerted attacks by fighters, the mission was aborted before getting anywhere near their targets and with over twenty holes in its fuselage and wings 1G + BH was so badly shot-up it barely made the French coast and made a forced-landing at Lisieux.

Even though they experienced ten-tenths cloud and reported heavy flak defence over the airfields, the failure of nine aircraft to drop their bomb loads did not bode well for any future daylight forays over in England by I Gruppe of KG 27. It was the level of fighter resistance that was most alarming and, even though no planes had been lost to the guns of the RAF, they knew they wouldn't always be so lucky. But there was some limited success. In addition to claiming to have attacked Netheravon, they also reported that three planes had bombed Old Sarum and lone raiders had attacked Boscombe Down and Hullavington.

The sixteen high explosive bombs destined for Boscombe Down had drifted about 2 miles off target landing harmlessly at Winterslow, almost the same distance away from the secret Royal Ordnance Laboratory at Porton. If this establishment had been hit who knows what chemical horrors could have been inflicted on the surrounding countryside. Any contamination could have spread even further by wind or water, and the possible release of such toxins as a result of a bombing raid must have been a continuing worry to the authorities.

The effect of the bombs dropped on Old Sarum was not observed owing to the thick cloud obscuring the target but, whichever aerodrome they bombed, it certainly wasn't Old Sarum. This airfield didn't suffer a serious attack until the spring of 1941 and perhaps the bombs unloaded over this area were part of the large parcel of explosives dropped in and around Middle Wallop and Andover, as both were hit late in the afternoon.

On the morning of 14 August, RAF Andover was still licking its wounds after an attack the previous day when Air Marshall William Mitchell called at the station to inspect the damage. Satisfied that the necessary repair work was being undertaken he didn't stay too long, which was just as well as late in the afternoon another enemy aircraft was inbound carrying a full bomb load.

LAC Alex Davidson attached to the Station Armoury at RAF Andover also worked on the Blenheims used by No.2 School of Army Co-operation and, during an emergency, he manned one of the Vickers gas-operated machine-guns – sometimes known as a Vickers 'K' gun – that had been rigged up by the Armament Section to augment the .303 Lewis guns which formed the backbone of the airfield's defence. Mounted on tripods they were more accurate and had a longer range than the often hand-held Lewis guns, and being belt-fed they were also capable of rapid, continuous firing. But in reality both type of guns lacked the firepower to even scare off a raider, let alone bring it down.

As the Heinkel He 111 made its run over the airfield, coming in low beneath the clouds from the west over the Andover–Weyhill Road, a barrage of fire went up from the Lewis gunners positioned on the edge of the airfield and from the two posts above the officers' mess. The Vickers gunners also opened up and, as the trail of tracer bullets sped skywards, the Heinkel could have only been hit by spent slugs because it still kept coming.

LAC E.C. Charlesworth of the RAFVR had been posted to Andover at the beginning of June 1940 and was part of the gun crew billeted in Rothsay House, on the north side of the airfield. He was off duty on 14 August 1940 and was on his way back from the mess hall when he noticed an aircraft approaching from the direction of Salisbury and, as no alarm had sounded, he assumed it was one of their Blenheims practising low flying. Then, just as the staccato of the machine-gunners reverberated around the airfield, he noticed black crosses on the underneath of the aeroplane and saw black blobs tumble from its belly.

Undeterred by the bomb bursts, he raced back to the billet to pick up his rifle and side arms but before he could make it to his gun post the last bomb exploded. Taking up position he helped change the empty ammunition drum on the Lewis gun and waited for the next attack, but it never came.

Alex Davidson had opened up at the raider as soon as it appeared out of the clouds but he didn't think he was having any effect in arresting its relentless approach to the airfield. The first bombs fell short, missing the vintage First World War hangars but some drifted off-line and landed in the centre of a group of W/T masts destroying a transmitting set and killing the civilian wire-less operator H.G. Read. However, because Andover was a grass airfield it absorbed the force of the explosions though huge, chewed-up clumps of earth were thrown into the air and clouds of smoke drifted across the airfield as the bombs cratered the ground. When the smoke cleared a lone airmen was found dead with his body twisted out of shape and his tunic shredded. Caught in the open, Aircraftsman First Class Alfred Warnes Clarke had been blasted to pieces by the anti-personnel bombs and was barely recognisable. He was subsequently buried at Andover cemetery. Sgt Dennis Butler was also thought to have been killed during this raid but he had actually died as a result of the attack the previous day when the headquarters and the officers sleeping quarters were hit and two officers killed. He is also buried at Andover cemetery and his gravestone is correctly dated 13 August 1940.

At 16.45 hours a 'Red' air raid warning was received at RAF Hullavington but no warning flag was hoisted on top of the watchtower, and only a fraction of the civilian employees making their way back to the main block to 'clock off' were made aware of the alert. But the warning soon spread and there was a sudden mad scramble to board the buses waiting to take them to Chippenham. Over 100 workmen got away from the station but those working on the outlying sites, along with the men working overtime, were forced to take shelter as best they could. And there they waited impatiently, for over an hour, until approximately 17.55 hours when the attack alarm was finally sounded and three enemy aircraft were observed almost directly above the aerodrome. The Ground Defence crews, swiftly springing into action, took up their battle stations and two of the three Hurricanes of the local defence flight, manned by the pilots of the No.9 Service Flying Training School (SFTS), took off in hot pursuit.

As evening approached, Evan White, the time-keeper for the A & B Flights of No.9 SFTS that had been flying circuits around the aerodrome, was watching the last of the landed aircraft being checked and refuelled prior to being moved to the dispersal points and tied down when an air-raid warning came through, followed by the ear-piercing shriek of the siren. The duty crews started to move the parked aircraft away from the hangars as the flying instructors grabbed their parachutes and raced across the dispersal fields to the Hurricanes but Evan, having no other duties, fastened on his tin hat and hot-footed it to the safety of the slit trenches. Smelly and cramped, the narrow slit trenches were not the best places to seek safety but at least they not as unbearable as the air raid shelters on the road from the north end of the Barrack Square that were under 2.5ft of water. As they splashed into the water it was too late for the airmen to make a hasty retreat, and every minute spent in these conditions was made even worse by the continual moans of the civilians who had already decamped to the safety of the shelters.

A rota system operated at the maintenance hangar used by No.9 SFTS, and as Mervyn Jones and his friend Don Fowler were working the late shift they intended going down to the local hop in the village hall. Shaved and spruced up they were just putting on their best blues when the air-raid warning sounded and grabbing a tin hat, rifle, bandolier and gas mask, they fled in a mad scramble to the slit trenches. As they squeezed in they caught sight of the two station defence aircraft, which they believed were obsolete Boulton Paul fighters, take-off. But as the minutes ticked by and there was no sound of any action they started to think that the instructor pilots were merely 'stooging around' to chalk up some extra flying time in combat aircraft. With the all-clear they rushed back to the barrack block just as the bombs exploded across the airfield and they dived for cover under their bunks.

On hearing the Merlin engines roar into life, Evan White poked his head above the edge of the slit trench and watched the Hurricanes, which were stationed on the far side of airfield, bump along the grass runway and lurch into the air and thought 'Now for some exciting action' but nothing seemed to happen. No gunfire could be heard overhead and, after what seemed ages, the Hurricanes

Leading Aircraftman Armourer
Alex Davidson outside the
Station Armoury at Andover in
the summer of 1940 holding a
Browning .303 machine-gun.
(Photograph: A. Davidson)

landed for refuelling just after the all-clear had sounded. By the disappointed
look on their faces, Evan could tell that the pilots had failed to make contact
with the enemy.

Group Captain Edwin Shipley, the acting station commander, had dealt with
three airmen charged with disorderly conduct in Bath and was busy showing
Flying Officer Watson of the Ministry of Aircraft Production, who was on a fact
finding mission, around the aerodrome when the red alert was received. Calling
on Squadron Leader Birbeck to assist with the emergency proceedings, he was
quietly satisfied with the rapid response of the Ground Defence teams and the
speed at which the Hurricanes went up to investigate. Expecting an attack at any
minute, the camp siren was sounded but the immediate threat seemed to have
receded when a 'White' message was received from the Home Office and the all-
clear was sounded at 17.45 hours.

Everyone rushed up from the shelters in double quick time and the airmen
not on duty headed for their billets or to the cookhouse for a hot cup of tea,
while the weary civilian workers finally headed off for the buses that were still
waiting to take them away from the station. But there was no relaxation for the
duty crews who had been called out to refuel the three Hurricanes that were
parked alongside the watchtower, and they were busily at work when the enemy
raider commenced its run over the airfield. As the first bomb blew the roof off the
maintenance hanger they dived for cover beneath the petrol bowser.

Airmen with 'empty' beer bottles at RAF Hullavington, summer 1940. Back row: LAC Kneale, LAC Groffman. Front row: LAC Murray, LAC Dawson, LAC Boyd. (Photograph: D. Kneale)

With the initial emergency over, LAC Norman Henry, as duty storekeeper at No.10 Maintenance Unit for the evening, had been called out from the front office of the main stores to help refill a petrol bowser from the nearby bulk petrol tank. This was located less than 600ft away and, after manoeuvring the bowser into position, they were in the process of pumping petrol from one container to another when suddenly, from somewhere behind them, there came an almighty thunderclap.

With their backs to the action they didn't see what the first bomb had hit but smoke was billowing from the roof of the maintenance hangar used by the Flying School, which was located some distance away on the other side of the main stores. The rest of the bombs were detonating one by one across the airfield but seemed to have fallen well short of the hangars used by No.10 Maintenance Unit, but some could have exploded amongst some of the training aircraft parked out in the open. They had been caught completely on the hop, having neither seen nor heard the approach of the enemy aircraft, and quickly disconnecting the bowser they fled to safety in case another raider followed up the attack.

When Henry finally made it back to the stores office he discovered that during his absence a jagged lump of curved shrapnel, weighing a couple of pounds or more, had crashed through the window and embedded itself in the floor on the other side of the room. It had flashed straight over the chair he normally used while awaiting telephone calls, and call-outs, and would have decapitated him in a second.

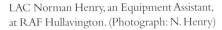

LAC Norman Henry, an Equipment Assistant,   LAC Doug Kneale, 1941. (Photograph: D.
at RAF Hullavington. (Photograph: N. Henry)   Kneale)

Doug Kneale, an LAC at 10 Maintenance Unit, was the duty runner and, in
the event of an air raid, had to report to the adjutant at headquarters and then
wait outside his office. Should telephone communication be impossible because
of bomb damage the adjutant would hand his written messages to the runner
who would deliver them around the station on a bicycle, regardless of any danger.

When the attack alarm sounded, Doug duly reported for duty and waited nervously outside the adjutant's door for almost an hour before the all-clear was heard,
then started to make his way back to his comfortable billet which originally had
been part of the married quarters. Taking a short cut along a country lane, then
through a gap in the hedge and across a small field to his quarters, the air was still
and scented with the smell of wild flowers and newly mown hay from the surrounding fields and hedgerows, and for a brief moment he was lost in thought.

He was about halfway along the lane when he heard the sound of an aircraft
overhead and glancing up caught a glimpse of a plane as it passed from one cloud
to another at about 5,000ft and thought 'That's a big one, but it must be okay as
the all-clear has gone!' Just a few moments later he heard the sound of aeroplane
engines getting louder and louder and again he looked up to see a plane pop out
from under the cloud base and watched a small blob fall from it, and then another,
and another. At first he thought they were parachutists in training until he heard
the all too familiar sound of bombs whistling through the air. He dived head first
into the overgrown ditch by the road.

The raider had been dead in line with him when it commenced its bombing run and as it bore down on him and passed overhead the whistling sounds got ever louder. Knowing they were going to land too close for comfort, he buried himself deeper and deeper into the ditch.

The first thump came as a huge relief because after that he knew the rest would fall further away. But the bomb had landed only about 130ft away and 'the ground came up and hit me like a sledge hammer' as the force of the explosion threw mud and turf into the air showering him with debris as it fell back to earth. One by one he heard the bombs detonate right across the airfield but he couldn't see a thing for all the swirling dust and choking cordite fumes. He hurried back to headquarters barely bothering to brush off the dirt and clay clinging to his tunic.

Large plumes of thick black smoke were wreathing skywards from several areas around the aerodrome and outside headquarters someone was frantically clanging the fire-bell but the fire engine could not leave its station, despite the desperate emergency. Only five fire fighters were on board but regulations dictated that they should not proceed unless they had a full complement, so they remained on high alert awaiting the missing member. Realising he was serving no useful purpose, hanging about in an empty corridor waiting for orders, Doug left his post at headquarters and climbed aboard the fire engine which then set off in search of a fire.

As they rattled along they passed a 'C' type hangar that had a huge hole in its roof and though it had taken a direct hit, it was not on fire but inside several bi-planes, that were undergoing repair, looked badly smashed. About 1,000ft further on they could see that two of the four trainers lined up alongside a petrol tanker were on fire and nearby an airman lay badly injured crying out for help. Parking the fire engine up-wind they started hosing down the burning aircraft but Doug was more concerned with the fate of the wounded airman as he wouldn't stand a chance if the petrol tanker exploded. No one seemed to be in any hurry to rescue the airman so Doug ran forward to check on his condition. He had been hit by shrapnel, his face was a bloody mess and his clothing was shredded and smouldering. Grabbing him under the armpits, Doug tried to drag him clear but he screamed out in agony. Though he was too heavy to carry, Doug managed to pull him about 150ft out of the immediate danger zone.

The fires were still proving difficult to extinguish and a stray spark from one of the burning planes could easily ignite the petrol bowser. Realising the peril they were in, Doug then raced back and, grabbing one of the burning trainers by the tail, pulled it out of harm's way. And with another mighty effort he tackled the other trainer and dragged it across the field away from the bowser as the firemen continued to try and dampen down the flames. Doug then left them to it and returned to the badly injured airmen, who was still moaning loudly, and tried to comfort him as best as he could until the ambulance arrived. But despite his efforts the poor chap died a few days later.

After helping the wounded into the ambulances there was little else Doug could do, so he thought he had better get back pretty quick to the post he

Airmen at the rear of the main stores at RAF Hullavington, summer 1940. Back row: LAC Maskell, Sgt Preucil, Cpl Ranelow, LAC Groffman, LAC Warne, LAC Boyd, LAC Kneale. Front row: LAC Murray, LAC Dawson. (Photograph: D. Kneale)

had deserted. But he hadn't been missed. Covered in filth and splattered with blood he presented a sorry sight and when the adjutant finally emerged from his room he took one look at Doug and thought he had been injured in the attack. This puzzled him somewhat as the Maintenance Unit had escaped the worst of the bombing, with damage confined largely to the apron area and hangar occupied by the Flying School, with the rest of the bombs falling on open ground in the direction of Hullavington village. Doug quickly blurted out what had happened but, completely unfazed by this tale of daring-do, the adjutant dismissed him with a nonchalant remark that he should clean himself up before going to the mess for tea. Without a word Doug took his advice and headed back to his billet.

Back at his quarters he came face to face with Corporal Demer, a general duties NCO, who because of all the grime and blood also thought that he had been injured during the bombing. Doug quickly put him in the picture. 'Eh Lad' he said, 'You should tell the adjutant what you did; you should get a medal for that.' In reply Doug could only mutter to himself, 'Since when did one recommend themselves for decorations?' But then he never felt this corporal was particularly bright.

In fact his heroism was soon forgotten as a few days later he was put on a charge for the serious offence of walking on the grass. Seven days 'Confined to Barracks' and, as an extra punishment, he was made to do one hour's square bashing in full kit on the parade ground each day.

LAC Ernest Graham, an armourer with 9 FTS, and 'Boy' Bennett had been undertaking their pre-flight inspections of the Hart and Audax trainers and fitting wing-tip flares for night flying when the German bomber burst out from beneath the clouds. Taking cover under the canvas wings of the aircraft, they watched as it attacked on a line about 300–450ft to their right, coming in from due north. The bombs fell short of their position but a hot splinter from one had set a petrol bowser alight and with sparks shooting into the air a couple of the trainers also went up in flames. Being 'regulars' they knew that their experience would be needed once the raid was over and, as the last bomb exploded, they rushed towards the scene of devastation.

Flt Mechanic Doug Gardener was detailed to play football that evening and, having already put on his red football jersey for the game, was making his way towards the pitch when he heard overhead the unmistakeable sound of unsynchronised aircraft engines getting louder and louder. Within seconds the enemy aircraft was out of the clouds and, with its front machine-gun spitting fire, was heading straight for him. Wearing a red shirt against a green grass background he was convinced he was their target and looking for somewhere safe to hide he ran into the nearest hangar and threw himself to the floor. It was one of the worst decisions of his life.

As the first of the contact bombs ignited on hitting the roof the blast picked him up and threw him forcibly across the floor into the brick wall. Almost simultaneously a second bomb blew a hole in the roof and slammed him even harder against the wall, covering him with falling debris and parts of damaged aircraft. But miraculously, except for being momentarily stunned and badly bruised, he was unharmed. Dusting himself down he strode purposely out of the hanger much to the amazement of his fellow airmen. But he was still a bit groggy and unable to go to the assistance of the men who were trying to push two of the bomb-damaged Hurricanes away from the burning petrol bowser that was well alight. A pilot was still sitting in one of the Hurricanes but he didn't seem to be moving though Doug didn't think he was dead as airmen were swarming over the aircraft trying to lift him out of the cockpit. The injured airman was Flt Lt Arthur Ridler who had suffered shrapnel injuries to both his legs, and he was gently eased from the cockpit by Ernie Graham and 'Boy' Bennett who were now helping to get the injured to Station Sick Quarters. Immediate medical assistance was at hand in the shape of a WAAF medic who tidied and bandaged the badly wounded before they were hoisted into the ambulances. For her timely and professional assistance, Cpl Major was later awarded the British Empire Medal.

Evan White had now appeared on the scene and it was here that he saw his first dead person lying by the petrol bowser, probably having been hit by shrapnel. It was not a pretty sight and, with all the confusion and coming and goings, he felt quite lost and unable to help Mervyn Davies and Don Fowler who, along with Squadron Leader McKay, were loading the wounded onto stretchers. Like many of the other young airmen this was his first taste of the nasty side of war and he was scared and left wondering what to do. He didn't like to admit it but he was quietly relieved when over the tannoy came the order for non-essential personnel to clear the airfield.

One of the dead was LAC Morley Hunkin, who only the previous weekend had married his sweetheart Joan Matthews at the picturesque little church in Hullavington village. In a daze a wounded airman, who had been the best man at the wedding, was seen to pick up the dead body and, sobbing and crying, carried it round and around in circles until he collapsed with grief. He finally gave up the body and it was later interred in the churchyard at nearby Stanton St Quintin.

Amid all this shambles Flt Lt Waters, a flying instructor with No.9 FTS, sprinted out of the watchtower and shouted at one of the ground crew to connect the surviving Hurricane to a 'Chore Horse' to start the engine. In his hurry to get airborne he dropped his parachute and leapt into the aircraft without bothering to check if it was damaged, and took off straight across the airfield from the parked position. Without the parachute acting as a cushion it was going to be a difficult and uncomfortable flight but, on his return, the rumour went around that he'd caught the raider and shot it down over Bristol.

By now Group Captain Edwin Shipley was at the scene and directing the rescue operations. After the all-clear had sounded he had been strolling leisurely back to his quarters when he noticed an aircraft come out of the clouds that he didn't take to be hostile until it unloaded its bombs. Momentarily mesmerised at the antics of the tumbling bombs he quickly took cover behind the Cotswold stone wall that surrounded his garden once the bombs had stabilized in flight, and were heading straight down. He watched as the bombs detonated across the airfield with the first and possibly the second one hitting the maintenance hangar, the third and fourth landing amongst the parked aeroplanes on the tarmac and hangar apron, with another exploding close and narrowly missing the watchtower. A few straddled the perimeter road but the rest exploded harmlessly on open ground throwing up a line of deep craters in the direction of Hullavington village.

Arriving at the Maintenance Hangar he could see that a gaping hole about 160ft wide had been punched in the roof, and inside damaged and buckled aircraft were skewed all over the place and covered in the dust and rubbish from the collapsed ceiling. But the open door had dissipated the full force of the blast and, briefly checking that there was no one buried beneath the piles of rubble, he hurried away as he was anxious to get to the main disaster area and the fire raging on the apron.

The fire team were busily hosing down two bi-planes but no one was tackling the flames shooting up from the burning 450-gallon petrol bowser parked on the apron, and he called for a tractor and a long length of rope to tow it out onto the aerodrome out of harm's way. 'I'm not towing that!' cried the civilian tractor driver. 'I haven't asked you to do so yet,' replied Shipley as he crawled along the floor and passed one end of the rope through the triangle bar at the front of the bowser. Fortunately the flames were bursting out from the pumps at the rear of the bowser and he was able to attach the rope to the tractor. The burning tanker was then towed out onto the aerodrome by the still protesting civilian.

It was left burning on the grass and Shipley told the fire crew not to waste any more time trying to extinguish the flames, but to wait in case anything else went up. Several of the aircraft were leaking fuel and they were moved to safety while the bowser continued to burn well into the following day when it finally burnt itself out. Surveying the damage he wasn't too worried about the number of obsolete Harts and Audaxes that were written off or damaged as they were scheduled to be re-equipped with Miles Masters, and the loss of some of their bi-plane trainers might hurry this along. In fact, not one aircraft had been lost and of the fourteen damaged by bomb splinters only four had to be returned to the contractors for repair. The rest were repaired at the station, including three twin-engine Avro Ansons that were used for general aircrew training.

Shipley was more concerned with the four dead, and the five wounded airmen and one officer from the Service Flying School. A civilian working on the roof of the Maintenance Hangar had also been wounded, as well as four soldiers of the Royal Artillery who were manning the ground defences. All the damage had occurred in and around the vicinity of No.7 Hangar occupied by 9 FTS with No.10 Maintenance Unit emerging unscathed, except for the damage to the Hurricanes it had loaned to the instructors of the flying school. This *ad hoc* arrangement was cancelled three days later.

Back at his office, the medical officer gave Shipley a brief report of the condition of the seven severely wounded, especially of those who might have to be treated off station. Satisfied that the medical and rescue services had generally worked very well together, he decided that the clearing up of the shattered hangar could wait until the following day and hopefully, with the return of the commanding officer, he would be spared the harrowing task of writing to the relatives of the dead airmen. In addition to LAC Hunkin those killed were AC1 Bertram Holt, later buried at Townstall Churchyard; AC2 Ivor King, buried at Bristol (Arnos Vale) Cemetery and, at only nineteen years of age, AC1 Glyndwr James Prior who was interred at Christchurch Cemetery in the presence of his father Hubert James Prior and his welsh mother Bronwen Prior.

As the raider sped away it was spotted by Pilot Officers Allan Wright and Desmond Williams, of 92 Squadron, who were on patrol over the Bristol area and had already exchanged gunfire with another Heinkel 111 over Hullavington some ten minutes earlier before it disappeared into the clouds. Not giving up on the fight, Wright, in his Spitfire R 6546, pursued this elusive bogey into the swirling grey murk and caught sight of it again in a patch of clear sky. Closing to within 1,200ft he fired a long burst at it expending over 800 rounds before it was again lost to the cloud. This time it did not return fire and Wright, believing it was probably done for, claimed it as half a kill.

Turning his attention to the Hullavington raider he dived to attack but it must have already noticed the Spitfires hovering above because it also swiftly headed for the clouds and, before Wright could open fire, it disappeared from view.

Finally giving up on this second chase, and low on fuel and ammo, Wright flying as Green 1 landed back at RAF Pembrey at 18.42 hours with Sgt Peter Eyles who, as Green 3, did not engage the enemy.

But 'Bill' Williams now flying alone as Green 2 was not yet willing to give up the hunt and a burst of AA fire in the distance drew his attention to the bandit as it dipped in and out of a layer of cloud at 5,000ft. It was now heading towards Bristol and he immediately closed to within 150ft. With the Heinkel firmly in his sights he made a beam attack, firing a short but deadly burst. Attacking from above he again let rip a volley from close in but the raider, seemingly unharmed, again hid in the clouds.

'Bill' had still not given up and he dropped back below the cloudbank in search of the enemy and after a couple of minutes he spied a Heinkel 111 approaching Bristol from the north. Closing from 1,200ft down to 150ft he made a head on attack giving it a quick burst, followed by another short burst of fire as he closed again to within 150ft. The Heinkel seemed to absorb all this punishment without any visible effect and in desperation Bill gave it yet another short burst. Obviously in trouble the raider now jettisoned its bombs in a desperate attempt to rapidly gain height and, relieved of its heavy load, it lurched up into the safety of the clouds.

Bill was sure it was finished and, on landing back at Pembrey, he confirmed the destruction of a Heinkel and for good measure claimed a half-share in another. But even though the local AA batteries and ARP units were reporting enemy aircraft down it is doubtful whether these were the ones claimed by Wright and Williams as other Spitfires of 92 Squadron were in the air, notably Blue Section led by Stanford Tuck.

CHAPTER SIX

Middle Wallop in their Sights

It was late afternoon, around 5 o'clock, when a tired Eddie Gray finally reached the head of the tea line of the mess hall at RAF Middle Wallop and, with his china mug filled to the brim, he looked around the hall for somewhere to sit. Spotting a vacant seat amongst the men from his billet he wandered over to where they had gathered, with some friends, in the centre of the room. After a hard day he was absolutely shattered and a place to park his feet and relax was his top priority. As he approached the group a rising tide of laughter shattered any hope of a quiet evening. The hut comic was in full swing and pulling up a chair Eddie, somewhat reluctantly, joined in the fun.

Someone offered him a cigarette but before he could light it the main door burst open and in rushed Pilot Officer Hookum, a veteran of the First World War, who shouted out dramatically 'Men of the Ground Defence, to your posts.'

Immediately there was a mad rush for the exits. Tables were pushed aside and chairs overturned as the men scrambled over one another to be the first to the billets to collect their rifles and equipment. Bringing up the rear, blowing whistles, cursing and swearing the NCOs urged them on, screaming that the Germans had landed paratroopers and gliders.

As they raced to man the gun posts, the sirens blared out incessantly, fuelling the confusion, if not panic, that quickly spread through the aerodrome. Men seemed to be running in all directions and somehow Eddie found himself being swept towards his position in the firing trenches outside the main gate. Then, without any warning the man in front, fellow aircraftsman Les Brooks, pulled up sharply to adjust his gas mask. Eddie pushed him roughly in the back and shouted 'Come on Brooksy, there's others behind.'

'Bugger off,' came the reply. 'There's not a Jerry within a hundred miles.'

Eddie silently agreed with him but at that moment he heard, above the jumbled noise of sirens and whistles, the unmistakable sound of an aircraft in a dive. Looking up Eddie froze momentarily as he watched a Junkers Ju 88 swoop out of the clouds and release a stick of bombs. Everyone ran for cover.

Eddie Gray, pictured on his second day in
uniform, Blackpool 1940. (Photograph:
Eddie Gray)

Those not near the shelters or slit trenches threw themselves flat or made use
of whatever cover was available. Some hid under the RAF lorries that the drivers
had swiftly abandoned, others cowered beneath the fire tenders and a few, not
thinking too clearly, dived under the petrol bowsers. The shelters were filled to
overflowing as the fleeing airmen piled in behind the civilian workers who had
downed tools and sprinted for safety the moment the sirens had sounded. The
raider had caught Middle Wallop on the hop.

Originally planned as a bomber station, RAF Middle Wallop, located some 5
miles west of Andover, was still under construction when it was taken over by 11
Group Fighter Command in June 1940. Subsequently transferred to the newly
formed 10 Group based at Box, Wiltshire, it quickly became a Sector Control
Station and the home of three fighter squadrons flying Blenheims, Hurricanes
and Spitfires. Another squadron was based at the forward airfield at Warmwell to
defend the naval base at Portland.

For an important fighter station it was poorly equipped to deal with an enemy
air attack. Except for a few machine-gun posts scattered around the perimeter, its
only AA weapons were four old 20mm Hispano cannons. Drum-fed, they could
bring to bear hardly enough firepower to scare off a lone raider, and against a
concerted attack their inadequate rate of fire would leave the aerodrome almost
defenceless. Later the station would receive six Bofors guns, manned by the Royal
Artillery, but on 14 August 1940 it was wide open to an all-out attack. The Ju 88s
seemed to sense this vulnerability and came down way below the low cloud base
in search of their target.

Junkers Ju 88As of I/ LG1 heading across the Channel, August 1940. (Photograph: Kurt Sodemann)

Junkers Ju 88A of I/LG1 heading for Middle Wallop, August 1940. (Photograph: Kurt Sodemann)

Without fighter escort, seventeen Ju 88s of I/LG 1, between 13.42 and 14.10 hours, had taken off from their base at Bricy, near Orleans, heading for targets in the west of England and South Wales. Briefed to attack aerodromes and aircraft component factories, they were also to carry out reconnaissance and to report the movement of any shipping in the Bristol Channel.

According to the weather reports they were likely to encounter poor visibility over their designated targets, in which case the pilots were instructed to act on their own initiative. If they were unable to locate their main or secondary objectives, they had a roving commission to bomb any military or strategic targets including ports, railway stations and even road junctions.

` Operationally, the Luftwaffe was out to test Fighter Command's ability to track and intercept swift, scattered raiders in heavy cloud. The Ju 88A *Schnellbomber* was ideal for this purpose. Fast and mobile, capable of 290mph and more, it could carry a 1,800kg bomb load and in a dive, once the bombs were released, it could often outrun a Hurricane. Could the RAF pinpoint the location of small groups of these planes approaching at high speed?

Convinced that the British radar system was of such a rudimentary design that it could not determine the actual size of a formation, the bombers divided into small groups, of two to three aircraft, and advanced over the Channel on a broad front. The aim was to split and hopefully confuse the fighter defences, forcing them to keep their squadrons on full alert and mount standing patrols. The Luftwaffe believed that such a rather simple ploy would take a toll of the RAF pilots. From their own experience they knew that weariness could sap morale as much as combat. After a while even Benzedrine has a reverse effect.

Once the bombers had crossed the coast, radar would cease to be an advantage to the defenders. Located around the coast, virtually on the sea walls, the radar masts could monitor the build-up of aircraft over the Channel but could not plot their path inland. The responsibility for this fell to the volunteers of the Observer Corps, often only equipped with binoculars and an aircraft recognition manual.

On a dense, overcast day the observers were completely blind and could only plot incoming aircraft from the sound of their engines as they passed overhead. This would give neither the height nor size of a formation, let alone distinguish between German planes or the RAF with any degree of certainty. The information that was available was filtered back to Fighter Command and then to the Sector Controllers, but often it was of limited use. On a day like 14 August 1940, with nine-tenths cloud over most of Britain, the Luftwaffe believed they held all the aces. But not quite. Rudimentary or not, the Chain Home (CH) station monitoring the Cherbourg Peninsula had detected the build-up of aircraft by Luftflotte 3. Throughout the late afternoon the WAAF operators had diligently plotted twenty-seven raids coming in on a broad front, stretching some 72 miles, from Lyme Bay to the Isle of Wight. Except for Raid 19, of over six aircraft, the raids appeared to be a series of small formations of two to four aircraft, intermixed with a sprinkling of lone raiders

Olt Kurt Sodemann and the Staff Car carrying the emblem of the III Gruppe/LG1.
(Photograph: K. Sodemann)

Some raids even failed to make landfall, and many were lost once they had crossed the coast, but Raids 1, 23 and 24 were picked up by the Observer Corps and tracked inland, heading north in the direction of Middle Wallop. The Spitfires would be waiting.

Led by Hauptman Wilhelm Kern, the Ju 88 As of 1/LG 1 assembled above the clouds and flew the 150 miles north-west to the French coast in loose formation. Approaching the Channel they broke up into small groups and fanned out on a broad front to cross into England between Portsmouth and Weymouth. As he peeled his *Schnellbomber* away from the formation, Obltn. Kurt Sodemann (the pilot of L1+AS) checked that the Ju 88 of his wingman Fw. Heinrich Boecker was still in touch as they set off in search of RAF Hullavington near Bristol and Swindon. These cities were sure to be protected by fighters and he was well aware that his was a potentially hazardous mission but, as he had only recently taken on the role of Staffelkapitan, he was determined to show that he was worthy of the title.

About halfway across the Channel Kern broke radio silence to wish his pilots luck and gave the order to decrease altitude into the dense bank of cloud below. They would now be relying on their navigators to bring them through the heavy cloud to their designated targets while hoping that the rolling dark clouds would also protect them from any RAF fighters that were waiting.

The previous day Kern had stumbled across Middle Wallop when I/LG 1 had attempted to carry out an attack on Andover. Owing to fierce fighter resistance and intermittent cloud, the Germans had failed to find Andover and, coming

Hptmn Wilhelm Kern after returning from a raid on 13 August 1940. (Photograph: K. Sodemann)

Operations Room of LG.1 Left to right: Hptmn O. Hoffman, Hptmn V.Eichhorn, unknown, unknown, Sodemann. (Photograph: K. Sodemann)

down low over the countryside, searched for an alternative target. Almost immediately an aerodrome appeared but the bombs were released without any real accuracy.

On returning to Bricy, the Germans checked the target files and reconnaissance photographs but they couldn't find any trace of an aerodrome matching the one attacked. Reluctantly Kern reported that they had bombed an unknown airfield in the south-west of England, without observing whether any damage had been caused. Luckily this problem was soon resolved as a journalist with the rank of *Sonderführer* had taken part in the raid and photographed the aerodrome. The film was rapidly developed and rushed to headquarters where it was identified as the unknown airfield as Middle Wallop. As it was a relatively new RAF station, the relevant data had not yet been distributed to all Luftwaffe units and reconnaissance pictures were still not available. But Kern now had the satisfaction of knowing his target and its precise location. Next time Middle Wallop would not get off so lightly.

During the pre-flight discussions on the morning of 14 August, Kern had outlined his plan for a repeat attack on Middle Wallop. Two other *Schnellbombers* would accompany his aircraft and, with the benefit of cloud cover, such a small force should be able to sneak through the fighter screen undetected. By diving out of the clouds at the last possible moment, they would loose their bombs onto the hangers and be away before the AA gunners could retaliate.

The *Sonderführer* couldn't resist such an opportunity and was again given per-mission to accompany the raid. This time he was hoping to have something significant to report and to capture on camera. He was not to be disappointed.

As the alert went to amber the twin-engine Blenheims of 604 Squadron were among the first planes away from Middle Wallop. Notoriously slow to scramble, they were not going to be caught on the ground if the alarm turned to red and most of those on readiness were sent into the air. However, their presence would soon confuse some of the Spitfires pilots of 234 and 609 Squadrons who were already airborne and flying a defensive circle around the station. As they waited patiently to intercept any raiders, the poor weather conditions made contact very much a hit and miss affair. Occasionally there was a break in the swirling cloud but, with vapour streaming across their windscreens, visibility was almost down to zero. Some of the fighters searched above and below the thick clouds but there was no sign of the elusive enemy. But if he did appear, ghostlike out the mist, he was in for nasty shock.

Unaware of this activity, the Ju 88s flew straight through the protective ring of fighters and closed relentlessly on their target. Kern's navigator indicated they were almost over their target as he prepared to take up the bomb-aiming position in the belly of the aircraft, while Kern looked for a gap in the clouds and swung the bomb-diving sights into position. This partially obscured his view but out of the corner of the canopy he spotted a small gap in the clouds and lead the forma-tion in a steep dive-heading straight for Middle Wallop.

When the alarm sounded one of the Ground Defence crew, Aircraftsman Jimmy Workman, a canny Scot from Glasgow, was having a quiet smoke in the

Returning crews reporting to Hptmn Wilhelm Kern. (Photograph: K. Sodemann)

Attack on Middle Wallop by I/LG1 showing the bombs exploding between No.4 and No.5 Hangars. (Photograph: Kurt Sodemann)

A line of bombs exploding on ARF Middle Wallop showing a direct hit on No.5 hangar

latrines and, literally caught with his trousers down, fled the building in a blind panic. Clutching his gas mask, tin hat and rifle in one hand, and holding up his trousers with the other, he headed towards his position alongside Eddie Gray in the firing trenches.

He was halfway up the road, still trying to fasten his tunic, when he heard the sound of an aircraft overhead. Looking up he saw what appeared to be a Blenheim coming straight for him and he instinctively let go of his trousers, which fell to the ground, his battle equipment clattering all around him.

There was a huge roar of laughter from the Station Police (SP) inside the main gate but this was immediately silenced as a stick of bombs tumbled from the aircraft. Forgetting everything, they sprinted for cover leaving Jimmy to collect his dignity and equipment.

The sight of the SPs fleeing up the road brought howls of derision from the men in the crowded firing trenches as Jimmy, red-faced, scrambled over the sand bags. They watched the hated SPs running in disarray and for a brief moment ignored the falling missiles. But they were brought back to reality when the first bomb exploded just behind the hangers, sending up a huge pall of smoke and debris.

Coming out of the clouds, in the van of the attack, Kern could see no sign of the airfield and swore at his navigator who, in reply, merely smiled and pulled aside the anti-dazzle curtain, pointing to the rear starboard window. Craning himself around Kern could just make out the shape of an aerodrome about 3 miles to the right. He levelled out and gently nosed the aircraft in its direction.

From the unusual layout of five hangars (two pairs set diagonally either side of the central hangar) at one end of the aerodrome and a circular road construction at the other end, he recognised it immediately as RAF Middle Wallop. His wingmen were still in touch but some distance behind, and not waiting for them to close up he commenced his bombing run.

The navigator was now in the bomb-aimer's position in the cramped forward section while the rear gunners, in the turret and ventral fairing, cocked their MG 15 machine-guns and scanned the sky for fighters. In a shallow dive the Junkers rapidly closed on the airfield and dropped three 250kg high-explosive bombs, one 250kg incendiary and five 50kg fragmentation bombs crashing down on the exposed airfield.

The first high explosive bomb erupted just short of No.3 Hangar, sending up a terrific pall of smoke and dust that rained down on the airmen who crouched even lower in the trenches. The second and third bombs were right on target but at the last moment inexplicably swung slightly sideways, landing directly between No.4 and No.5 Hangars, blowing out the windows and hurling a shower of splinters across the airfield. The crash and fire tender bays took the bulk of the blast, but though badly buckled and scorched remained intact. The incendiary and anti-personnel bombs drifted off to the right, away from the barrack blocks and transport yard, detonating harmlessly on open ground. Kern cursed his luck and, as the ground gunners opened up, he headed back to the safety of the clouds.

Obltn. Wilhelm Heinrici. (Photograph:
M. Kramer, *née* Heinrici)

Kern was unaware that his wingmen had almost closed up the gap between them and, as he pulled out of the dive, he was taken by surprise as the starboard Junker unleashed its bombs. The pilot had either not observed Kern's bomb pattern or dispatched his missiles too hurriedly because they fell even further to the right, completely missing the buildings and the dispersed aircraft of 604 Squadron. The *Sodenführer* had been furiously clicking his camera and then, still hoping for a definite photograph of the destruction of an RAF fighter base, he focused his lens on the remaining aircraft as it closed rapidly on the target.

The pilot, Obltn. Wilhelm Heinrici, watched the bombs from both the lead planes drift away from the hangars and, slightly correcting his course, he brought his aircraft around for a more direct run on the airfield. But because he was now heading due north his escape route south was becoming increasingly precarious with every passing second. He would have to bank sharply to the right, while at the same time try and gain height. At that point, hanging sluggishly in the air, the Ju 88 would be an easy target should it run into one of the patrolling Spitfires.

At only twenty-one years of age Heinrici was young for a bomber pilot and perhaps it was his relative lack of combat experience that caused him to ignore the danger presented by such a manoeuvre. Most likely it was his youthful sense of immortality, sheer bravado and a sudden rush of adrenalin that caused him to throw caution to the winds and bring his aircraft down to less than 2,000ft to press home the attack. Keeping the aerodrome firmly in his sights, the 250kg bombs slung beneath the wings were released straight at the hangers as the 50kg fragmentation bombs tumbled towards the barrack blocks. The first high explo-

Pilot Officer Eugene
'Red' Tobin of 609
Squadron

sive blew the corner off No. 4 Hangar but the second landed directly on target, crashing through the roof of No. 5 Hangar that housed reserve aircraft of 604 and 609 Squadrons. Detonating inside such a confined space magnified the effect of the explosion and, as the roof disintegrated skywards, the massive steel doors were blown clean off the upper guide rails collapsing to the ground in a twisted heap.

The force of the blast slammed the Spitfires and Blenheims against the sides of the hangar and the leaking tanks sent the place up in a sheet of flame. The raging inferno would leave No. 5 Hangar a shattered, burnt out shell that wasn't repaired until long after the war.

Strolling over to the mess hall two pilots of 609 Squadron, 'Paul' Edge and the American 'Red' Tobin, were caught in the middle of the aerodrome when the Ju 88 broke out of the low cloud. All around them frightened airmen were flinging themselves flat and, with the plane seemingly chasing him, Edge started to run wildly away. But, on a warning yell from 'Red', he turned and they both ran directly beneath the aircraft and dived headlong to the ground just as it released a stick of bombs.

As the bombs burst close by the earth erupted violently covering them from head to toe in chalk dust, turning them deathly white. Though badly shaken and with a ringing in their ears, they were unharmed. When the dust cleared Edge saw that a row of craters lay directly across his original line of escape. He had just avoided certain death.

To the men in the trenches the SC 50kg bombs seemed to fall out of the sky in slow motion and, covering their heads, they listened for the telltale crump of bursting bombs. One hit a shelter packed with Irish civilian workers killing three, though one unofficial report listed six dead, after which they would never trust

Damaged Bleinhem inside the remains of No.5 Hangar. (Photograph: Peter Foote collection)

a shelter again. At the first sign of any trouble they'd jump off their ladders and head for open country, sometimes even before the alarm had sounded. Another bomb exploded dangerously near the Station Headquarters rocking the flimsy wooden building that housed the fighter Operations Room, and the last landed in the centre of the main barrack blocks.

The men of Ground Defence were throwing everything they could at the raiders as, one by one, they swooped down on the aerodrome. The machine-gunners were blazing frantically away, and there was even some very coordinated rifle fire, but the best chance of bringing down any of the attackers lay with a shell from one of the 20mm cannons. One of these guns was mounted in an isolated spot on top of the guardroom roof and the gunner, 'Lofty' Raines, was sure he had hit one of the raiders when it was attacked, and finished off, by a lone Spitfire. At least this was the story he would tell – which he maintained was confirmed by the Spitfire pilot – to anyone willing to listen.

The clouds of debris, smoke and dust rising from the crippled aerodrome was an awesome sight from the air, and even though the *Sonderfuhrer* had some impressive photographs the damage from the fragmentation bombs was largely superficial. Within a few days – except for the destruction of No.5 Hangar, which was a complete an utter wreck – the craters had been filled in and levelled off, the Station Headquarters had been rehoused and most of the buildings repaired or made good. But immediately after the attack there was much to be done.

Throughout the initial bombardment some airmen had remained resolutely at their posts despite anxious pleas from their comrades to join them in the relative safety of the shelters. Even as, one after another, the bombs exploded across the

Shattered remains of No.5 Hangar after the attack of 14 August 1940. (Photograph: Peter
Foote collection)

airfield a maintenance crew of 609 Squadron did not abandon its position at the
entrance of No.5 Hangar.

Ignoring the flying glass and sheets of orange flame, the members continued
to crank shut the hangar doors in a desperate attempt to save the stranded aircraft
from the lateral blasts. But this valiant action came to an abrupt end as the direct
hit blew the heavy steel-plated doors off the upper runners, sending them crashing, in a ninety-degree arc, down onto the working party.

They tried to save themselves but Henry Thorley and Ken Wilson had hardly
moved before the massive doors smashed their bodies into the ground. Corporal
Bob Smith also died instantly as the leading edge of the door caught him on the
shoulder with such violence it severed his arm from his body and almost cut
him in two. Corporal F.H. Appleby was severely wounded, losing an eye, and the
whole area was awash with blood and gore.

Eddie Gray had been tossed in the air by the force of the explosions, but as
soon as the all-clear sounded he sprinted to No.5 Hangar to see how he could
help. By the time he arrived on the scene some of the blood-splattered survivors
were already fighting to jack up the doors in a vain attempt to save the lives of
the crushed airmen but Eddie could see that it was hopeless. A limp, mangled arm
sticking out from the side of the doors was enough to convince him that no one
could have survived the force of such an impact. The sight of one of the survivors,
slumped against the side of the hangar, crying uncontrollably at the fate of his
friends, confirmed this belief.

Inside the shattered hangar he could see a badly buckled Blenheim and a
Spitfire wing sticking out of the mass of burning wreckage. Another member

of the ground crew was hysterical, and kept repeating over and over that two of his best mates were under the doors. One had grabbed hold of his pal's arm and tried to pull him to the safety of a nearby shelter but, at that instant, the bomb exploded and the collapsing doors killed them both.

Red Tobin had felt the shock wave of the blast flash over the top of his body as he lay there flattened to the ground. And though his head was still spinning when he scrambled to his feet, his first instinct was to head full pelt towards the hanger that had taken a direct hit. At the hanger he was shocked by the carnage. There was an airman with his foot and half a leg blown off, one with an arm missing and another with a red patch on his chest from which a load of mess was hanging out. It was a sickening sight.

The door of the hanger was half closed and just inside he could see the bodies of the three mutilated men, overalls singed and shredded, laid out on the ground with one seemingly splattered against the edge of the door. Red felt sick, and almost threw up there and then. But as other air force men came into the hanger they just seemed to go about their business in a respectable and calm manner, with no sign of panic. Then he remembered what he had been told about the British: 'no matter how bad the situation, they will always keep that stiff upper lip'.

Meanwhile, an unexploded bomb had lodged in the side of a nearby workshop having bounced off the corner of the hangar and burrowed into the join of the floor and sidewall. The top of the fin was clearly visible, sticking out about 2ft but no one gave it a second glance as they worked feverishly to clear the tangled wreckage and jack up the doors. But the rescue work was more in desperation than hope: the bodies were crushed beyond help. Eddie, realising there was little he could do, quietly slipped away.

There were also many wounded, both civilians and servicemen. At Station Headquarters ten airmen had been injured mainly by flying glass, and back at the 'decontamination centre' Ernie Woodger waited for a report of the casualties from the orderlies who had gone out to attend the wounded. The news that filtered back was not good and additional bed space would have to be found. Their medical training would be tested to the full.

Up in the sky, Obltn. Heinrici pulled back hard on the controls to send the dive-bomber, engines screaming on full power, back to the safety of the clouds. At the same time he banked sharply around to head south and home but this combined movement dangerously reduced the rate of climb and the Ju 88 seemed to stand in the air. It was an inviting target.

Heinrici had lost sight of the two lead aircraft when, at about 8,000ft, they disappeared into a dense layer of cloud and there was now little hope of regaining close contact. Shorn of the collective firepower of the *Kette* the lone, lightly armed *Schnellbomber* would have to rely on its speed and the clouds to evade any RAF fighters.

Once into the clouds they would be invisible again and, with luck, the homeward journey would be as uneventful as the inward flight. But the clouds seemed to remain elusively out of reach and Gefreiters Heinz Stark and Freidrich Ahrens nervously fingered their MG 15 machine-guns as the aircraft struggled to gain height.

Earlier that afternoon at 16.50 hours the Spitfires of A flight, 609 Squadron, had taken off as instructed to patrol in the area of Boscombe Down and, at 15,000ft, they formed a loose defensive circle around Middle Wallop. They had only been in position for about five minutes when they were surprised by a twin-engine aircraft approaching them head on from the south. At first they thought it was one of the Blenheims circulating over the aerodrome but, as it passed overhead, they noticed black crosses on the wings and identified it as a Ju 88 or possibly a Me 110.

Flying Officer John Dundas, flying 'Yellow 1', wheeled his Spitfire around sharply and immediately gave chase to what he incorrectly took to be a Me 110. Closing to 900ft he managed to get in two quick bursts without any noticeable effect before losing sight of the enemy aircraft as it dived through the top of the clouds.

The Me 110 was in fact Kern's Ju 88 and his ever-alert rear gunner fired off a couple of warning shots hoping to deflect the attacking Spitfire just long enough for them to make the safety of the clouds. And as the thick, dark clouds rolled over their plane he heaved a huge sigh of relief. There was still a long, dangerous journey home but they could make it unscathed.

Sgt Alan Feary, flying 'Yellow 2', had plunged Spitfire L 1065 straight through the clouds hoping to intercept the fleeing raider in the first clear layer but was forced down below 8,000ft before he broke free of the murk. There was no sign of the enemy plane, which he believed was a Ju 88, and realising it had stayed hidden amongst the clouds, he was just about to rejoin his flight when, off to starboard, he glimpsed another raider bombing Middle Wallop and immediately dived to the attack.

Seeming to sense the impending danger, the Ju 88 had already started its slow climb away from the airfield when Sgt Feary gave chase at full throttle, quickly closing to within 750ft astern. As the enemy plane loomed large in his sights he pressed hard on the gun button firing an intermittent ten-second burst at the Junkers as it banked sharply away in a desperate attempt to escape. The burst of fire had used up most of Feary's ammunition but there was little sign that the fleeing raider had suffered any serious damage, even though it had ceased to return fire.

The top rear gunner, Freidrich Ahrens, had spotted the danger almost immediately and he shouted out that a fighter, possibly a Spitfire, was closing fast. Already on full power Heinrici knew he could not out-climb any of the RAF's front-line fighters but he might just be able to outrun it, especially if he could put some distance between them by causing the attacker to overshoot their plane. As the attacking aircraft, now clearly identified as a Spitfire, closed and commenced to fire he banked the Junkers sharply to the right and watched the fighter shoot straight overhead. For a brief moment he thought this desperate manoeuvre had been successful but the Spitfire was swiftly back on his tail and the bomber shuddered violently under the hail of fire from eight machine-guns.

Although the Ju 88 was a difficult plane to knock out of the air at such close range, it should have disintegrated under the sheer weight of bullets from the

Browning .303s but, somehow, it appeared unharmed. The engines at least should have been shot away but they were still functioning and even though bits had been seen flying off the plane it was not aflame. Such an intense salvo should have torn the bomber in two but it seemed to have a charmed life.

As it went into a steep dive it seemed possible that, despite absorbing such heavy punishment, it might yet make its escape. Feary was not going to let this happen and he closed again to less than 750ft.

Feary's first salvo had in fact torn an ugly gash in the rear of the fuselage and shattered the cowling over the port engine that started to slow and splutter ominously. A few stray shots had crashed through the top of the canopy and Ahrens let out a yell as a bullet whizzed past his head. Amazingly, though badly shaken and superficially cut from the flying glass and metal, not one of the crew was seriously hurt.

With the damaged engine slowing to a stop Heinrici desperately scanned the countryside for somewhere to land. Almost immediately he spotted some open heath directly ahead and told the crew to prepare for a crash-landing. As he steadied the plane it was rocked by a second blast which knocked out the starboard engine and set it ablaze. A sheet of flame shot along the wing and, with black smoke pouring from the shattered port engine, the plane was clearly finished and losing height at an alarming rate.

There was a cry of pain from someone in the rear but it was too late to bale out and the crews only hope of survival rested on the skill of the young pilot. In the cockpit Eugen Sauer turned to him for reassurance but before he could speak the plane crashed through the top of some trees at the edge of the heath and instinctively he closed his eyes and threw up his hands to protect his face.

As Feary fired again smoke started to pour from the bomber's engines and then suddenly the whole tail section ignited under the intense hail of fire. The plane came down in a shallow dive, attempting to level off, as if the pilot was looking for somewhere safe to land and then it crashed into the ground and disintegrated. Following it down Feary did a victory roll over the crash site and hurriedly returned to base to rearm and refuel. There was still other enemy aircraft to be dealt with.

Below, in the rolling English countryside of south-west Hampshire the rural way of life on the farms, clustered around the villages of Redlynch and North Charford, seemed to move timelessly along even though the war was almost 12 months old. There was a shortage of labour of course and food rationing had been introduced, but the latter was having less of an effect on the rural communities than on the population of the cities and industrial towns, where food coupons were already being traded as currency. The war had yet to make its mark on the villagers but that was about to change.

Miss Edith Dear, who worked the smallholding at Lower Windyeates Farm, was standing by the iron five-bar gate of the field close to the electricity pylon ready to let her cows out to graze when the bomber came in low from the north. Ablaze at the tail it took the top off a pine tree at the edge of the forest, and was heading straight for her and the overhead cables.

Pieces of black, evil-smelling fabric were falling off and it was so close she could clearly see the swastika on the tail. She thought her end had come but at the last moment the burning plane veered to the right of the pylon and just scraped over the wires before smacking into the ground at Turf Hill, opposite Deadman Hill, and cartwheeling across the field in a ball of flame.

Bits of airframe and what looked like seats or bodies shot out of the disintegrating plane, spreading mangled and burning wreckage over a wide area. Edith's immediate reaction was to rush to the scene of the crash, but first the cattle that had been frightened by the explosion would have to be penned in. From the force of the impact it was unlikely that there would be any survivors but, in the distance, she could see that some other villagers were already racing to help.

Among the first to view the devastation up close was young Jim Long and a friend who had been working in the fields of Windyeats Farm when they heard the sound of machine-gun fire coming from somewhere to the north. Then from over the top of the farmhouse a twin-engine aircraft appeared – Jim initially thought it was a Blenheim – trailing smoke and with both engines on fire. Coming in low it scared the wits out of Cliff Rex who was working on a hayrick, causing him to leap off the top almost breaking an ankle.

Equally afraid was Willie Cook, the estate keeper, who had been driving his horse and cart along the Millesford road when the Junkers smashed through the tops of the trees. He thought he saw part of the undercarriage shear off or someone bale out, but he was more concerned for his safety and he pulled the horse to a halt, jumped down and dived under the cart. Then he was out and, with a few others and his son Sidney, was hurrying to join Jim Long who was standing over a badly wounded German airman who was groaning in pain. Having no first-aid experience there was little they could do to help but someone did at last bring some blankets.

Luckily a lady with a smattering of German was quickly on the scene but the wounded airman didn't seem to understand her. Making best use of her rudimentary knowledge of first aid, she tried to make him as comfortable as possible but he continued to cry out in pain and for some reason refused a sip of water. She became upset that her efforts were to no avail but, nevertheless, wrapped a blanket around him, hoping this would show she meant no harm.

Sid Cook was horrified to see bits of human flesh lying around and what appeared to be the remains of two, or possibly three, badly mutilated bodies with their hands and feet burnt to a crisp. One airman, lying in a twisted heap, had both legs burned off at the knee and a wound in his back that could have been caused by a bullet. An engine, torn off on impact, had bounced across the field scattering pieces of airframe and a wing in its wake. The fuselage and remaining wing of the blazing plane had skidded almost 900ft cutting a flaming trail through the dried grass before finally coming to rest in a twisted heap. It was a fearsome sight. One that young Sid would always remember.

About 90ft from the main wreckage they found an aircraft seat, wrenched off on impact, with a crewman still strapped inside but he was not moving and appeared to be dead. But they were all unwilling to touch the body and left it to be collected by the ambulance crew.

Police Sgt Young, soon on the site, methodically marshalled the emergency services with the dignity and authority expected of a senior officer. The few men under his charge had attempted to keep the morbidly curious at bay but, with the wreckage spread over such a wide area, it was a nigh on impossible task. And, as help would soon be needed to contain the grass fire that was spreading out of control, he did occasionally relax his vigilance. Certainly he turned a blind eye to the RAF pilot who drove up and looted the rubber dingy as a souvenir. Young lads were also hunting for souvenirs and many pieces went missing, not all taken by young boys.

Amazingly, the airman still strapped in his seat was found to be alive but with severe concussion and a bruised and battered face that was bleeding slightly. He couldn't possibly survive. But survive he did and make it home.

Eugen Sauer, after being in a coma for five days, came to in a small room to see two soldiers with fixed bayonets at the foot of his bed. There was also an officer present who acted as an interpreter, and Eugen asked the reason for such high security. In his crippled condition he could barely move and was hardly capable of an escape attempt.

With just a hint of menace the interpreter replied that the soldiers were there for 'his protection' as the British people hated German airmen. This comment did alarm him but only momentarily. He couldn't image that the British would harm a POW, especially one so badly wounded. Despite his terrible injuries his morale was still high as he was convinced Britain would surrender in a few months. Even if he could walk there was no immediate need to escape. With German victory assured he would soon be released just like other captured German airmen, shot down over the Low Countries, had been after the fall of Belgium and France.

In fact the would be home in Germany long before the end of the war. Despite receiving medical treatment for over three years he was still classed as unfit for active service and, in 1943, was repatriated through Geneva in a POW exchange administered by the Red Cross. Initially taken to the Luftwaffe hospital in Munich for assessment, he was subsequently transferred to a local 'cottage' hospital where he would receive treatment for another year before being finally discharged and making it home. Just in time to spend Christmas 1944 with family and friends.

The villagers watched in silence as the two wounded airmen were carried on stretchers to the ambulance that had arrived to rush them to Salisbury Infirmary. One was still groaning loudly and even though he was the enemy they showed by their silence that they had some sympathy for his wretched condition. But despite the best efforts of the doctors and nursing staff, Freidrich Ahrens died the following day.

He was buried on 17 August in the City of New Sarum Cemetery, Salisbury, in Section 6, Grave 108, alongside his fellow airmen in Graves 109 and 110. But the grave markers of all three said that they were 'unknown airman'. Later a white wooden IWGC cross was erected in the name of F. Ahrens, although it incorrectly showed his date of death as 13 August 1840.

Even when their bodies were exhumed in April 1963 and reburied in the German Military Cemetery at Cannock Chase, only Ahrens was correctly identified and buried in Block 7, Grave 42. It was remarkably lax of the German authorities that the remaining 'unknowns' were not identified as Heinrici and Stark until 1999. They are now listed as being buried in Graves 38 and 41, Block 7.

Feary had landed back at Middle Wallop at 17.25 hours but within fifteen minutes his Spitfire had been refuelled and rearmed and, as the base had again come under attack, he took off in pursuit of the raiders. Rapidly climbing to 6,000ft he noticed six Spitfires attacking a lone Junkers 88 but he resisted the urge to join in and continued to 11,000ft above the clouds. After scouting around for a few minutes, he sighted about 5,000ft higher four Ju 88s flying in a diamond formation, heading south-west and he rapidly gained height to attack from above and behind. But at that moment he heard over the radio that a further enemy formation of three plus bandits was heading for Salisbury, and he decided to delay his attack and hope for re-enforcements from the rest of the squadron.

But when the formation turned south he didn't hesitate for a moment and swept down on the starboard Junkers firing a four-second burst and raked the other bandits with such ferocity that all his ammunition was quickly used up. An ammunition box holding 300 cartridges fed each of the Spitfires eight machine-guns but the Colt-Browning's rate of fire was so rapid – 1,200rpm – that it used up the 2,400 rounds within just fifteen seconds.

In the heat of battle Feary had forgotten the 'fifteen-second rule' and expended all his ammo in two fierce bursts. He thought he must have scored some hits but the formation just sailed straight on not bothering even to return fire. Annoyed he sped away to land and rearm.

Refuelled and rearmed, Dundas was back in the air within twenty minutes but this time he was scouting alone. He had also received the message that two or more bandits were approaching Salisbury at 15,000ft and he climbed to 17,000ft to intercept from out of the sun. He soon spotted four bandits, in a box formation, flying south but as his aircraft recognition was not that good he took the raiders to be Dornier Do 17s, or even Do 215s, but once again they were Ju 88s.

As he dived into the fray, Dundas caught a brief glimpse of another Spitfire just as it veered away after making a stern attack on the trailing raider. But Feary did not notice the late arrival flying to his assistance and, as his guns fell silent, he was forced to break off the engagement, leaving Dundas to continue the running battle alone. The odds were again 4-1 against but Dundas was not deterred.

Attacking beam-on, he opened fire on the lead Ju 88 from 2,400ft but was dismayed as he watched his shots pass harmlessly in front of the aircraft's nose. His second beam attack also failed to register any hits and after the third attack he broke away far too steeply and momentarily blanked out.

Flying Officer H. M. Goodwin of 609
Squadron. (Photograph: Chris Goss)

Coming around, he found himself in dense cloud and thought he had lost the
enemy formation but it had doggedly stayed on the same course heading south.
He caught them up just as they reached the coast but, before he could close in, a
lone Spitfire made a short attack from directly below before disappearing into the
clouds. It did not return.

Determined that at least one of the enemy would not make it back to France,
he now fired on the fourth member of the formation, which had not yet
come under attack. Pressing hard on the gun button he sent out a continuous
six-second burst and, as he broke away, he managed to see the bomber leave the
formation and glide into the clouds.

It was clearly badly damaged and, although Dundas tried to follow it down
through 10,000ft of thick cloud, he did not pick it up when he broke out of the
other side of the murk. There was absolutely no sign of an enemy plane, damaged
or otherwise, and even though he didn't see it crash or splash into the sea, he
nevertheless claimed a Do 17 destroyed.

After the initial attack on Middle Wallop, all the remaining serviceable Spitfires
of 609 Squadron were hurriedly started up by the pilots who had been caught
on the ground. Eager for revenge they took off without orders, but most were
unlucky and did not catch even a glimpse of the enemy, let alone engage them
in combat.

Pilot Officer Michael Appleby who, along with a few other pilots had noncha-
lantly watched the bombing while sitting on top of a slit trench, took off twice in
the hope of catching one of the elusive Germans but on both occasions he drew a
blank. Thick black clouds were the best camouflage a bomber could have and the

fighters would mainly lose the games of hide and seek. Fighter pilots often lacked the patience to play a long waiting game.

Pilot Officer David Crook who had watched in amazement as the Ju 88 made its devastating pass over the aerodrome also took off straight away and was soon in contact with a couple of Heinkels, but he lost them in the heavy clouds. He had managed to get off a couple of shots but he wasn't sure if they had struck home. Flying over the crash site of Feary's kill he later reported that he had never seen an aeroplane so thoroughly wrecked: it was a terrible mess.

The few Blenheims of 604 Squadron still on the ground were also sent up and Sgt Pilot Eric Poole entered in his logbook that he'd 'intercepted a Ju 88 over Andover drome gave chase but could not close. Bloody old Blenheims!' But he was probably lucky that he didn't cross the path of Crook whose aircraft recognition was not too good. The following day he would pepper Sgt Cyril Haigh's Blenheim L 6610, forcing it to crash-land back at Middle Wallop, inflicting some painful 'rear' injuries on his wireless operator/gunner Sgt George Evans. The observer Sgt Walter Fenton was unharmed but the aircraft was damaged beyond repair.

Also up was Flying Officer Henry MacDonald Goodwin in his Spitfire N 3024, PR-H. He had been shot-up in combat with *Zerostorers* on 12 August but gained some consolation the following day by shooting down a Ju 87B Stuka dive-bomber and seriously damaging another.

At this point I need to make a quick detour and tell the story of 'Mac'. He lived at 'Palmers Hill', the large family home set in 5 acres in West Hagley, near Stourbridge. His father was the prominent local businessman Laughton C. Goodwin who, in the early 1920s, had been a partner in the Castle Motor Company that produced the 'Castle Three-wheeler' and now owned a garage in Kidderminster.

Mac had a sister Elisabeth, the youngest, and his brother Barry who raced cars and had competed in the Shelsley Walsh Hill Climb, and as his father was one of seven children there were also many cousins. Their mother, Jess, was a member of the wealthy Palethorpe family who were also prone to making impromptu visits and the house was always full of fun and laughter.

Mac and his brother were witty and amusing – Mac particularly so – and perhaps for the time possibly a bit wild. With their fast cars and a small, if somewhat old, monoplane at the bottom of the garden they were considered spoilt by some of the family.

But to their young female cousins they were romantic, heroic figures and Mac would fly the plane down to Rhosneigr, on Anglesey, and land on the beach at low tide to join in one of their summer picnics. He would squeeze them into the cockpit and, one by one take them up for a spin before the tide came in.

He would also take them for a drive in his Bentley sports car which though old, with a leather strap holding down the bonnet, was still one of the faster cars around and the girls loved to wave to their envious friends as it sped along the country lanes.

Mac and his brother Barry joined the 605 County of Warwick Squadron, Royal Auxiliary Air Force, well before the war when the squadron was stationed at Castle Bromwich, to the west of Birmingham. At the outbreak of war they decided, for family reasons, not to remain in the same unit and Mac transferred to 609 Squadron that, by the commencement of the Battle of Britain, was equipped with the latest Spitfires.

In contrast 605 Squadron still had to make do with worn-out Hurricanes and even the ones that they were given to replace those lost over France, in the hectic last days of May 1940, were old fabric-winged aircraft. They were told there was absolutely no chance of them being supplied with upgraded fighters in the immediate future and, possibly in compensation, the squadron was posted to the relative quiet of Drem in Scotland. But on 24 June 1940 one of these dilapidated, out-of-date Hurricanes failed to pull out of a dive, killing Barry, still only twenty-three.

A few days after Barry was killed Mac was at home, thoughtfully fingering a gold cigarette case that had been a twenty-first birthday present to Barry, when his pretty eighteen-year-old cousin Mary Goodwin called round to keep him company and to see if she could help in any way. She found him alone, sitting on the edge of a large, square, footstool and, for a while, he was his usual cheery, clowning self. Suddenly he became very serious and looking straight at her said, 'Keep the Goodwins laughing Mary'. She never saw him again.

The last anyone saw of Mac and his Spitfire was a report from the Royal Observer Corp that a friendly fighter had been hit and that the pilot had baled out 2 miles south of Boscombe Pier at 18.14 hours. The Boscombe Lifeboat was launched but, despite a through search, there was no sign of the ditched airman.

His body was washed ashore on the Isle of Wight some ten days later and he was buried alongside his brother in the north-west corner of Chaddesley Corbett Churchyard, Worcestershire. Within a few weeks their father was found dead, in a spinney, from a shotgun wound.

Before joining 609 Squadron Mac had swapped his Bentley for a more economical MG sports car – since known as the standard mode of transport of an RAF officer during the Battle of Britain – as the advent of petrol rationing drastically restricted private motoring. But for those serving in the forces, especially those in the RAF where aviation fuel was easier to misappropriate, it was not impossible to obtain an illegal gallon or two, and many ingenious alterations were made to the petrol tanks to fool the random roadside checks.

When the squadron was on forward patrol at Warmwell, some of the pilots allowed their cars to be used by the ground crews in exchange for the cars being thoroughly cleaned and washed, but most importantly for the tanks to be topped up with petrol. It was not always easy to get petrol out of the bowsers without being noticed, so Stan Waterson, who looked after Mac's car, took to keeping a couple of cans filled with 100 per cent octane fuel hidden in the lockers as his own private reserve. So when it was neatly parked, awaiting Mac's return, the spruced up MG always had a tank full of petrol.

Huge crater at Middle Wallop caused by a 250kg bomb

The MG was kept in this pristine condition and in its usual place until after his death was officially confirmed. Even though he had failed to return to base no one had seen a Spitfire shot down, or witnessed one in difficulties, and it was probably assumed that he had landed safely at one of the nearby airfields and had not had the opportunity to report in. Certainly they did not seem overly concerned, and neither the Station Operational Record nor the 609 Squadron Log for 14 August mentions his loss.

As almost all the reported engagements had taken place virtually within sight of Middle Wallop, the loss of Pilot Officer Goodwin over the coast was puzzling. He was thought to have probably been chasing an enemy bomber out to sea when he was caught by some accurate, or lucky, return fire and was forced to bale out. No Mayday message was received and it seems that he had made a hurried exit from the plane, which would rule out engine failure though this does remain a possibility. When his body was eventually recovered, Mac was found to be still wearing his 'Mae West' and that suggests he had been afloat for some time and that the search pattern was inaccurate. But remember that in 1940 civilian lifeboats were not fast enough to locate downed airmen adrift in the choppy waters of the Channel, and that they didn't get any help from spotter aircraft. The RAF had still to address the vexing question of air-sea rescue but, as the air battles raged on and the losses mounted, this would become a priority.

By the end of July a rudimentary, but primarily local, service using high-speed launches, some naval boats and a few borrowed Lysanders had started to evolve but it wasn't until an Air Ministry meeting in late August that the organisation

Mike Boddington (left) enjoying a 'sing song' later in the war

was put on a formal footing. The RAF was to mount air searches leaving the actual rescues to the naval launches. But, like Mac, many more fighter pilots were to perish in the Channel before the organisation was fully operational.

Even then, for some inexplicable reason, no use was made of seaplanes or flying boats. The Germans, on the other hand, had a first-rate air/sea rescue service deploying, throughout the Battle of Britain, some forty He 59 float planes that regularly patrolled the North Sea and the English Channel. Painted white and bearing Red Cross markings they were nevertheless considered fair game by the RAF.

But back to 14 August and the skies above Middle Wallop. On his third sortie, Feary again spotted a twin-engine enemy aircraft bombing the aerodrome and he immediately gave chase but, before he could close in, it disappeared into the clouds. Keeping on the same course he continually peppered the elusive bandit as it peeped in and out of the clouds but seemingly to no effect. Then he received instructions to return to base and reluctantly he broke off the engagement even though, this time, he had ammunition to spare.

After landing back at base, Feary took time out to view the terrific amount of damage caused by the raiders and was completely taken aback by the total devastation to No. 5 Hangar, the damage to No. 4 Hangar and the barrack blocks, and a large hole where a shelter had been. The 50kg fragmentation bombs had, in the main, merely pock-marked the concrete but the 250kg bombs had chewed huge craters in the ground big enough to swallow a couple of lorries, and he was glad he had been airborne when the airfield was attacked.

Being the only sergeant pilot with 609 Squadron, the post-flight banter and informal tactical discussions in the Officers' mess was barred to him and he cut a lonely figure as he wandered into the Sergeants' mess. With 238 Squadron having decamped that day to St Eval it was unlikely there would be any fighter pilots at the bar that would help him celebrate his victory. Fortunately, a bunch of sergeant pilots from the recently arrived 234 Squadron had breezed in and were already toasting Sgt Mike Boddington's victory claim – he had also claimed a Ju 88 – and immediately it became a double celebration.

Later, some of the sergeants in charge of the advanced maintenance party that had followed 234 Squadron down from St Eval also turned up, and they proceeded to hog the rest of the evening's conversation with tales of their own dangerous exploits.

They had set off before their fighters in a couple of old transport planes, and had arrived over the station just as it was being bombed and in the middle of dog-fight between German bombers and Spitfires. To watch the action they rushed excitedly from one side of the plane to the other, causing it to rock alarmingly. Their Polish pilot shouted at them to settle down as he steadied the plane in the first of two courageous, if foolhardy, attempts to bring it in to land.

The bombs continued to rain down on the aerodrome and, in the midst of all the explosions, someone bravely ran from the control tower firing red signals into the air to warn them not to land. With this, much to the relief of the passengers, the daredevil pilot abandoned any further attempts at landing and headed for the safety of nearby Boscombe Down. But once the all-clear sounded they returned to their transports and finally landed at Middle Wallop without any further trouble. It had been an exciting time and the stories would get better as the night wore on. But the flight sergeant pilots of 604 Squadron were plainly not in the mood to join in the party because, again, a Spitfire had fired on one of their Blenheims. The celebrations were therefore somewhat muted but at least Feary got to know some of the combat pilots of 234 Squadron.

However, he would never really get to know the officer pilots of 609 Squadron. They mixed well enough at dispersals, and during the days at the forward base of Warmwell, but relations between officers and other ranks were actively discouraged and, off duty, there was little social contact. Feary wasn't exactly excluded from their beer parties at The Swan (known to the pilots as the 'Mucky Duck') in Monxton, or the long nights out at the Square Club in Andover, but not having been to public or officer school, he knew they had little in common.

Before the war Feary had worked as a clerk in the Derby Borough Treasurer's office and had learned to fly in his spare time as a volunteer with the RAF Reserve, which he joined in 1937 at the age of twenty-five, receiving the rank of sergeant. He had been a bit unfortunate to be posted to 609 Squadron in June 1940 as this was an Auxiliary Air Force Squadron that, before the outbreak of war, was considered the home of the wealthy and the well connected.

Even though their ranks had been thinned out during the battles over France and Dunkirk, the pilots of 609 Squadron had still managed to retain a Corinthian spirit and cavalier attitude that was the mark of the Auxiliary Air Force. The squadron was not really the home of a working lad from Derby, the son of a horse inspector for the Midland Railway.

By the inverted snobbery rules of the 1940s he was, therefore, virtually forced to keep his distance. This enforced exclusion was something that the American adventurers, especially Pilot Officer Eugene 'Red' Tobin, were uncomfortable with and couldn't really understand as they were all combat pilots facing the same risks.

Though they carried the rank of a pilot officer the Americans couldn't march, could hardly salute and, not having attended officer school, were not familiar with the niceties of the Officers' mess. They were completely reliant on the services of a batman who advised them of the correct protocol and looked after all their daily needs, even darning their socks, when they were on the ground.

But they did enjoy the socialising, especially when they could get up to London and visit the Eagle Club in Charing Cross Road, the only place in London where they were guaranteed a coke and a hotdog. The club did not serve alcohol but it was the ideal jumping off point for the drinking dens of Soho were they would party until the money ran out.

Even though they were always uneasy, this did not stop the three Americans on 609 Squadron from behaving like officers, if not English gentlemen, when on duty at Middle Wallop. Just over a month later on 19 September the squadron would lose these colourful characters when they were transferred to become the vanguard of the first Eagle Squadron, but within less than fourteen months they would all be dead.

Pilot Officer Vernon 'Shortie' Keough was the first to go. Out on patrol on 14 February 1941, his Spitfire mysteriously plunged straight down into the North Sea. Tobin survived a further six months but perished during a sweep over France on 7 September 1941 – his squadron was overwhelmed by Me 109s – and Pilot Officer Andy Mamedoff crashed in bad weather on 8 October 1941 when coming into land at Ronaldsway, on the Isle of Man. Only a few weeks earlier he had married Penny Craven, of the Craven cigarette family, at a Christian ceremony in the quiet church at Epping.

Sgt Alan Feary did not even survive the Battle of Britain. On 7 October, patrolling over Weymouth, 609 Squadron attacked a combined force of Me 110s and Ju 88s when Me 109s, providing top cover, attacked them from above. Feary's Spitfire was hit and sent spinning out of control. For some reason he baled out too low and his crumpled body, covered by his half-opened parachute, was found at Watercombe Farm, near Warmwell.

The Squadron Diary recoreded that, 'He seemed to regard his Spitfire with the kind of jealous care that some others bestow on animals.' In a way this probably explains why he did not abandon the uncontrollable aircraft at the earliest opportunity. He was not taken home for burial and he lies in the military plot at the Holy Trinity Church, Warmwell, a few miles east of Dorchester.

An ace with at least five victories to his credit, his bravery was never honoured officially. He was not recommended, even posthumously, for any award. It's an odd fact that by the end of the war only four sergeant pilots of 609 Squadron had been decorated, compared with forty officers.

The three Americans who served
with 609 Squadron during August
1940. Left to right: Pilot Officers E.
Tobin, V. Keough and A. Mamedoff

Tragically when he was killed in action Feary's young fiancée, Joan Drake,
was four months pregnant. Even though Feary, a six-footer, was well spoken and
polite, for some reason her parents were strongly opposed to the match and, as
she was under twenty-one, their wedding plans had been put on hold. When,
on Feary's death, she told them of her pregnancy they virtually disowned her.
Ashamed of the stigma attached to an unmarried mother she agreed not to keep
the child and, when a son was born on 6 March 1941, he was sent to a children's
home in Australia. In later life David Drake-Feary, still living in Australia in the
small agricultural town of Horsham, Victoria, would become aware of his father's
daring exploits during the dangerous days of 1940. He was proud to find that his
father was a Battle of Britain pilot – one of 'The Few'.

A dinghy rescued from the crashed Ju 88 was donated to the Mayor of Derby's
War Fund and placed on exhibition in the town but, for the next forty years,
Feary was largely forgotten by the town until 1981 when interest was revived
by the archaeologist Barry Marsden. His in-depth research into Feary's early
life and wartime adventures was officially rewarded when, in 1987, a perma-
nent memorial to this Battle of Britain pilot was opened to the public at Derby
Industrial Museum.

As 14 August drew to a close, Eddie Gray, forgetting how tired he was, had
volunteered to stand guard over a crashed aircraft that had come down not far

Airmen from Middle Wallop and Old Sarum standing guard over the wreckage of the Ju 88 of 1/LG1 that crashed and disintegrated at Turf Hill, North Charford at 17.00 hours on 14 August 1940. Left to right: Eddie Gray, with bandaged hand, Cpl Jim Stevens, Jimmy Workman and A/C Harrison. The four airmen on the far right are part of the guard from Old Sarum. (Photograph: Peter Cornwell)

from Middle Wallop. He had done crash duty before but this had always been on British planes that had come down as a result of engine failure or had been involved in flying accidents. This was the first time he had been ordered to stand guard over a crashed enemy aircraft and, along with six other volunteers, he piled into the back of an RAF service lorry.

It was nearing dusk when they set off and the lorry bumped its way along the winding, unlit country roads for about 10 miles before arriving at the scene of the crash just as daylight faded. The devastation was a picture never to be forgotten. Illuminated by a grass fire, that seemed to be burning out of control, the smouldering, tangled central mass of wreckage was a terrible sight, and the long shadows cast by the armed men already standing guard only added to the eerie spectacle.

For some reason a 'crash guard' had also been dispatched from Old Sarum and they had already secured the area by the time Eddie's crew arrived on the scene. Their corporal said one of the Germans was still unaccounted for, having possibly baled out, and everyone was told to keep a sharp look out as he may yet find his way to the crash site. A double guard was posted in the unlikely event of this happening but no one really expected him to turn up.

As night wore on it became quite chilly and Eddie, having been woken up by the cold, brewed up some cocoa for himself and the boys out on 'stag'. Even though the grass fire would occasionally flare up it was a fair way off. The wreckage strewn all over the ground was hidden in darkness.

Eddie gingerly picked his way around the obstacles as best as he could in the dark but his foot caught something that sent him sprawling. He came down heavily cutting his left hand on a splinter of blackened aluminium sticking out of the burnt grass. The wound bled profusely but a makeshift bandage stemmed the flow and, after a hot drink, Eddie again drifted off to sleep.

In the early morning Eddie was up and about checking over the remains of the burnt-out Ju 88 when something caught his attention in the middle of the wreckage. In the half-light he thought it was just a molten seat but, as he peered closer, he was horrified to see that it contained a stump of badly charred flesh barely recognisable as a human being. He had found the missing airman, or what was left of him, and together with Corporal Jim Stephens they recovered as much of him as they could and covered the grisly remains with a blanket. It was not a sight they wanted any one to see, and certainly not the army of villagers arriving to put out the burning grass. It had flared up again and it would take most of the day to bring under control.

Eddie never forgot the cold night he spent on Turf Hill though, as the war dragged on, the memory did start to fade. During the next five years he would witness many other crashes and similar scenes of destruction but, except for the crash of a Lancaster bomber, he would never again see such carnage. And periodically that terrible image of death would come clearly back into focus. It would haunt him for most of his life.

Many years after the war, when Eddie found out that one of the crew of the Ju 88 had survived the crash, the number of bodies they had recovered puzzled him. Could there in fact have been five men aboard? Was one of the crew still unaccounted for? Or were the body parts so badly shredded that two bodies became three in the failing light?

The contemporary RAF 'K' report, probably compiled immediately after the crash, is so brief it only adds to the mystery:

14.8.40   18.00   Salisbury Plain   Ju 88   (1/ LG1)   (L1 + -H)   5186   Rennes(?)
A/c badly smashed.   2 of crew killed, 3rd very badly injured in crash.
Identification from Disc.

This seems to suggest there were only three men on board the plane but the report was probably filed before the body was found the next day. However, it is odd that no mention is made of a probable fourth member of the crew.

A further 'K' Report based on information passed to the admiralty was far more detailed but throws little light on the make up of the crew. It incorrectly gives the date of the crash as 15 and not 14 August 1940, and again only a partial aircraft code number is shown but some interesting facts do emerge that are worth repeating:

Ju 88. Crashed on the 15.8.40. at Redlynch, Nr. Southampton.
One black H is the only identification letter decipherable. Engines: two Jumo 211.

One airscrew marked VDN Hamburg-Gr. Borstel. Petrol mark on fuselage, yellow triangle with white outline, E.87 marked beneath. Aircraft destroyed by fighter action and burnt out on impact. No guns, ammunition or instruments salvable. Crew probably four.

So even this later report only suggests, rather than asserts, that the aircraft carried a crew of four, presumably because some of the bodies were in a bit of a mess. The best interpretation of the body count is that when Eddie arrived at the scene only one cadaver was still on site – the one with the legs burnt off – and this was removed shortly afterwards. Having been told by the Old Sarum guard that two bodies had already been taken away he assumed these were corpses when, in fact, both airmen were still alive even though one would die the following day. These three, plus the one found the next day, gives the correct crew number of four but Eddie, believing that they had all perished, added the one survivor to this figure resulting in an incorrect total of five. But Eddie was never really satisfied with this interpretation.

However, there is a entry in the War Diary of the 35th Anti-Aircraft Brigade that sheds some light on this enigma. It records that 'Searchlight Site 5244 observed fighters engaging a Ju 88 that crashed at map reference U 671361, 5 miles NE of Fording bridge.' Two of the crew were burnt and the two others seriously injured. The plane containing a collapsible rubber boat, together with rations, including wine and cigarettes. These figures confirm the crew number as four, though the presence of wine seems to indicate the rather casual attitude of some of the bomber crews on their sorties over Britain.

There is also a bit of a mystery surrounding the number of aircraft destroyed on the ground at Middle Wallop when No.4 Hangar was damaged and No.5 was completely gutted. According to Chris Goss, in his book *Brothers in Arms*, three Spitfires – R6692, R6977 and P9322 – of 609 Squadron were written off, and it's probable that the two 604 Squadron losses shown for 15 August, of Blenheims L6723 and L8676, in fact occurred on 14 August.

The attack on Middle Wallop by Lehrgeschwader 1 can be viewed as a limited success. For the loss of only one Ju 88 it destroyed five planes – three being front-line Spitfires – on the ground and accounted for another Spitfire and its pilot during aerial combat. The tally of dead was also in the Germans' favour.

Later in the year, at the beginning of October, Ron Newman was helping with the harvest in the fields behind Windyeates Farm when he stumbled across the lower gondola of the Ju 88 lying on a bank at the edge of the woods. Complete with an MG 15 machine-gun, ammunition and leather pouch, it had remained unnoticed for almost two months even though many villagers had seen something fly off the aircraft as it crashed through the tops of the trees.

Ron had been living at Windyeates for some time but, on the day of the crash, he was working at the Royal Naval Armaments Depot, at nearby Dean Hill, and only picked up the sequence of events on his return home. He did visit the crash site but the heavy RAF presence kept everyone at bay and he didn't linger.

His friends had many a tale to tell about the crash but as he had also witnessed the destruction of an enemy aircraft – a Heinkel bomber no less – at roughly the same time he was not outdone in the story stakes. Someone said that one of the crew had baled out and was still on the loose, but no one mentioned that part of the aircraft had come down in the woods and finding the gondola was a great surprise. Many people might have been tempted to keep a machine-gun from the Ju 88 but Ron had no hesitation in handing it, and the ammunition, to the police.

The gondola remained undisturbed on banking, near the Keepers Cottage on Matchains Estate, east of Windyeats Farm, for many years. It was certainly there in the early 1960s but when the late Peter Foote made a detailed search of the site in October 1965 it had vanished. It was probably removed for scrap and won't be seen again but there is the remote possibility that its historical value was recognised and that someone saved it for posterity.

Incidentally, at the same time that the last Ju 88 of LG 1 took off from Orleans, an unusual confrontation was taking place about 200 miles west-north-west of Londonderry when an Fw 200 Condor of I/KG 40, fed up with being tracked by two Sunderland flying boats, turned and drove them off by firing a heavy salvo at one of them. Though the Sunderland did not appear to be visibly damaged it had, in fact, suffered hits in the starboard wing and fuel tanks from the Condors 20mm cannon and it was forced to return to base.

Gefr Eugen Sauer

CHAPTER SEVEN

Schnellbombers over the South-West

Late in the afternoon of 14 August 1940, as the south coast of England faded behind them, Obltn. Kurt Sodemann grew increasingly uneasy as his small formation of two Ju 88s penetrated further and further inland. A holder of the Iron Cross, he was no stranger to danger, having fought in the skies over Poland, Norway and Dunkirk, as well as taking part in every raid undertaken by LG 1 against England, but he was well aware of the inherent dangers of a daylight-bombing mission. Even with fighter cover it was a perilous task and, as they flew onwards in clear blue sky, just above the clouds, he knew how vulnerable his unescorted bombers would be to a sustained attack by RAF fighters.

A Luftwaffe career officer, he had been transferred from the 'Kreigsschule' of the army to the Fliegershule at Celle in 1935 and, in 1937, after completing flight training he was posted to III Gruppe of LG 1, then stationed on the Baltic at Greifswald. By the summer he had seen action on all fronts and in July 1940, at twenty-nine years of age, he was transferred to the I Gruppe/LG 1 to take command of the 3rd Staffel.

Now he had to acquaint himself with the whole Staffel, and not just his own crew, but as he soon found out he had inherited a 'very reliable and efficient crew' to whom he could leave all the pre-flight preparations. Quickly he familiarised himself with the men under his command and checked out their ability to fly the Junkers Ju 88. He put them through intensive training because, having flown Ju 88s for over a year, he was well aware that they remained difficult planes for the inexperienced. He was also critical of the puny defensive armament of only three drum-fed machine-guns, and he made them practise changing the magazines time and time again.

But, in reality, their best form of defence was the heavy cloud base below. By skimming through the tops of the clouds they should, with luck, be able to dive into the protective murk before the fighters could close to within firing range. Then flying in and out of the clouds they could use their speed and agility to dodge the fighters. Combat was out of the question. He didn't relish the thought

Kurt Sodemann (far left) and fellow officers of 3rd Gruppe of LG1, June 1940. (Photograph:
K. Sodemann)

of a running battle with any of the RAF fighters, even on a one-to-one basis.
However the next day, during an attack on Middle Wallop, he did encounter a
twin-engine aircraft – probably a Blenheim of 604 Squadron – that he engaged
in a brief exchange of fire before his Ju 88 managed to outrun it, with his gunners
seeming to get the better of the action. The extra gunnery practice paid off.

Each aircraft carried three SC 250kg high explosive bombs and one *flam-
mbombe* (a 110kg oil-bomb in a 250kg casing) under the wings and five SD 50kg
fragmentation bombs inside the fuselage. The 'Flambo', if dropped on a sensitive
and ignitable target, such as an RAF workshop or crowded hangar, was capable
of causing the greatest amount of destruction, and Sodemann hoped his present
crew would be up to the task of accurate bombing, unlike some of the inexperienced crews he had had to put up with in the past.

During the Norwegian campaign he had attacked a cruiser in the Molde-
Fjord crossing so low over the ship – not more than 200-300ft above it – that
they couldn't miss. It was an easy target, but his navigator/bomb-aimer made a
serious mistake with the bomb release mechanism and the bomb plunged harmlessly into the water almost half a mile from the cruiser. And over Dunkirk he had
attacked a ship packed with evacuated British soldiers as it steamed at full speed
away from the beachhead. The bombs splashed into the sea either side of the ship
but they did not explode because his bomb-aimer had stupidly set the fuses on an
eight-second delay. When they did detonate, sending up huge columns of water,
the ship was out of the danger zone, well away from the impact of the bombs.

After only five weeks in charge he was unable to gauge which of his pilots
would make his ideal wingman for this mission, but he knew Fw. Heinrich

Fw. Heinrich Boecker. (Photograph: Frau L. Boecker)

Boecker and his crew would be more than up to the mark as they were all expe-rienced airmen. He was sure that they would give a good account of themselves once they had arrived over the Maintenance Unit at RAF Hullavington, their intended target that day. Having been lucky enough to somehow elude the defending fighters he led the formation through a break in the clouds to check out their bearings as, according to his navigator Otto Bergstrasser, they should be almost on top of their target. And as they emerged beneath the low cloud base they were surprised to find themselves directly above an aerodrome but it cer-tainly wasn't Hullavington.

Sodemann gave a telling look at his navigator and drew the aircraft back up into the safety of the heavy clouds, as he was sure their presence had set the alarm bells ringing in the aerodrome below. The RAF fighters if not already in the area would now be climbing to intercept and he ordered the crew to prepare for a bombing run. As they took up their attack positions Sodemann circled the unknown airfield a couple of times and then sent the Ju 88 into a shallow dive to give them a perfect bombing platform.

As he hurriedly shuffled through his briefing sheets and target maps there came an excited cry from Bergstrasser. The unknown airfield they had acciden-tally stumbled upon was in fact RAF Kemble, the home of No.5 Maintenance Unit and luckily their secondary target for the day. Having flown too far north they were a long way off Hullavington but at least they had another prime target that fell within their overall battle plan. Sodemann gained some small comfort from this even though, in reality, he had once again been let down.

RAF Kemble was a large aircraft storage unit located some 4 miles from Cirencester and, since the late spring of 1940, was also the home of No.4 Continental Ferry Pilots' Pool. All of its hangars were crammed to capacity and the overspill – mainly bombers – were picketed out amongst trees near the

Tetbury Road. Though not a front-line station Kemble was still a major target and the incoming Ju 88s, even with their limited bomb load, could inflict massive damage on the aerodrome, especially if one of the congested hangars took a direct hit.

It was around 16.30 hours when J.C. 'Les' Jones climbed down from the gunnery post perched on top of the water tower at RAF Kemble. Having spent most of the day 60ft up in the air manning twin Lewis guns, he was glad to be relieved and grab a well earned cup of tea and a sandwich.

Only nineteen years of age it was lucky he didn't suffer from vertigo, and even in the height of summer it wasn't the best place to be. For the Ground Defence team it was probably the worst location on the station, but at least the duty roster ensured that the men shared the jobs. They were never stuck at one post too long and no ground gunner was ever permanently selected for 'mid-air' duties, though one or two airmen did seem to spend an inordinate amount of time at this post – it was never wise to annoy the warrant officer.

After a quick wash Les collected his knife, fork and spoon from his billet and was walking to the mess hall with Vic Gardiner, Reg Voisey and Bill Cruise, three friends from Cardiff, when Fed Allen and Bert Lydiart, two boys from the Welsh Valleys, stopped and looked up at two aircraft that had popped out of the clouds. The strong light made recognition difficult but as no alarm had sounded the lads thought that they must be friendly. But the next moment the earth shook and clouds of debris and dust shot into the air. They hadn't seen the bombs fall but they certainly felt the explosive blasts that tore great holes in the concrete and grass and shredded the trees surrounding the aircraft parked on the edge of the airfield. Dropping to the ground they let go of their equipment and cutlery and covered their heads with their hands.

No.4 Continental Ferry Pilots' Pool at RAF Kemble, 1940. (Photograph: W. Morgan)

The tented mess hall was almost blown over but no one was injured and none of the buildings or hangars had been hit. The Luftwaffe had failed to inflict any serious damage on the aerodrome but as wings and pieces of airframe flew up out of the trees they realised that the falling bombs had landed right in the middle of the parked aircraft.

Amazingly, as the bombs rained down there was no return of fire from the Ground Defence crew. Not one gun had opened up on the raiders. Then Les remembered. So as not to give their positions away to the enemy they had been warned not to return fire until the official order to do so was received by the field telephone. As the ground erupted around them someone had either forgotten to send the order or had dived for safety before doing so, and that's why the guns stayed silent. He couldn't believe that not even one gunner had thought to disobey the order and open fire as the Germans flew low overhead.

Sodemann quickly surveyed the aerodrome as it spread out before him. The hangars presented the obvious target but then, out of the corner of his eye, he caught a glimpse of some planes parked on the ground. Half-hidden by trees they seemed to be a mixture of fighters and bombers and were an easy target, and anyway the hangars could well be empty. Oddly they hadn't experienced any flak, not even light AA fire, and the chance of an uninterrupted bombing run was too good to miss. Without any further hesitation he bore down on the static targets. The trees wouldn't offer much protection. They would be blasted to matchsticks.

The large bombs were laid directly on top of the parked aircraft but one or two of the 50kg bombs drifted away and exploded on the edge of the buildings, cratering the hardcore, throwing up a huge hole in the grass runway and blowing out some windows. Most of this damage was largely superficial and easily made good but the thought of an unexploded bomb kept everyone well way from the area. Just as Sodemann pulled the Ju 88 back into the clouds he caught sight of a broken wing whirling skywards and realised that a wing from an operational aircraft couldn't possibly fly that high in the air. Had he been fooled by dummy aircraft? And as there was no AA fire was this in fact a decoy airfield. Momentarily his heart sank.

As his wingman shot past also heading for the aircraft amongst the trees it was far too late for their radio operator, Werner Lorenz, to signal him to abort his bombing run and to concentrate his attack on the hangars. Their rear gunner, Ernst Bossert, watched Boecker's bombs land right in the middle of the trees, uprooting them, sending branches and pieces of airframe high into the air. A direct hit. But on what?

Back up above the clouds a fighter appeared in the distance and Sodemann ducked back into the protective veil of vapour but, during this manoeuvre, he lost visual contact with his wingman. Repeatedly they sent out radio signals but there was no reply and he feared that the worst had happened. Had the RAF downed a Schnellbomber?

Heading home his spirits were lifted somewhat when his crew assured him that they had without doubt dropped their bombs on top of real aircraft and not onto cardboard replicas. His rear gunner had had the best view and he was sure they hadn't been duped. The wings and metal pieces that shot into the air were real.

Landing back at Bricy he was relieved to learn that Boecker had returned safely some minutes earlier but was surprised to hear that he was only claiming to have badly damaged about four or five of the planes parked in a wood beside the airfield at RAF Kemble. And although Sodemann was sure he had completely destroyed at least one or two and had damaged beyond repair many others, he went along with this assessment and submitted a similar claim. In their records the Luftwaffe would record that about ten aircraft had been destroyed or damaged on the ground but, for some reason, the target airfield was incorrectly listed as Flugplatz 'Hamble'. This mistake was presumably a typing error, not poor identification.

The RAF later admitted that nine Armstrong Whitworth Whitley twin-engine bombers had been damaged in the attack and, although out of date by 1940, the Whitley still formed one of the main strike aircraft of Bomber Command. But at this stage of the war the loss of bombers was not a significant worry for the RAF.

Dusting himself down 'Les' Jones checked out the damage to the airfield but, except for a huge crater, there was nothing that would cause the repair party any problems. But he had a problem; he couldn't find any trace of his canteen cutlery. How would he explain the loss during the next kit inspection? A loss through enemy action was probably not an acceptable excuse but, with the help of his room-mates and a bit slight of hand, he managed to pass muster. There was a long war before him but never again would he lose his entire cutlery in one go.

Aircraftman Leslie Sansom had also casually glanced up at the approaching aircraft and, as he shielded his eyes from the sun's glare, he saw two bombs falling out of the sky and dived for cover in the nearest slit trench, his only means of shelter. From here he watched the two stand-by Hurricanes that were armed and ready for local defence quickly take-off, ignoring the usual warm-up time, before the all-clear sounded. On their return Sgt Chandler disappointedly reported that their chase had been in vain as they had failed to make contact with the enemy bombers that had used their speed to climb back up and hide amongst the clouds.

Ordered to fill in two of the bomb holes that had just been made in the grass take-off and landing strip, Leslie pocketed a large piece of shrapnel that, in 2007, he still had in his possession. Then aged ninety-four he was still sharp enough to write to the *Daily Mail* concerning the hours he spent in 1940 with the British film director and then Ferry Pilot Arthur B. Woods, who went on to win the AFC as a night fighter navigator.

Throughout the following crucial weeks of the Battle of Britain, Kurt Sodemann continued to lead his Staffel during their daylight forays over Britain, again mostly engaged in armed reconnaissance and nuisance raids against coastal targets. Always with the same crew but sometimes in other Ju 88s, he would take part in every raid undertaken by the unit only for his luck to run out on 21 September 1940, ironically, after returning from another raid on Middle Wallop.

H. Lonicer (with
bandaged arm) and
K. Sodemann at
Euston Station on
7 October 1940. In
the background are
O. Weckeiser (with
cap) and H. Berthel
(bare-headed)

As he headed for home, his Ju 88 (L1+AL) was harried all the way to the coast by the Hurricanes of 238 Squadron and the Spitfires of 602 Squadron. The fighters seemed to come at them from all directions and bullets pounded into the aircraft wounding him slightly. After taking so many hits the plane started to shake and shudder and to lose height rapidly, and Kurt realised they would never make it back across the Channel. He considered giving the order to bale out but then, just before they ran out of land, he decided to try and bring the stricken aircraft down. And against the odds he made a comfortable belly landing at Mudberry Farm, Bosham, Sussex, almost within sight of the sea.

Of the four RAF pilots who attacked Sodemann's aircraft not one survived the war. Sgt Eric Bann would be dead within a week after he baled out and his parachute failed to deploy and Pilot Officer Archibald Lyall would perish before the year was out when he baled out too low. Early in 1941 Pilot Officer Charles Davis came to grief and Pilot Officer Osgood Hanbury did not survive the summer of 1943.

After being captured Sodemann was separated from his men and taken to Cockfosters for interrogation. There he was housed with his Gruppencomander Major Heinz Cramer who had been shot down a few days earlier, and British Intelligence was presumably hoping that they would inadvertently divulge some Luftwaffe operational secrets. Whether they did let slip some vital information Sodemann could not be sure, but they were both well aware to the dangers of hidden microphones and always steered their conversations away from military matters.

After two weeks at the interrogation centre he was sent to a holding camp near Hyde Park for a couple of days before being transported by train to the officers' POW Camp No. 1 at Grizedale Hall, near Windermere, in the Lake District. From there, like most other Luftwaffe officers, he was subsequently shipped to Canada

The crew of Ju 88 (L1+AL) at their fiftieth birthday reunion on 21 September 1990. Left to right: Ernst Bossert, Otto Bergstrasser, Kurt Sodemann and Werner Lorenz. (Photograph: K. Sodemann)

where he was caught up in the infamous 'Battle of Bowmanville' on which the film the *Mackenzie Break* was loosely based. He was brought back from Canada at the end of the war and spent the winter of 1946–47 at the POW camp at Llanover Park near Abergavenny. He managed to visit the site during a family holiday to Britain in 1973, but the only thing that remained from his time there was an insulating knob fixed to a tree on which a telephone cable had been attached.

After this one nostalgic visit, thoughts of his wartime exploits were largely pushed to the back of his mind until, completely out of the blue, he received a phone call from his navigator on 21 September 1989 wishing him all the best for their birthday. A tradition had arisen amongst Luftwaffe airmen that if they survived an aeroplane crash they called that date their 'second birthday'. And although his crew had not been in contact with one another since their crash in 1940, Otto Bergstrasser proved once again to be a fine navigator for he tracked them all down and a reunion was held at Kurt's home on 21 September 1990 to celebrate their 'fiftieth' birthday.

The operational roster for the I Gruppe of LG 1 for 14 August 1940 was armed reconnaissance, primarily against the RAF aerodromes of Maintenance Command in the west of Britain, with aircraft factories, military installations and railway terminals in and around the Bristol area as secondary targets. But because of the poor weather conditions they also had a roving commission to attack any opportune target that presented itself if the main and secondary targets were obscured by cloud. The bombers fanned out in all directions all over the west of England and Wales in search of attractive objectives. Most foraged on their own for an unwary airfield.

Penetrating as far north as Worcester and even crossing to the other side of the Bristol Channel, where they bombed the airfield at Pengam Moors on the out-

Construction work being undertaken at RAF Colerne in 1940. (Photograph: P. Osmand)

skirts of Cardiff, the raiders concentrated their attacks on military and industrial complexes rather than easy civilian targets. An isolated attack was carried out on Weston-super-Mare where hits were observed on the quayside, and an airfield that they thought was probably Whitchurch, near Bristol, was also bombed but, owing to bad visibility, the extent of the damage was not observed. The airfield bombed was in fact RAF Colerne, which was hit by one of the two Ju 88s of Raid 148 that, a few minutes earlier at 17.45 hours, had dropped eight high-explosive bombs on the huge underground Royal Ordnance ammunition and explosive depot at Monkton Farleigh, but no significant damage was reported. And luckily no one was killed or injured.

At the time of the attack RAF Colerne was still under construction, with the runways being laid out by the construction company B. Sursley & Co. Ltd where Peter Osmand was employed as an assistant civil engineer. The station had only opened as a maintenance and aircraft storage unit the previous May and work, under the supervision of the Air Ministry Directive, was still in progress.

As the alarm sounded Peter saw two aircraft, which he incorrectly identified as Dornier Do 17s, approaching from the direction of Box village and even though he dropped his half-eaten sandwich he didn't immediately dive for cover. He stood transfixed as the bombers, coming down to less than 4,000ft, headed in his direction and as they flew overhead one of the bombers released its deadly load that landed in the distance near the Station Headquarters.

Only eight bombs fell on the airfield and they were clustered in an area of about 180ft with one scoring a direct hit on an old disused barn, taking its roof off. The civilian canteen was a bloody shambles having also taken a direct hit, as well as catching the blast from two bombs that exploded just outside, killing LAC

Obltn. Kurt Sodemann with Hptmn Hoffman and Obltn. Horst Beeger in the Briefing Room of I Gruppe/LG1. (Photograph: K. Sodemann)

Bernard Walton and mortally wounding AC2 Fred Sharrocks and injuring seven other airmen. Many more suffered slight wounds from the debris and flying glass from the shattered windows of the headquarters and stores, while five civilians were also wounded, two of them seriously.

Due to rolling clouds over Little Rissington they were unable to report the result of the attack on the railway station or to see whether any bombs had strayed off target and fallen on the town. The Ju 88s that couldn't find their targets, or were forced to abort their missions because of concerted attacks by fighters or heavy AA fire, jettisoned their bombs and some of these possibly did accidentally fall in municipal areas but most fell on open ground or in the sea. At this stage in the Battle of Britain the bombing of purely civilian targets was still forbidden. Hitler had yet to authorise the Luftwaffe High Command to commence terror bombing.

Because the prevailing heavy cloud in the south-west obscured many of their primary objectives, the reconnaissance results yielded little information. Three merchant ships of 5,000 tons were sighted in Portsmouth harbour and many aircraft were seen on the ground at the airfields of Weston Zoyland and Weston-super-Mare, but nothing of any real interest to Luftwaffe Intelligence was obtained.

On their return to Orleans, the pilots of LG 1 reported being attacked by twenty fighters near Netheravon and by four more near Salisbury, and that they were also fired at by two Bristol-Blenheim 'Destroyers' over Bournemouth. Heavy flak and barrage balloons had disrupted the attack on Pershore (Throckmotton) and, instead, the lone raider dropped a full bomb load over a factory layout and railway junction at Blackpole on the edge of Worcester airfield. Barrage balloons were also reported over Southampton, Portsmouth and Bournemouth. Such a concerted defence was not expected and resulted in three of the bombers aborting their missions due to attacks by fighters. Amongst other transmissions the Ground Station at Avord picked up a faint message from L1 + CH that it had dealt with an in-flight emergency and was heading back to base. It landed safely at 17.30 hrs.

The barrage balloons over Southampton forced the bombers to fly just too high, and most of the bombs destined for the docks and ships at anchor fell on the town causing damage to shops and houses, missing any target of military value. The heavy AA barrage put up from the batteries on the west side of the River Trent also affected the aim of the two Ju 88s as they ranged over the city, and the bombs landed in the St Denys area between Cobden Bridge and the railway bridge that crosses the River Itchen. The bombs missed the shipbuilding yards alongside the river but the main railway line was hit, ripping up the tracks and causing damage to a stationary train and rolling stock. But the line was back up and running in the morning.

Initially it was thought that three of the Ju 88s had been lost during the afternoon raids over Britain, but this was later downgraded to two when it was learned that one aircraft had made a forced-landing at Cherbourg with battle damage. Repaired on site, it was subsequently flown back to the LG 1 headquarters at Orleans. Other than the Schnellbomber shot down by Sgt Alan Feary after attacking Middle Wallop, the only loss suffered by I/LG1 on 14 August 1940 was the Junkers Ju 88A-1 of the 2nd Staffel flown by Lt Werner Stahl that failed to return from operations over Britain. There is no record of it crashing on land so it presumably came down in the Channel, but which one? The English or Bristol?

In the book *Fly for your Life*, which details the exploits of the famous fighter ace Flt Lt R.R. Stanford Tuck, there is a dramatic, if somewhat fanciful, account of an engagement over the Bristol Channel between a flight of Spitfires of 92 Squadron and three Ju 88s. During this action one of the raiders was badly shot-up and went straight down to crash on the outskirts of Cardiff, with two survivors being pulled from the wreckage. Another, after taking a phalanx of bullets in a head-on attack, finished up on the south bank of the Bristol Channel and the third, streaming oil and glycol, came down someway inland.

Though the information given in Tuck's combat report is a bit less subjective, he nevertheless claimed to have engaged Ju 88s even though Sgt R.E. Havercroft, who was flying as Blue 3, was sure they had engaged Heinkels 111P. He clearly saw the telltale cut-out at the trailing edge of the wing as he dived into the attack. He was surprised that Tuck had already submitted his intelligence report claiming the destruction of Ju 88s, but not wanting to cause any dissent he went along with his flight commander's report.

However, no Ju 88s was reported to have crashed in this area on the afternoon of 14 August 1940. The only enemy planes known to have been shot down over Cardiff and the Bristol Channel were Heinkels 111P but when Tuck was approached on the matter in 1983 he was adamant that his aircraft recognition

Bomb damaged Southern Railway line at St Denys, 14 August 1940

was correct. The squadron commander of 92 Squadron had approved the entry in his logbook and he did not wish to be drawn into any controversy on the subject.

Anyway, his mind was quite clear. They had engaged and shot down Ju 88s and there was no way he would alter his statement. Even when it was pointed out that Blue Flight had probably accounted for three Heinkels and not just two 88s, which would raise his victory tally, he still would not discuss the matter any further, and it was thought best to let things lie.

However, the Ju 88s of LG 1 did forage the other side of the Bristol Channel and at least one had orders to attack the airfield at Cardiff, as the surviving service book of Gefr Karl Neff, the radio operator in Stahl's aircraft, shows this was their intended target. The mystery is whether they were shot down into the sea before they could carry out an attack or after they had accomplished their mission.

It was just after 17.30 hours when Malvina Lowe cycled towards the small humpback bridge, opposite the tram depot, that was the only entry and exit point from the airport at Pengam Moors onto Newport Road, Cardiff. Pengam was a busy commercial airport that served the city of Cardiff but and it was requisitioned and taken over by the RAF. Occupying reclaimed land commonly called 'The Tide Fields', it subsequently also came to house No.43 Maintenance Unit that acted as a packing unit for aircraft being shipped overseas. Initially there was only one large hangar and a few small outbuildings and the conditions were somewhat cramped, but private business and the military seemed to coexist without too many problems.

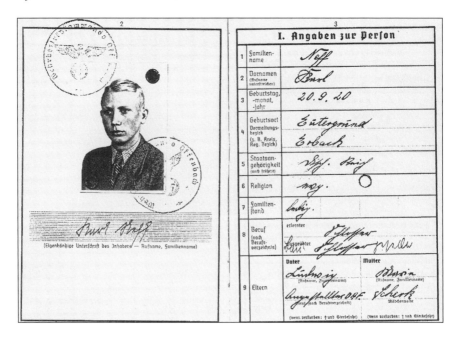

The Service Book of Gefr Karl Neff, showing Cardiff as the target. (Document copy: J. Neff)

The leaden clouds had blown away and it was now a pleasant evening with a clear blue sky as Malvina left, and there was no thought of any danger as she turned to look up at an aircraft she could hear approaching. No air-raid sirens had sounded so there was nothing to fear but then, to her great surprise, a stick of bombs fell from the low flying plane and they were heading straight for the ground between her and the queue of men outside the hangar. Jumping off the bike, she flung herself to the ground and said a quick prayer.

Having hitched a lift in a lorry, Ken Evans was coming home to Cardiff for a short spell of leave from the army. As he was driven down Rumney Hill he suddenly saw, flying low across the road from north to south, no more than 600–900ft away, with its markings plainly visible, a German bomber. And as it passed over the main railway line, to the left of the road, it released its bombs. Ken and the driver were out of the lorry in double quick time and, like everyone else in the vicinity, dived for cover as the bombs whistled down.

The bombs landed in a straight line just missing the hangars and buildings, burying themselves so deeply into the marshy ground that the sound of the explosions was almost completely muffled. Everything went completely quiet and there was an eerie silence and, if it wasn't for the large craters left behind, there was nothing to indicate that they had suffered a Luftwaffe attack. There were no causalities, no material damage and the silence was so unreal that Ken thought the bombs had failed to explode.

Malvina could feel her heart throbbing as she remounted her bicycle and peddled madly over the bridge to get back home, to warn her family of the impending danger. She thought there would be more bombing but, except for a stray bomb during the night of 27 February 1941, the aerodrome saw out the war without further incident.

However, an unexploded bomb did land in the garden of 62 Willows Avenue and Elizabeth Rooney and her family were forced to evacuate their home until the bomb was deactivated. With the police, army and civil defence all in attendance, it was a rehearsal of what was to come. For the streets of nearby Tremorfa and the city of Cardiff would suffer severely during those long winter months of 1940–41.

Despite being fired on by the guns of the 45th Heavy AA Brigade – twenty rounds being expended – the raider made it safely back to France and filed a report claiming hits on the buildings and the hangar. A row of three SC250 bombs, one Flambo, and five SD50 across the buildings and one SC250 direct hit on hangar. Even if the report is somewhat optimistic it nevertheless proves that the Cardiff raider returned to base, so what became of Karl Neff's aircraft flown by Obltn. Werner Stahl?

After taking-off at precisely 15.52 hours the seven Hurricanes of B Flight of 43 Squadron, Tangmere, had been in the air for about an hour, on patrol over the Isle of Wight above Bembridge, when they received an order to vector 270 degrees to intercept an incoming bogey the other side of the island. Over the Needles at 8,000ft there were patches of loose, drifting, clouds, billowing up like great dark balls, making visibility a bit of a hit and miss affair so Sgt Jim Hallowes, flying Green 2, was sent to

Gefr Karl Neff
(on the right).
(Photograph: Jakob
Neff)

check above and below the clouds. Almost immediately he gave the 'tally-ho' as he
spotted a Ju 88 about 2 miles away, not more than 500ft above them, flying north-
west. This must have been Stahl's aircraft heading for Cardiff airport.

The Hurricanes must have been seen as soon as they gave chase because the
raider quickly dived for a protective layer of cloud some 1000ft below. Even
hitting speeds approaching 250mph it couldn't shake off the seven Hurricanes
that had lined up astern and delivered a devastating No.1 attack. Then after
breaking away they came back around, this time in no fixed order, and attacked
again and again.

All the attacks were from astern but with a sudden change of tactics
Sgt Hallowes flashed in front and made a quarter deflection from head on, and
oil immediately gushed from the German's starboard engine as the salvo blew it
full of holes. As the oil poured out in a continuous stream, the fighters now concentrated all of their fire on this engine. And trailing clouds of black smoke it also
appeared to Squadron Leader John Badger to be on fire.

The gunners in the Junkers were valiantly trying to mount a defence but, with
seven attackers swarming all over them, they were in a hopeless situation. As
soon as the Hurricanes had been sighted Obltn. Werner Stahl, probably react-
ing instinctively, turned and headed for France and home, but then realising this
would be a journey too far he almost immediately brought the plane back around
and once again headed for England, almost certainly signalling surrender.

Sgt Hallowes had opened fire from 900ft, and now closed to 300ft, getting in three good bursts. The whole of the flight attacked at least twice, some
pilots three or four times, until in the words of the Intelligence Officer of 43
Squadron, the fuselage, tail unit and wings 'resembled a flying sieve'. It was shot
to pieces but, showing no mercy, the fighters continued relentlessly to strafe the
stricken aircraft.

In a further act of submission it came down to less than 1,000ft and jettisoned
its full bomb load into the sea to show that it no longer presented any possible

threat. By now its gunners had ceased to return fire and were either dead or wounded, or had been ordered to desist in the hope that the attackers would recognise this as a further signal of surrender and cease their relentless pounding.

But these acts of submission went largely unheeded or unnoticed, and the Hurricanes continued to fire blast after blast against the defenceless bomber. They were still firing at the shredded aircraft as it followed its bombs down into the sea and crashed, in a plume of foam, about 20 miles south-west of St Catherine's Point, less than 15 miles from land and safety. No one was seen to bale out.

Just as Hallowes fired his final burst the cockpit filled with blinding, acrid smoke. Had he been hit? It seemed like it and he climbed hard to gain height notifying Green Leader that he was possibly on fire and was preparing to bale out. One of the Hurricanes then detached itself to stay with him and report his position should he hit the drink. He undid his Sutton harness and oxygen leads, opened the hood and jettisoned the quick release panel. He steeled himself for a leap into unknown.

But, as there wasn't any sign of any flames flickering around the aircraft, and the engine continuing to function perfectly – the instruments showing no loss of oil or overheating – he quickly decide to stay with the Hurricane until it showed signs of severe stress. Flying north back to base at 5,000ft the cold air dispersed the acrid smoke but he was still worried there could be something wrong with the aircraft, even though there was now no visible sign of any damage. When he landed safely back at base the cause of the smoke and fumes in the cockpit was found to be an explosion of a round of de Wilde ammunition in the breach of one of the machine-guns. These incendiary bullets, though very effective against enemy aircraft, were also volatile and sometimes went off unexpectedly with unfortunate results.

Of the attackers, Sgt Hallowes, Sgt Montgomery and Pilot Officer du Vivier expended all of their 2,400 rounds of ammunition in a five-minute fury of firing. Pilot Officers Van den Hove and Upton shot off about 1,600 rounds each, with Squadron Leader Badger using slightly less. Only Sgt Dennis Noble, a young twenty year old, seems to have shown some compassion and shied away from the savagery, firing only 400 rounds at the enemy. And they were probably fired in the initial attack from astern when his adrenaline was in full flow. Either way it seems that he didn't want to be involved in such a one-sided conflict and held off from the slaughter.

Where the bombs exploded into the sea there was a brown oily stain on the water but when Badger brought his Hurricane down to sea level, to check for possible survivors, he couldn't see anything to indicate the demise of a crippled bomber. But he had definitely seen it splash into the sea… or had he? Shaking off this brief moment of apprehension he subsequently filed a victory claim on behalf of the whole flight.

Of the seven RAF pilots involved in this action only three would survive the war, 'Jim' Hallowes, Hamilton Upton and one of the two Belgians, D. Le Roy du Vivier. With a year the latter rose to be the Commanding Officer of 43 Squadron.

However, after only four weeks with the squadron Sgt Dennis Noble was shot down and killed on 30 August and Squadron Leader Badger, after being grievously wounded in the same mêlée, finally died from his injuries some ten months later on 30 June 1941. And the other Belgian Pilot Officer Van den Hove was shot out of the air and killed on 15 September 1940. This only left Sgt Herbert Francis Montgomery who would not even see out the day's end.

He had only joined 43 Squadron from his training unit on 3 August, and had flown just four operational sorties before 14 August 1940 when he failed to return from the last mission of the day. According to his mechanic he had trouble starting his engine because he had overprimed it, and he took off about ten minutes after the rest of the Squadron that left at 18.05 hours. In Hurricane L 1739 he was flying Blue 3, Sgt Hallowes was Blue 2 and Squadron Leader Badger was Blue 1, but on full throttle he managed to catch up with the flight before it engaged the enemy.

They had been vectored to intercept a lone raider on a line between Winchester and the Isle of Wight, but here was no sign of the enemy so they widened their search to patrol off Selsey Bill. Then they hard a conversation in German on the radio and, as they turned and headed south, the signal became ever louder and Hallowes was given permission by Blue Leader to proceed above the clouds to investigate. He put the Hurricane into a steep climb and, as he broke through the cloud and levelled off, he sighted a Heinkel 111 about 10 miles to the south.

But he had been seen and the enemy bomber dived for cover with Hallowes in hot pursuit. By a stroke of sheer bad luck it ran straight into the two Hurricanes below who immediately went into the attack with all guns blazing. On closing Hallowes also let rip, and large pieces of metal were seen peeling off the Heinkel as the hail of bullets tore into the fuselage.

But it now started to put up a fight and some concentrated return fire was aimed at the attackers from the upper rear gunner, and also something that looked like a coil of wire was thrown back at them. Whatever this was it didn't deter them and they continued to harry the Heinkel, but they now ran into some really bad weather and Blue Leader ordered them to break off the attack and make their way back to base. The Heinkel 111 was probably from KG 27 and one of the many that limped home with battle damage.

But Sgt Herbert F. Montgomery failed to return from this engagement and what became of him is something of a mystery. Neither Blue 1 nor Blue 2 saw what happened. The clouds had been down almost to sea level and, even though it is possible his Hurricane may have been hit by return fire from the Heinkel, it's more likely that he lost control of it in the squally cloud and crashed into the sea. He was a very average pilot having trained on bi-planes (Hawker Harts) with rudimentary blind flying equipment, and had previously spent only about twenty-five hours' flying time on Hurricanes.

He had been posted to 43 Squadron on 3 August 1940 straight from No.6 Operational Training Unit and first flew operations on 11 August, but he had been airborne for just fifteen minutes. He flew two patrols again the next day managing eighty-five minutes but the day after he logged only thirty minutes.

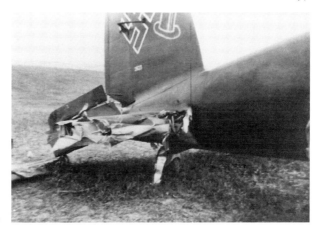

Battle damaged Heinkel
111P of KG 27 after
crash landing at Rennes.
(Photograph: H. Rodder)

Even taking into account circuits and bumps when with 43 Squadron, it's unlikely that he accumulated enough flying time to have mastered the art of flying a Hurricane in stormy weather.

Montgomery was born on 16 December 1913 at Chorley Wood, and was considerably older than his fellow trainee pilots at Shawbury and Sutton Bridge. Short, with fair hair, he was a jolly and extrovert and, having run a boarding house in Bournemouth, kept people amused with tales of his weirder lodgers. But with only twelve days at Tangmere, he had insufficient time to make much impression in the Sergeants' mess.

His body was subsequently washed ashore on the other side of the English Channel and today he lies buried in France in Senneville-Sur-Fecamp church-yard, Grave 6. The simple headstone has no epitaph.

But why was Lt Stahl flying alone and what became of him and his crew? On the morning of 14 August, after kicking their heels at Bricy for over three weeks, the 2nd Staffel of LG 1 finally received the orders that they had been eagerly awaiting. They were to attack targets on the English mainland. When the weather permitted they had spent day after day on dive-bombing practice and their skills were now to be tested. Every third day they had been told to stand by for action but now the alert seemed for real and the crews could hardly contain their excitement. For most of them this would be their first opera-tional flight over the English Channel and as their targets were read out, and the flight routes were discussed and examined in detail, they were eager to start up their aircraft.

The start was scheduled for 9.40 hours and all the machines were lined up and prepared for take-off when, almost at the last moment, they received orders to stand down as there was bad weather over the south of England. Disappointed they headed back to the barrack rooms to sit, play cards and wait; they remained on full alert. For five long hours they waited but then the attack order was once again received and, at 14.40 hours, the Ju 88s of I Gruppe started to rumble along the runway heading at last for England.

The Staffelkapitan of 2nd Staffel Obltn. von Eichhorn, and his wingman Lt Stahl, had orders to attack a military target the other side of the Bristol Channel, on the outskirts of Cardiff. By daylight it was a difficult mission but they had been promised a Me 110 escort, yet as they crossed over the expected meeting point on the French coast there was no sign of the *Zerstorers*. They pressed on.

Then out over the Channel Eichhorn's aircraft ran into trouble. The starboard engine had started to splutter and clatter and, with the loss of power, they began to fall far behind the rest of the group. Lt Stahl was completely unaware of his Staffelkapitan's problems and took his aircraft down into the safety of the clouds as they approached the English coast. Out of the corner of his eye Eichhorn briefly caught a glimpse of Stahl's plane as it disappeared from view somewhere south of Portland. It was the last time there was a reported sighting of Stahl's aircraft. On his return Eichhorn logged the time of this sighting at approximately 16.00 hours, after which they were alone and completely lost but still flying northwards, hoping that a suitable target would somehow present itself.

As the starboard engine continued to malfunction Eichhorn considered aborting the mission and returning to base. What an inglorious end to their first foray over England. But then a stroke of luck, the engine mysteriously started to run smoothly and they increased speed in an attempt to catch up with the tail end of the Gruppe, and possibly make contact with Stahl. Flying almost on full power the plane managed to come up close to the remnant of the Gruppe, only to see the planes dive, one after another, through a large gap in the clouds that closed in behind them.

Once again they were alone and lost over enemy territory. Nothing for it but to blindly follow them down and they shot through the first small hole that opened up in front of them. Almost directly below them there loomed up a target on which they released their total bomb load and then quickly climbed back amongst the clouds. With their mission completed they now headed south for the Channel and home.

As they approached the coast they came under heavy flak attack and climbed high above the clouds to shake off the explosions that rocked their aircraft. Barrage balloons were also up but they didn't present any problems and they pressed on for France. Soon they were directly over the harbour at Le Havre and heading for Bricy where they touched down at around 19.00 hours. So ended their longed-for first flight over England.

Lt Stahl's was one of the three aircraft that failed to return to Bricy on that day and, for the next few days, Eichhorn waited in vain for some positive news concerning the fate of his wingman's plane. But, as time passed, he was forced to admit that it had probably been brought down by RAF fighters. He was now faced with the unenviable task of writing to the parents of the missing airmen.

On 19 August he wrote to the father of Karl Neff stating that it was his painful duty to inform him that his son had not returned from a mission over England. He had been hoping to hear that his aircraft had landed back somewhere in

France but five days had now passed without any news and, reluctantly, he was forced to accept that it was lost, and had now been officially listed as missing.

He also conveyed the sorrow felt by Karl's fellow comrades who were all hopeful that he was still alive and a prisoner in England. Information on POWs was provided to the German Red Cross in Berlin and, if that they gave any news about their son's whereabouts, he asked if they could relay it back to him, as such information was not quickly passed down to military units. He also supplied the names and addresses of the rest of the crew in the hope that perhaps their families had received some comforting news that they could all share.

Then, on 5 December, the family of Karl Neff received the communication they were dreading. It was a further letter from Obltn. von Eichhorn stating that sadly he had received information from the office of the OKW, responsible for War Casualties and Prisoners of War, that the body of their son Gefr Karl Neff had been found on 18 September 1940, washed up on the beach at Le Crotoy. Shortly afterwards he was taken to the cemetery in the nearby village of Le Crotoy and buried with full military honours. His aircraft was last seen crossing the Channel heading for England and was probably intercepted and shot down by enemy fighters.

His body was the only one of the four-man crew to be given up by the sea. The bodies of the other three still lie entombed in the wreckage of their aircraft, somewhere at the bottom of the Channel.

But those missing Me 110s did make a somewhat belated appearance. At approximately 17.30 hours Pilot Officer Harry Mitchell, while on patrol with 'B' Fight of 87 Squadron, stumbled across a large number of enemy aircraft, which he put at seventy plus, 5 miles south of Portland at 6,000–8,000ft. He identified them as mainly Me 110s with a sprinkling of J 87s. Climbing up to 11,000ft he attacked out of the sun and using full deflection fired a three-second burst at the Me 110 bringing up the rear, blowing off the tail plane. He pulled around in a steep turn and lined up another Me 110 in his sights, firing again with full deflection, and saw the tracers smash into the fuselage but he didn't stay around to watch the results of this barrage of bullets.

Below him he noticed a Ju 87 that seemed to be flying aimlessly in a circle but, as he positioned the Hurricane for an attack, he must have been spotted for the Stuka dived away into a thin layer of cloud. Playing cat and mouse with one another in and out of the clouds Mitchell finally caught up with the dive-bomber in a clear patch of cloud and, from dead astern, closing to within 900ft, he shot him down with a full five-second burst. Then with all his ammunition used up he turned tail and fled back to Exeter claiming two positive kills and one probable.

But as far as the Luftwaffe is concerned this combat is something of a mystery as there is no mention in their records of such an engagement. The Me 110s and Ju 87s could have been part of VIII Fliegerkorps flying out of Caen, either as a feint or on a routine patrol as far as the English coast, but if so why is there no mention of this conflict, especially as least two aircraft were supposedly lost? Another Battle of Britain mystery that will probably never be explained.

CHAPTER EIGHT

War over Wales

After the call to arms by Speck von Sternberg, the bomber crews of the III Gruppe of KG 27 had sufficient time to scrutinise the maps and photographs of their allocated targets. All twenty-five serviceable aircraft had been primed and ready for take-off since early morning, and the last-minute checks would be carried out just before take-off with the first *Kette* scheduled to be airborne at 15.50 hours. They checked the distances and flying time to their targets: most of the destinations, such as the airfields and factories in and around the Bristol area, the ports and docks along the Bristol Channel at Cardiff, Newport and Western-super-Mare, and even the daunting long-distance mission to the docks at Liverpool, were well known but some places were completely unheard of and almost unpronounceable. For example there was an industrial layout and a power station at Pontypridd, an aircraft component works at Blaenavon, both in the mining valleys to the north of Cardiff, and RAF Sealand, an aerodrome in the extreme north-east of Wales on the banks of the River Dee. An aerodrome that no one had ever heard of, and the intended attack at twilight, on the cusp of darkness, was still going to be just as dangerous and daring as any journey to Liverpool. Someone muttered 'a dangerous mission' and there were a couple of hollow laughs, but flying hundreds of miles over enemy territory without fighter cover wasn't a joke.

Everyone wondered who had drawn the short straw and it came as no surprise to learn that Obltn. Artur Wiesemann, the second in command of 8th Staffel, was the man chosen to spearhead a three-pronged *Kette* on this almost suicidal mission. He was a daring and resourceful pilot, having earned his spurs with the Legion Condor in Spain, and there was no one more qualified because he had flown such distances without fighter cover during the Polish campaign. But some of his crew had mixed feelings and his radio operator Uffz. Heinz Kochy hurriedly sought out his friend Bruno Gripp to make sure that his last wishes would be carried out should he not return.

For these daylight missions the Heinkel He 111 had to carry an extra crew member to man the MG 15 machine-guns fitted to the beam windows either side of the aircraft. It was a difficult and tricky role to cover two windows at

Obltn. A. Wiesemann (centre foreground) and aircrews studying target maps prior to take-off on 14 August 1940. (Photograph: H. Kochy)

once, and no one had received any intensive training with any real proficiency. Any spare crew member would do and Paul Walter was roped in to man the guns in Wiesmann's aircraft but, as an oberfeldwebel and radio operator, he thought such a duty was below him, an affront to his rank, and he successfully protested to the Staffelkapitan Hauptmann Hartmann. So Uffz. Gustav Ullman, one of the ground crew that had received basic gunnery training, was pressed into service as their air gunner much to his annoyance as he had never flown in combat before.

Born in Brazil he had something of a Latin temperament and looking at their Heinkel 111 (1G + FS) he said, 'If I get in that plane, it'll be shot down!' Their navigator and bomb-aimer Heinz Rodder gave a nervous laugh but, by the look on the face of fellow crew member Flt Engineer Walter Schaum, he could tell they were both apprehensive about this long and dangerous flight.

As they went through their pre-flight checks the mongrel that had flown with them many times before showed no interest in climbing aboard. This was unusual as he was normally to be found scampering around the plane and, except for high-flying sorties when he would let off a series of foul smelling farts, he was always welcomed aboard. Even though he was something of a lucky mascot no one gave it much thought that he hadn't scrambled up into the aircraft and anyway, they thought, as they were flying an operational sortie it was probably best that he was left behind.

Gustav Ullman and Walter Schaum. (Photograph: W. Schaum)

Both Wiesemann's wing men were experienced pilots and Feldwebel Oskar Dubral in Heinkel 111P (1G + CS) would be flying 'Caesar' the left *Kettenhund* (chained dog). The crew were all experienced except for the beam-gunner Uffz. Heinrich Schrage who had also been press-ganged into the job, but they were all well up to the task having flown in combat many times even though their Legion Condor veteran, radio operator Feldwebel Walter Gietz, had an indescribable feeling of uneasiness that settled in the pit of his stomach as he clipped on the parachute and boarded the plane. Two other Feldwebel, Flt Engineer Franz Knoblich, and Anton Wiesmeier (the observer/navigator) took the crew up to full battle complement.

'Peter' Oekenpohler, another battle-hardened Feldwebel would be flying 'Dora', Heinkel 111P (1G + DS), on the right of the formation and Wiesemann knew he could rely on this brave and resilient pilot who had already survived a couple of tricky situations during the French campaign. Also onboard was Uffz. Erich Frielinghaus (the radio operator) and Flt Engineer Uffz. Franz Losecke, both of whom were seasoned campaigners having flown together many times, while their observer/navigator was Fw. Erich Schreiber a worthy and reliable officer. Only their air gunner Gefr Zwelter was an unknown quantity as he had also never before flown in combat. The success of the whole mission could well come down to the performance of the untried and inexperienced air gunners, but no one dwelled on this negative thought.

Loaded with 50kg and 250kg blast bombs, the first machines of 9th Staffel were scheduled for take-off at 16.00 hours and, after they had made their final flying preparations and plotted their course on the flight maps and marked out the known fighter airfields along the route, the crews had over one hour to kill.

Time enough for a farewell party. The drinks were not exactly overflowing but there was the continual clink of glasses as they wished one another the best of luck.

Not everyone was in a confident mood. The two 20 year olds, Hans Ramstetter and Gerhard Rother, who would be flying in the first *Kette* away, as the observer and air gunner in the lead Heinkel 111P (1G + OT), were particularly nervous of the whole enterprise despite the reassurances given by their pilot Lt Otto Uhland. But when the old stagers, flight mechanic Josef Krenn and radio operator Edo Flick, made light work of the whole affair, having braved such feelings before every previous battle flight, they felt a little bit less apprehensive.

Knowing they would not be flying alone but as part of a *Kette* eased their fears, as three aircraft grouped together should be able to put up enough defensive firepower to see off any attacking fighters. At least that's what they were told. And anyway their machine was a lucky plane having survived unscathed from an air battle over Lille on 19 May 1940 when five accompanying He 111s of KG 27 were shot down by the Hurricanes of No.1 Squadron. During this action Pilot Officer Paul Richey was shot down and badly wounded by a gunner of one of the Heinkels and 1G + OT carried a small brass plate approximately 2x2in on the main fuselage, just aft of the port wing, featuring an RAF roundel with the date underneath in celebration of this victory claim. For a Heinkel 111 to have shot down a British fighter was no mean feat.

Obltn. Ernst Ohlenschlager would be flying Heinkel 111P (1G + NT) on the right of the small formation and his complement comprised of Unteroffiziers Kurt Sulzbach and Adolf Blumenthal as observer and radio operator, and Nicholas

Airmen of 8th and 9th Staffels of KG.27 at POW Camp X (Angler) in 1941. Left to right, standing: K. Kupsch, A. Blumenthal, D. Siebers, G. Rother, J. Krenn, K. Sulzbach, H. Kochy. Sitting: O. Dubral, W. Gietz, N. Jug, W. Schaum. (Photograph: W. Gietz)

Hauptmann Josef Riedl. (Photograph:
Frau W. Krause)

Jug a Feldwebel as flight engineer. The fifth member of the crew was Gefreiter
Kurt Kupsch, in reality a ground technician but he had also received intensive
training as an air-gunner and was the ideal choice to man the beam machine-guns
firing over the wings from the windows either side of the fuselage. At twenty-two
years of age he was the youngster of the crew. The oldest member of the *Kette* was
Hauptman Josef Riedl, the thirty-one year old in command of the left *Kettenhund*
who also had difficulty bringing his crew up to compliment as his usual observer/
navigator was unavailable; so Fw. Ernst Haumann was drafted in from the 7th
Staffel to fill this role. Another old-hand was Unteroffizier Hans Dolata who acted
as the radio operator and dorsal gunner with the defensive position in the bola
being filled by Flt Engineer Unteroffizier Adelhard Witt. But with such a paucity
of trained air gunners the fifth man vacancy as beam-gunner fell to the inexperienced Gefreiter Emil Wolf, who had only just turned twenty-two.

As the Daimler-Benz engines roared into life the Heinkels taxied into line.
They would be taking-off in small batches every ten minutes, spread over a time
frame of about two hours, with Weisemann's *Kette* scheduled at 18.10 hours to be
one of the last away. The *Kette* led by Lt Uhland was one of the first to take-off
at 16.00 hrs with the airfield at Cardiff, and the nearby industrial complex, as
their main targets. Other targets included the airfields at Blandford Forum and
Yeovilton, the hangars and buildings of the Bristol Aeroplane Company at Filton,
and the aircraft components factory of the Parnell Aircraft Company at Yate on
the outskirts of Bristol, as well as railway and transport services in the South-West.

Cardiff docks and its warehouses, and the surrounding manufacturing plants,
were also possible hits as well as industrial targets in the South Wales valleys, with
the new light industrial estate and power station at Upper Boat, to the south of
Pontypridd, well worth a visit. A lone raider would attempt to seek this out only

to be driven off by 164 Battery, 63rd Light Anti Aircraft Troop that opened up with their .303 Lewis guns, firing over 140 rounds at the raider as it swooped to attack from less than 2,000ft. Some of the bullets must have struck home because it swerved and banked sharply away, making off to the north-east in the direction of Blaenavon. The raider had come down so low that miners walking home could make out the face of the pilot and Fred Trivett, a sometimes taxi driver, would later swear that the pilot waved at them as it sped up the valley.

The iron and steel works of Blaenavon Co. Ltd was also a special objective for the Luftwaffe as the latest intelligence reports had suggested that the company was producing propellers and aircraft engine parts. Prior to the outbreak of war many Germans had worked for the company installing a giant press in the 'Black Shed', and they had probably provided intelligence on the layout of the site and the adjoining naphthalene coke works that was capable of producing high octane fuel. The by-product coke works also produced Benzol from raw Benzene held in four large storage tanks, as well as providing gas for the eastern and western valleys. The site was highly inflammable and an ideal target for a load of incendiaries.

In her multi-coloured pinny, Ena Harris was a typical war-time 'Welsh mam' and she was outside her house, emptying the dregs of the teapot down the drain, when she saw a plane coming up the valley and, thinking it was British, shouted out 'Come on down boys, come on down for tea.' To her amazement the bomb doors opened and clusters of incendiaries tumbled out of the aircraft, glistening like stars. They were landing amongst the industrial buildings on the far side of the valley, away from the town, and all over the hillside the dried grass was set alight and bursts of flames could be seen amongst the dense smoke. A few stray

A line of Heinkels 111P taxing for take-off, summer 1940

bombs straddled the houses in Chapel Row where prompt action by a couple of air-raid wardens saved the house of Ann Jones after a bomb burnt through the roof and lodged in a ceiling joist.

Having arrived home after a hard day's work, L.C. Browning had a dropped off to sleep in the armchair to be awakened by the two evacuees from Dover they were looking after, who came running in shouting 'Uncle! Uncle! Come quickly an aeroplane is dropping letters all over the place.' When he got to the doorway he saw thick clouds of smoke passing overhead in the direction of the town. He realised there was a fire at the naphthalene area and he sprinted over to the coke ovens where he joined some of the ARP wardens who were the first of the emergency services to arrive at the scene.

They needed urgent help in containing the burning incendiaries but the Home Guard were still assembling in the Drill Hall where they had to report for orders once the air-raid warning sounded. However, the ARP men were quick off the mark, even commandeering the town clerk's car to get them to the site from their headquarters at the council offices the moment they received the call that incendiary bombs had fallen on the plant of Wm Prestwick & Sons and on the gas work plant of the Blaenavon Co Ltd.

Flying up the valley just below the tip of Coity Mountain the plane was immediately recognised as an enemy Heinkel 111 by Hugh Ashman, a schoolboy aviation enthusiast, who was standing in his back yard as it passed overhead. The crosses on the wings were clearly visible and shocked at being so close to the enemy, he ran excitedly into the house to tell his mother that he had seen a German plane with 'millions and millions' of little black things falling from it. The shower of bombs were spread in an arc over a distance of almost 2 miles and fell just in front of the steelworks in the Black Shed and set fire to the waste naphthalene tip in front of the coke works, which almost escaped unscathed. The few smouldering bombs that fell amongst the by-product buildings were quickly dealt with by covering them with slag dust, but the fires from the waste tip were allowed to burn themselves out.

From the air the fires and the huge pall of smoke drifting over the town gave the impression that the works were aflame, but the damage was minimal and production was not halted. A daring, well-planned raid had come to nothing but as the raider once again circled the area before heading south, he must have been thought he had scored a direct hit.

At about 18.00 hours another lone raider homed in on the docks at Newport in the mistaken belief that he was attacking Cardiff, but it was met by a hail of AA fire from the coastal batteries and was forced to hurriedly dump its bombs that fell harmlessly into the River Usk. Taking evasive action, it was last seen heading back into the safety of the heavy cumulus cloud at 5,000ft.

Approaching from the north-west over the Bristol Channel at 10,000ft, the two Heinkels of Raid 179 dropped down to 3,000ft for their bombing run on Filton but they flew into a barrage of shells from the Bofors at the airfield and the heavy guns surrounding Bristol that forced them to break off the attack. The small arms gunners had also opened up but the all fire ceased when a fighter appeared on the scene with the Heinkels now quickly seeking safety in the clouds as they headed north in the direction of Yate.

Parnell Aircraft Ltd was located at the aerodrome, Yate, and was an important plant producing tail planes, rudders, elevators and gun turrets for the Air Ministry and had been well documented as a key target by the Luftwaffe. As they closed in on the factory the bomb bays opened but Yate was well defended, and the men manning the Bofors and light machine-guns launched a phalanx of missiles claiming a hit on the edge of a wing of one of the raiders. A large piece of metal flew off the plane but it still pressed home its attack though the bomb-aimers must have been seriously shaken as only three of the bombs released landed anywhere near the target, and they landed harmlessly opposite the entrance to the factory. But the nearby engineering establishment of Newman Industries Ltd., situated on the other side of the aerodrome. suffered serious damage having been hit by six of the bombs that had drifted off target.

The first bomb plunged through the roof of building No.5 and the resulting explosion rocked the Switch House causing structural and superficial damage leaving a shallow crater about 17ft across in the concrete floor. The blast from the second bomb resulted in superficial damage to the Machine Tool Shop in building No.11 and the Power Plant Repair Shop and store located in the adjacent building. The Machine Tool shop housed in building No.13 took the brunt of the third bomb and the roofs of buildings No.9 and No.12 were also badly battered by the blasts. The three other bombs fell in an open space in the south-east corner of the works enclosure. Production was curtailed for only three to four days though, and the casualty rate was surprisingly low with just four people being hurt by the blasts, though two of them suffered horrendous injuries.

Evading the approaching fighters, the raiders then flew due west to the Bristol Channel and then, as they turned south-east, they spotted a railway junction near Congresbury and their nine remaining bombs were dropped on this unsuspecting target. Three of the bombs landed within 60ft of the line, churning up the embankment and two unexploded bombs were found lodged in the fork of the GWR line that was closed, with traffic being only briefly disrupted. Then as they flew along the Channel coast the raiders were lost from sight.

Other hostile aircraft, mostly operating alone, dropped their bombs in what appeared to be random targets as they criss-crossed over the west of England and along the border of Wales even foraging as far north as Welshpool. In an eventful two-hour period running up to 19.00 hours over fifteen raids were logged entering the area but they were difficult to track as visibility was greatly impeded by the thick banks of low cloud.

The aircraft fired at by the AA batteries were reported to be Junkers 88s as well as Heinkels and, at around 18.00 hours, over ten bombs, probably intended for the nearby RAF station at Weston Zoyland, landed at nearby Edington Burtle damaging railway lines and telephones but there was no report of casualties. At the same time a total of twenty-five bombs were dropped over the town of Frome and at

Kurt Kupsch. (Photograph: K. Kupsch)

Rodden, about a mile to the south-east, but only the one that hit the GWR line near the station caused any delay. The bombs missed the buildings and, except for the eight strays that chewed up farm land, there was no material damage and the goods traffic was able to bypass Frome railway station without any trouble.

Bombs were also scattered over Shepton Mallet, near Cannards Grave, but they failed to hit the Southern Railway line and no damage was reported. Further south an unidentified raider dropped six high explosives on Yeovilton airfield that completely missed the target though a civilian labourer was slightly injured.

At Littlehampton bombs destined for RAF Ford drifted off target and fell on the golf course, luckily landing in the rough though one of the greens took a near miss much to the relief of the members who had taken shelter in the club house. The war had finally come to the golfing set though some thought that bombing a golf course was extremely unsporting!

As the Channel Islands came into view, Hans Ramstetter immediately went to high alert. He was sure no RAF fighters would be patrolling this far out over the Channel, but he was just that little bit on edge and he became even more nervous when over the intercom Lt Otto Uhland ordered everyone to keep a sharp lookout.

Flying at 180mph the *Kette* had quickly climbed to their operational height of just over 13,000ft and set a compass course of approximately 335 degrees. To the right, and through the haze, they recognised Cherbourg far below them and as they approached mid-Channel they knew they could soon be pray to any patrolling RAF fighters. But they reached the south-west coast of England without incident and, at Exmouth, they made a slight course correction to the north in the direction of Cardiff.

As they flew inland they encountered thick, rolling banks of cloud that were building up about 3,280ft below them but occasionally, in a clear patch, they saw the splendour of the evening sun lighting up the barrage balloons. It was a beautiful sight and, for a brief moment, they almost forgot they were flying over enemy territory but that moment quickly passed as their nerves started to jangle, and the further they penetrated inland the more jittery they became. The RAF must be out there.

Remarkably they still hadn't been discovered and with no flak being thrown at them everything was too quiet, suspiciously quiet, as if a storm was about to break and the *Kette* closed in even more tightly to provide a compact cone of fire against any attacking fighters. Each of the He 111s, now armed with five MG 15 machine-guns, had a good rate of defensive shots and with cool nerves and sharp eyes they constantly scanned the skies for enemy fighters, but deep down Ramstetter knew that against a concerted attack from all sides they were doomed to fail.

The *Kette* was now over the Bristol Channel less than 10 miles south of Barry and, with only four minutes flying time to the target, Ramstetter was already glued over the bomb-sight as the city of Cardiff grew ever nearer. Suddenly a cry, 'Fighter', and the machine-guns were simultaneously cocked and ready for action.

In the right *Kettenhund* the beam-gunner Kurt Kupsch caught a quick glimpse of a Spitfire high above him and shouted out to his commander 'fighters astern'. He didn't quite catch the reply but thought it was some thing like 'Hurricanes or Spitfires?' He wasn't sure but thought it was a pointless question as both were equipped with eight machine-guns and whichever planes they were, they would soon be sending a hail of lead in their direction. Behind his MG 15 he waited nervously for them to come into range rather than fire off some hopeful shots but, from the flashes coming from the other Heinkels, he could see that not every gunner had been so hesitant. With only seventy-five rounds per ammunition drum he held

Spitfires of 92 Squadron at Pembrey, summer 1940. (Photograph: A. Wight)

Senior NCOs at RAF Pembrey. (Photograph: A. Wright)

his fire until he could get in a telling shot and, as a fighter came at them all guns blazing, he let rip at it as it flashed overhead. A hit! He was sure he had scored a hit.

And they were Spitfires, the Spitfires of 92 Squadron. The squadron had been badly mauled covering the evacuation of the Allied troops from Dunkirk and had been transferred from RAF Hornchurch to RAF Pembrey in the afternoon of 18 June 1940 for the purpose of 'rest and refit'. The unit was down to only eight aircraft from an original sixteen. In other words, the defence of the whole of South Wales and parts of the Bristol Channel after the evacuation was in the hands of only eight serviceable Spitfires controlled from Filton near Bristol. Luckily the Luftwaffe stayed its hand and by 1 August the squadron was back to full strength.

The pilots were eager for action and even though things were beginning to hot up over the English Channel, only elusive reconnaissance machines were allowed over South Wales to check out the airfields and docks dotted either side of the Bristol Channel. The Spitfires went up after these lone raiders and scored a notable success when a Heinkel He 111P of KG 54 was attacked and shot down by Yellow Section on 4 July. It crash-landed the other side of the Bristol Channel, way inland, at Gillingham in Dorset.

The only other positive result came on 24 July when a Ju 88 of LG 1 was shot down in flames and crashed just the other side of the Channel at Lynton. Another Ju 88 of LG 1 was believed to have been shot down into the sea just off the coast near Llantwit Major on 17 July, but this was unconfirmed, and there were slim pickings for a squadron whose core of battle-hardened pilots included the redoubtable Stanford-Tuck.

The survivors of the original squadron had made their unofficial headquarters at the Stepney Arms in Llanelli where the landlord was a convivial Welshman of Irish descent who made them more than welcome, and promised to break open a bottle of bubbly for every enemy aircraft they shot down.

But in reality Llanelli was a dreary place best summed up by Pilot Officer Brian Kingcome in his book *A Willingness to Die.* Though appreciating the beautiful scenery and sandy beaches surrounding RAF Pembrey, he thought the pubs in the Llanelli area were 'appalling: utterly spit and sawdust hostelries with, around the walls, lines of chairs occupied by local ancients who ached to burst into song and seized on the slightest pretext to do so.' Even the happy-go-lucky Tony Bartley, who later married the actress Deborah Kerr was glad to be away from the 'sordidness' of Llanelli. Despite its solitude and miles of golden sand, Pembrey was not a glamourous posting.

So, it was on a rather grey afternoon at Pembrey on 14 August with clouds just touching the hilltops towards Kidwelly, and well past 16:00 hours when the three pilots of Blue Section, who had been on readiness since lunchtime, were looking forward to being relieved. In fact the pilots of Green Section had already ambled over to join Flt Lt Robert Stanford Tuck, Pilot Officer Bill Watling and Flt Sgt 'Tich' Havercroft, and they were lounging around awaiting the changeover when the field telephone in the dispersal hut tinkled faintly.

The line from Bristol was poor and the pilots fell silent as the airman strained to catch the words from the other end. Before he had even time to shout 'Scramble',

Tommy Thompson and 'Tich' Havercroft. (Photograph: A. Wright)

Best of tuck always, *Bob Stanford Tuck*:
O.C. 257 Sqdn:
1940—41.

Fl. Lt Robert Stanford Tuck

Tuck was already running fast towards his aircraft with Watling not far behind, with Havercroft bringing up the rear as fast as his short legs could carry him. All three were airborne and in loose formation in less than two minutes and climbing steeply eastwards towards the cloud base.

They broke through the top of the clouds at about 4,000ft and kept on climbing in dazzling sunshine. Havercroft now realized his radio was dead and had no idea what instructions Tuck was receiving, but he realized they were heading up the Channel towards Bristol. He fiddled with the radio controls and his headset trying to get a sound but to no avail, and he signaled his problem to Tuck by tapping his helmet and pointing a thumb down. Tuck understood.

They levelled out at about 17,000ft and opened out to a wide search formation. Havercroft had no idea what he was looking for or in what direction. Suddenly he saw ahead and far below, three specks in close formation proceeding in the opposite direction. Obviously neither Tuck nor Watling had seen them so he banged open the throttle and shot well ahead of them, rocking his wings violently to attract their attention and rolled over in a steep dive in the direction of the three black dots that were now far behind them.

His ears were popping with the rapid decrease in pressure and, although he was clocking well in excess of 400mph, Tuck whizzed past him. As they overhauled their targets he could make out they were German twin-engine bombers but at that distance it was not possible to identify the type. He switched on the reflector gun sight and took off the safety catch on his gun-button.

Pilots of 92 Squadron; Havercroft is the second on the right and Bill Watling is kneeling

Tuck went straight in behind them to receive a wicked cross-fire from the rear gunners but he managed to fire at the leader before breaking away. Making a diving beam attack Havercroft picked out the *kettenhund* on the right of the formation and closing down to less than 600ft he let rip a three-second burst with full deflection. His eight .303 Browning machine-guns sounded off and an acrid ammonia stench filled the cockpit. Puffs of smoke came away from the port engine of the enemy bomber but Havercroft had now come in so close he had to break away hard to the right and downwards to avoid a collision and, as he did so, he caught a glimpse of the cut-away where the wing joined the fuselage of the aircraft, an identifying feature of a Heinkel 111. Climbing back to attack height he came in on its left quarter and fired a three-second burst, again with no visible effect. The enemy formation refused to break up and by now had turned, and was flying back out towards the Bristol Channel.

Tuck's beam and stern attacks were having little apparent effect as the enemy formation continued to maintain its course and height. Watling was flying as Blue 2 and had made a diving beam attack from out of the sun, letting off a three-second burst and then at 900ft, closing in rapidly to 600ft, he fired, with double deflection, another deadly burst at the aircraft on the left-hand side of the formation. Much to Watling's annoyance these attacks were seemingly having no effect on the enemy as all three aircraft flew serenely on making a gentle turn to the left, eventually swinging south, going back the way they had come. He attacked again. This time from the right but the accurate return fire was forcing him to break away early and as he came in for yet another attack he watched the left *kettenhund* dive gently away from the formation with white smoke pouring from both engines.

Not realizing that Watling had seriously damaged his adversary, Tuck decided to break off these unprofitable beam and stern attacks and, with Havercroft, climbed and screamed ahead at full throttle. Turning around they were set for a head-on attack at the vulnerable glazed cockpits of the bombers. Throttling back hard to slow down they lined up their sights long before the enemy came within range. At a closing speed approaching 400mph Havercroft opened up on the right Heinkel and a large chunk of engine cowling flew into the air and puffs of smoke came from the port wing as the bullets struck home. As he flashed past the grey streaks all around him showed that the gunners were concentrating all their fire-power at his Spitfire but he was sure they had missed. Or so he thought.

As he rolled out of range he was aware of a pungent smell in the cockpit and he became uncomfortably warm. Quickly checking his instruments he saw that the radiator temperature was way above the top limit and rapidly going off the clock. 'Sod', he thought, 'the buggers have got me after all.' There was no option but to shut down the engine or it would seize and possibly catch fire. Things went very quiet as he levelled off to take stock of the situation.

Despite their outward appearance of immunity the bombers had taken many hits, and it was only the professionalism and battle experience of their pilots that kept the formation tight to maximize their defensive firepower. As soon as he heard the cry 'Fighter' Ramstetter knew they were in for a fight and, manning the forward machine-gun, he braced himself for the coming battle. With their combined firepower they manage to ward off the first attack but the fighters came again. First one, then two, and then five and they openeds fire at them as soon as they presented a good target. The fighters were coming in close, as near as 900ft, but as they banked away showing their underbellies the gunners were sure they had scored some hits.

So they kept coming in at them from all directions spitting out their shiny tracer bullets and, as the first fusillade hit home, all hell broke out amongst the crew of Ramstetter's Heinkel. The aircraft only shuddered slightly as the missiles spattered along the wings but it was the ones that crashed into the fuselage sending shards of metal spinning throughout the inside of the aircraft that almost shattered the nerves of the gunners. They had to hold their nerves.

Already they could tell from their tracers that they were forcing the fighters to break off their attacks and over the intercom Ramstetter shouted out to the radio operator and the rear gunner to open fire the moment a fighter filled their gun sights. Another attack was successfully beaten off and they thought that they must have shot down one of their tormentors as only four attackers were now circling them for yet another attack. For about five minutes they were able to withstand these ferocious assaults but then the left *kettenhund*, under the command of Hptmn Riedl, was seen to break away from the formation and head straight down into the clouds with smoke pouring from both engines.

Gefr Emil Wolf, the beam gunner aboard
Riedl's aircraft. (Photograph: E. Reif)

Uffz. Edo Flick. (Photograph: E. Flick)

Lt Otto Uhland. (Photograph: H. Rodder)

POWs in Canada. Ramstetter is third right, Josef Krenn second right and Flick far right

It had been hit by Tuck who, giving himself time to aim, had opened up as he came in head-on and somehow he was right on target with a dead steady burst ripping into the stricken bomber. Zipping directly over the formation he put his Spitfire into a steep vertical climb and, glancing back, he saw his target dive quickly away with heavy smoke pouring from both engines. He now turned his attention to the remaining Heinkels – which somehow he had wrongly identified as Ju 88s – and, as he circled, Ramstetter hurriedly changed the empty magazine of his MG 15 machine-gun. There was a chnace of escaping into the clouds far away, but the Spitfires were too quick for them and attacked again.

Their dorsal gunner and radio operator Edo Flick has a terrible time as the fighters came in from behind banging away mercilessly, and Ramstetter called him up again as he has ceased to return fire. 'Has he been hit? Hell No. His gun has jammed. Shit.' Quick as a flash Ramstetter was out of the cockpit and crawling on his bum along the fuselage, protected from behind by the armour plate, but before he could reach Edo another mighty hail of bullets crashed into the aircraft.

What of the pilot and the rest of the crew? Lt Uhland was bleeding from the neck but luckily it was only a grazing shot. Flick and the beam-gunner Gerhard Rother were also miraculously unmarked but the flight mechanic Krenn had a slight gash on his head that bled profusely, though it wasn't a serious wound. They were damn lucky. They had survived a terrible onslaught but their trusty He 111 was in a bad way and almost done for. Looking like a sieve with the right motor missing, and spitting and trailing a stream of white smoke, it was in a perilous state. It had taken numerous hits during the twenty minutes of air battle and lost height as they tried again and again to escape the fighters.

The bombs were now jettisoned and Lt Uhland slowly steered the shattered machine south, for home, on the one good engine. With some gentle coaxing they might yet make it back to France as the fighters had now disappeared and a quiet calm came over the crew. But this was short lived as the right motor juddered and shook before it caught fire and stopped. With flames licking along the wing the plane was doomed and, overcome by their hopeless situation, Ramstetter shouted, 'Bale out'.

His only thought was to get out of that hell hole and he tried desperately to open the cockpit door but the latch was jammed. 'Just my luck,' he thought, as with all his might he again tried to unfasten the latch. Lt Uhland shouldered him aside but he also failed to release the catch but, with a powerful joint effort, the door suddenly snapped open. As the senior officer, Uhland baled out first and he climbed out onto the left wing, gripped the rip cord of his parachute and was away in the slip stream.

Krenn and Rother jumped out of the floor tub. Flick, because of the danger from the tail plane, was also supposed to exit the same way but in a complete state of panic he leaped out of the top of the aircraft. A move he immediately regretted.

With no sign of the fighters Ramstetter was in no mood to be taken prisoner. He intended to return to France and sat in the pilot's seat where he took over the controls in an attempt to extinguish the fire in the right motor. He put the plane into a nose dive and slipped it from side to side but the flames continued to engulf the wing. The plane could explode at any moment and, taking it back up again, he left the growing inferno the same way as L. Uhland. Counting one, two, three, he pulled the ring on his chest parachute and all at once was free of the deafening death rattle of their dying aircraft. At a height of 6,000ft he hung helplessly to his parachute but, as he spiralled silently to earth, he realized that he was sinking too fast at about 20ft a second. Below, he could see that the parachutes of his comrades had fully opened out but with a sad heart he watched their fatally crippled Heinkel go down steeply in a cloud of smoke. It reared up one more time and then exploded as it crashed into the ground.

Tuck followed the damaged Heinkel down through the clouds but he had difficulty in keeping up. At the speed the machine was going he thought he had either hit the pilot or the engines were out of action, and gradually it disappeared into the murk. Breaking out of the cloud, Tuck came out about 15 miles south of Weston-super-Mare but there was no sign of the enemy. As he looked around a Heinkel came out of the clouds and dropped a stick of bombs that fell near the Highbridge–Glastonbury railway line.

He turned his Spitfire towards the raider but it climbed and tucked itself back into the cloud. It was now nearly 18.00 hours and, with fuel running low, he turned for home. The running battle had lasted nearly half an hour. The enemy had put up a terrific fight and as he sped westwards he wondered about the fate of Havercroft.

As Ramstetter floated down all was quiet but then a few shots could be heard coming from below. Someone was shooting at him. Scared that his 'chute might

Hans Ramstetter. (Photograph: Christine Mack)

become holed he tried to guide it by pulling on the lines in a swinging motion to present a poor target, but this was not a success. In a panic he pulled out his pistol and fired some shots downwards, which had the desired effect because the shooting stopped. Not far from him one of the crew had already landed and shortly after that he made a surprisingly soft landing in peaty ground on the edge of a water-filled ditch about 600ft from the rest of the crew.

Using the rapid-release catch he immediately freed himself from the parachute harness and attempted to make his way to where some roughly clothed men were standing over the injured body of one of the crew, but two burly farmers with shotguns at the ready stopped him in his tracks. One of them had probably already taken a pot shot at him and he was loath to argue even though he still had some live cartridges left in his pistol. In broken English he failed to make his concerns known and dejectedly he was made to sit down on the grass but, for some unknown reason, they later relented and escorted him to where Edo Flick lay moaning in agony. He was in a horrible mess with broken legs, a bloody face and badly bruised body having smashed into the tail plane when, in a blind panic, he had baled out from the top of the Heinkel. After a short while he fell unconsciousness.

Ramstetter was so worried about Edo's condition that he had failed to notice the arrival of Rother and Krenn amongst the large crowd that had now gathered around them. The pair seemed to have appeared out of nowhere but then he noticed that the police had also arrived and that his comrades were under arrest. Rother had been subjected to a barrage of sticks and stones from a bunch of Irish navvies working in the grounds of the Royal Ordnance Factory and was glad when he was arrested and given police protection. But there was no sign of the pilot Lt Otto Uhland. Had he evaded capture?

At about 18.00 hours Dave Morgan, a young fourteen year old, was standing on the lawn of his home at The Vicarage in East Huntspill when he heard the unmistakable rattle of machine-gun fire and, a few minutes later, the stuttering sound of a plane in trouble. From the corner of his home looking towards the solitary barrage balloon on Pawlett Hill he could see a Heinkel heading in the direction of South Wales but, as he watched, it began to turn back, on fire. Four men were seen to bale out and were drifting on their parachutes in the direction of the Royal Ordnance Factory being constructed on the Puriton Levels. One was seen to be falling faster than the others and, keeping them in view, he ran to where the channel for the Huntspill River was being dug and arrived at the same time that an airman splashed into the water. It wasn't deep or in spate but he had difficulty in standing up as the parachute kept pulling him over. Dave was only about 150ft away but he was so overcome with the excitement of the occasion that he could only stand and watch as the airman struggled to free himself. At last he did so and on hearing people talking in an adjoining field he headed off in that direction.

Trailing a safe distance behind, Dave followed him into the field where four men were gathered around an injured airman, possibly the one who had come down too fast. As he got up close and stood over him Dave could see that he had a broken leg and had suffered severe bruising to his body. His face was contorted in pain and he had a helpless look in his eyes. One of the four was doing everything he could to make him as comfortable as possible but one of the others, a big hunk of a man, menacingly wielded a shovel and said, 'Lets finish the bastard off.'

To a young lad brought up on the chivalrous deeds of Biggles in the First World War such a malicious remark came as a profound shock. He couldn't quite gauge the mood of the crowd but he was sure it wasn't pleasant as some, carrying pitchforks, were making threatening gestures and it wasn't until the police arrived and took charge that he felt the injured airman was safe. He had now been joined by a school friend, and together they set off in search of the crashed aircraft unaware that one of the enemy airmen was still unaccounted for.

By now the police had arrived in numbers and with drawn Webley revolvers they ushered the three enemy airmen through the throng of agitated villagers towards the waiting police vehicles for transportation to the local police station. Later they were collected by the military and spent an uncomfortable night camped on a hard cold floor.

Provided with food and oversweet tea to soothe their shattered nerves (or make them more amiable), they were soon interrogated by someone from the intelligence service. Even in their demoralized state they were sure they hadn't given away any worthwhile information and the following morning, under heavy guard, they were put on the London train for the 'POW Cage' near Hyde Park where they were again briefly interrogated before being sent to POW Camp 2 at Oldham.

An ambulance soon took Edo Flick to Bridgwater Hospital where, after emergency treatment, he was placed in a bed in Poole Ward and guarded overnight by four armed policemen. In the next bed was Trevor Solomon, who had just had the middle finger of his left hand amputated, and who thought the security arrangements a bit heavy handed as, with a couple of broken legs, the enemy airman could hardly make a dash for freedom. Other patients on the ward also objected to the oppressive presence, so after a few days only one policeman remained on guard. Nicknamed 'Fritz' by the inmates and nursing staff, Edo was something of a celebrity and given sweets and cakes and fussed over by two nurses, 'Dizzy' Mullard and 'Blacky' Bell, though the dour but efficient matron Miss Dakin took a dim view of all the attention given to an enemy airman. She was glad when he was sufficiently recovered to be transferred to the Royal Herbert Hospital in Woolwich.

As Dave and his school friend jogged along a rough drove in the direction of Puriton they were halted in their tracks by a loud shout and were surrounded by three angry soldiers pointing rifles at them in a rather unfriendly manner. The soldiers couldn't possibly have thought that two innocent young schoolboys were enemy agents, but they were nevertheless given a severe dressing down before being sent on their way. Warned that during an emergency they should stay indoors and not be running out and about, the boys, though shaken, continued their search for the crashed aircraft. It had come down almost in the centre of the village in an orchard at the end of Cann's Lane and they could see flames leaping from the wreckage and hear ammunition exploding but a cordon of police, the Home Guard and soldiers prevented them from getting too close.

Chris Fright had been transfixed as he watched the burning Heinkel spiral down and then lurch up one last time before crashing into the ground, exploding not 600ft from where he was standing. In its final dive it had knocked a chimney off a house at Waterloo Terrace and its blazing trail had set a hayrick and Dutch barn alight. Glued to the spot, Chris didn't move until the very last moment as he had been distracted by the descending parachutist, then all hell broke out as the ammunition ignited sending bullets flying in all directions. The airman, who from his insignia appeared to be the pilot, had landed heavily only a few feet away and was immediately surrounded by a crowd of irate locals and workmen who threaten to lynch him if he moved so much as a muscle.

The orchard was in the care of a farmer who had already fired at one of the descending airmen and he was not best pleased that his crop had been ruined. Things could have turned very nasty if it wasn't for prompt action by the village constable and a lone Local Defence Volunteer (recently renamed the Home Guard) who bundled the bemused airman into a lorry and drove him off at top speed in the direction of Bridgwater. Lt Uhland, being an officer, was kept well away from his crew and interrogated separately but, later that evening, they were told he had come down in one piece and that his neck wound was only superficial. Yet they did not see him again.

People had swarmed to the scene of the crash by car, cycle and on foot but the military cordon and exploding ammunition had kept the souvenir hunters at bay and would do so until the smouldering mass was brought under control by

Tscheplak. Obltn. Ernest Ohlenschlager Weinrich. (Photograph: H. Rodder)

Remains of Heinkel He.111P that crashed at Puriton

the fire brigade. RAF crash investigators arrived to sift through the wreckage to see if they could uncover any secret or new enemy equipment, but not before a nineteen-year-old Flt Sgt had arrived in an MG Sports car to bag as a prize, and to celebrate his first victory claim, the swastika on the tail plane of the Heinkel.

He had landed his Spitfire at nearby Weston Zoyland and, in his haste to get from the airfield to the crash site, the car was seen coming round corners on two wheels. At the crash site he proudly told one of the villagers that he done the distance in only eight minutes. The only RAF pilot involved in the air battle to fit this description is young Bill Watling of 92 Squadron who was twenty years of age, and even though he was a 'snotty-nosed' pilot officer he is the most likely candidate. He was killed on 7 February 1941 some two weeks short of his twenty-first birthday.

As he watched Riedel's aircraft roll over and go down trailing a pall of smoke, Kurt Kupsch's euphoria in shooting down a British fighter quickly evaporated. Even before he had time to ponder on his comrades' fate, bullets were smashing into his aircraft as Bill Watling made another angled beam attack. They success-fully fought off this attack and Kupsch called for more ammunition as the fighters now came at them head-on. Again they beat off their attackers but with the second head-on attack their left engine suddenly started to spew out oil and, alarmingly, two Spitfires continued to circle for the kill, remaining tantalizingly out of range of their machine-guns.

Over the intercom he heard Obltn. Ohlenschlager call for the flight mechanic Fw. Jug to rim the plane and at that moment it broke sharply out to the left and a

Front section of Heinkel 111P (1G+NT) that
crashed at Charterhouse on 14 August 1940.
(Photograph: Ivor Sydenham)

Ivor Sydenham in the Home Guard in 1940

despairing thought went through Kupsch's head that both Heinkels were 'hanging very lonely in the air like apples ripe for the picking'. Frantically everyone tried to stabilize the situation but then the second engine spluttered and gave out. Kupsch was now really scared as a fighter was still on their tail and circling for another attack, but it held its fire and with a waggle of its wings was gone. They were lucky. Watling had run out off ammunition. Diving through a gap in the clouds he came out 3 miles north of Cardiff and headed back to Pembrey.

After a brief consultation Obltn. Ohlenschlager decided against baling out and told the crew to keep quiet and to brace themselves for a crash-landing. He would try and get them down safely. He ordered the observer Kurt Sulzbach to jettison the bomb load and, coming down through the clouds, he scoured the countryside for a suitable landing site.

He had hoped to make it to a large flat wheat field that he could see in the distance, but the Heinkel fell faster than expected and he hurriedly looked around for another landing site. Just ahead he could see a softly rising meadow and though not ideal he had no alternative but to put the battered bomber down quickly before it plunged out of control. With the under-carriage up and the flaps down, he held the aircraft in a straight line and told the crew to hold on to whatever they could. Like some giant plough it cut a huge furrow in the field as it careered across the meadow, crashing through the low stone wall at the end and finally coming to rest straddled across the Charterhouse Road, near Cheddar, Somerset.

Amazingly no one was injured and the crew scrambled from the broken air-craft in case it caught fire. Obltn. Ohlenschlager, however, was suffering from slight shock and he sat down on the wing of the plane as the others hurriedly tried to burn the maps and target pictures. Everyone was very nervous and, as Kurt Kupsch looked up, he could see two civilians advancing towards them with what looked like hunting rifles. With a sudden sinking feeling Kurt realized that for him the war was well and truly over. But that feeling didn't last as he was sure he wouldn't be a POW for very long. Surely the English would soon be pleading for peace and he'd be released.

Cecil Upton was just leaving work when he saw the crippled raider land in a field about 1 mile away. He got out of his car, picked up a rifle and told one of his colleagues to phone for the police. He reached the scene within three min-utes after picking up Mr Walters, an air-raid warden, on the way. The plane was lying across the road blocking their path with the crew milling around burning papers. Jumping out of the car they levelled their guns at the German airmen and ordered them to put their hands up and get away from the plane. The Germans obeyed and handed over their pistols.

Soldiers from a nearby unit then came running through the wheat field and surrounded the frightened airmen, pointing their rifles at them. A British offi-cer then strode into the circle, saluted and asked if anyone was wounded. The Germans shook their heads but he could see that Obltn. Ohlenschlager was in a dazed state so he offered him a cigarette and asked him to take a seat in Upton's car. The remainder of the crew were ordered into an army lorry and driven to the nearby barracks where they gratefully received tea, bread and bacon and eggs. An hour later they were taken to a Bristol prison for interrogation – the first leg of their long journey to a POW Camp in Canada.

As the stricken Spitfire glided down into the clouds, Havercroft had no idea whether he was over land or the sea. He would have little chance of surviving if he ditched in the Bristol Channel and he remembered with apprehension that on take-off the cloud base had been barely 600ft. The Welsh mountains could be just below. Perhaps he should bale out. He threw back the cockpit hood but the blast of cold air made him think again. Spitfires were expensive things and if he could get it down without too much damage then, with luck, it could be repaired and back in action. Anyway he had never baled out in a plane before and he didn't intend to start now.

Flying at 140mph he entered the tops of the clouds and tightened his straps for the inevitable impact. Moisture dripped onto his knees and streamed over the windscreen as it hurtled through the clouds. There appeared to be no break in the clouds and he had visions of a mountain suddenly leaping up in front of him when he was in the clear at about 4,000ft. Below he could see rough countryside with deep valleys and high moorland. A curving road climbed out of one valley winding its way over the top of a heather-covered hill and dropped back into another valley. He decided to put the Spitfire down on top of the hill as near as he could to the road.

A final check: speed 120mph, undercarriage up, fuel cocks off, guns safe and magneto switches off. Then with the altimeter winding down rapidly he banked to the right and put the flaps down. As he braced himself a line of power cables loomed across his path and, climbing steeply over them, he pushed the Spitfire hard for the ground before it stalled. Clods of earth and heather flew up as it slid violently to a halt. The deceleration threw him forward against his harness and the hood, which he had forgotten to lock back, almost took off the top of his head as it slammed shut with a bang. In the silence he sat very still and tried to calm down. A few sheep looked up, bleated then promptly ignored him.

Senses regained he pulled back the hood, undid his harness and climbed out. The cool breeze was sweet and scented and he lay face down in the heather to inspect the battle damage, and looking into the radiator he could see that at least two bullets had smashed straight through the matrix and gone out of the top of the wing. He gave the German gunner top marks for accuracy, slung his parachute and helmet over his shoulder and started to walk across the mountain towards the road.

An air-raid warning sounded in the mining village of Maerdy, in the upper reaches of the Rhondda Valley, as the battle raged overhead. Spent cartridge cases cascaded down onto the grey slate rooftops and the Local Defence Volunteers were ordered by Captain Melhuish to muster at their headquarters in St David's Hall where they had an armoury. Ivor Sydenham, then only sixteen years of age, was issued with a rifle, three rounds of ammunition and told that a German raider had come down on the mountain between Maerdy and Aberdare. Along with the captain, another volunteer and Sgt Lloyd from the local police station he was bundled into a car and they set off to investigate the crash and to capture any Germans who might have survived.

Wearing a flying jacket and a 'Mae West', which hid his RAF uniform, Havercroft walked along the embankment bordering the road and watched a car struggle slowly up the hill. It stopped a short distance away and out jumped out four men of the Home Guard who rushed forward brandishing their rifles and shouting words he couldn't quite catch. Captain Melhuish pulled out his revolver and in German ordered Havercroft to put his hands up. Taken aback by their aggressive attitude he put down his parachute and had a right go at them, not realizing that they had every reason to be cautious. Amongst the torrent of swear words he finally managed to blurt out, 'I'm a bloody British pilot.' Private Ivor Sydenham felt slightly foolish. His first German had turned out to be an RAF pilot and he immediately offered his apologies.

Things were quickly sorted out and everyone laughed at the farcical confrontation. Squeezing his small frame into the car, Havercroft was driven to Maerdy Police Station where Mrs Lloyd, the wife of the police sergeant, made him welcome and gave him a cup of hot sweet tea. That evening after a wash and brush up, Sgt Lloyd took him down the main street of Maerdy where they called in at the Maerdy and Royal Hotels and a working man's club. Everyone made him welcome and people came out of their houses pushing packets of cigarettes into

Dennis Hampton Jeffrey. (Photograph: D.H. Jeffrey)

Fw. Ernst Haumann – Observer/ Navigator on board Riedl's aircraft. (Photo; Frau E. Gerke)

his hands, many of them talking in a language he couldn't understand but their meaning was unmistakeable. It was a memorable evening.

He spent the night in the police station, not in the cells but in one of Sgt Lloyd's comfortable spare bedrooms. He was up very early and caught the 06.00 hours bus for RAF St Athan, about 30 miles away where some of the local men were building a new runway. From there he was picked up and flown to RAF Pembrey to be reunited with his squadron. As the bus weaved its way down through the twisting streets, he could see that the valley had been untouched by war.

Ivor Sydenham was later to stand guard over the crashed Spitfire N3285 that had its engine cover left open, presumably by Havercroft when he inspected the damage, and with its hood still pulled back and open to the elements. The salvage crew soon arrived to recover the buckled machine but Havercroft had made such a good forced-landing that it was repaired and flew again during the latter stages of the Battle of Britain.

On the seafront at Barry, the sound of machine-gun fire overhead was interrupted by the roar of engines as a German bomber, coming from inland, swept low out of the clouds heading in the direction of Steep Holm. Arthur Dite, the first mate on the salvage tug the *Standard Rose*, which was anchored about 600ft out, mid-way between Barry harbour and Sully Island, hit the deck in terror as the bomber came straight at him. The rest of the crew also scurried for safety expecting to be machine-gunned any minute.

Uffz Hans Dolata the Radio Operator aboard Riedl's aircraft. (Photograph: Frau H. Liebchen)

Wooden grave marker of Hans Dolata showing the wrong date of death. (Photograph: A. White)

In the spring of 1989 Hedwig Liebchen, the sister of Hans Dolata, and her husband were finally able to lay flowers on his grave. (Photograph: A. White)

A poor photo of 1G + NT down at Charterhouse, but it shows the censored unit code. (Photograph: A. Wright)

On the morning of 14 August, Dennis Hampton Jeffrey and his parents had set off by car from their home in Cardiff for a day out at Southerndown, but the weather was very dull and overcast with light showers so, instead, they decided to drive to Barry Island. They parked the car in front of the putting green at Nell's Point next to where the path led to the sand and rocks below, but there were very few people on the beach and those who were their had their backs to the sea wall sheltering from the weather.

So they ate their sandwiches on top of the wall that overlooked the winding path that led down to the sands when they heard the sound of an aircraft overhead. As a member of the school cadet corps he was very keen on aircraft recognition and, though he could hardly believe it, he immediately recognized the plane that dipped below the cloud ceiling as a Heinkel 111. Coming from inland it flew over the fairground at about 500ft and, as it bore down, he thought it was going to strafe the beach but almost instantly it turned to run parallel with the coastline but then turned again and headed out to sea. It was zigzagging to and fro as if trying to shake off an invisible attacker: there was no sign of any RAF fighters.

Although it was leaving a thin stream of smoke in its wake, Reidl's aircraft did not appear, to the few people on the sea front at Barry, to be in serious trouble. It was flying straight and level but, to some, it did seem to be gradually losing height as if the pilot was positioning the aircraft to ditch in the sea. Somehow it had survived the heavy barrage of gunfire from the ships in Barry docks and from the guns of the local TA unit of the 77th Heavy AA Royal Artillery on the hill opposite Sully Island. It now gained a couple of feet as if it was making one last effort to get back up into the clouds when suddenly there was a rapid rat-tat-tat that sounded like machine-gun fire and it flipped right over and with a roar from its engines went straight in. The wings folded up like a cormorant as it hit the water.

Such was the steepness of the nose dive that many of those on the ground thought that the pilot must have been mortally wounded by the ferocious AA fire, and had fallen forward onto the controls sending the aircraft into an uncontrollable dive. It was all over so suddenly that none of the crew had a chance to bale out.

As the *Standard Rose* sped to the scene of the crash, a Spitfire appeared out of the clouds, briefly circled and then quickly disappeared. Many small boats were also putting out to sea from Barry harbour but they were disappointed in their hunt for trophies as only papers and maps were floating up to the surface, but Arthur Dite did manage to fish out a pair of zipped-up flying boots. They, along with everything they recovered, were confiscated by the RAF Sea Rescue Launch that quickly took command of the situation once it arrived on the scene. When the tug reached its berth at Barry Pier the authorities were waiting, and the members of the crew were subjected to a rigorous interview and warned not to discus what they had seen with anyone, especially the press. Some small pieces of wreckage were later washed up on Sully Beach, enough for Police Superintendent James to be satisfied that the plane that crashed into Sully Bay was in fact German.

Almost one month later on 11 September the body of the radio operator Hans Dolata was washed ashore on the other side of the Bristol Channel at Portishead. As he was manning the open-air dorsal machine-gun position his body was probably thrust out of the plane as it powered into the water. He was quietly buried in the cemetery at Weston–super-Mare where he lies to this day in a small plot set aside for Germans who were killed during the war. The small wooden cross originally erected over his grave incorrectly showed the date of death as '11.9.40', and when a stone headstone was substituted for the worn-out wooden one the correct date of death was still not entered alongside his date of birth. His was the only body of the five-man crew to be recovered from the aircraft that went down in relatively shallow water less than half a mile off shore.

Owing to some official hesitation by the German authorities, Hedwig Liebchen, the sister of Hans Dolata, was not made aware of his place of interment until 1988 and she now made plans to visit his grave. In the spring of 1989, accompanied by her husband Gerd and their daughter, she finally made a pilgrimage to the cemetery and, placing flowers on his grave, said a silent farewell prayer.

CHAPTER NINE

Last Raiders of the Day

As the Daimler-Benz engines roared into life, the airmen of the last *Kette* away were waved into the sky by the ground crews as the remaining Staff Officers of III/KG 27 lined up and saluted their departure. The flight leader Obltn. Artur Wiesemann, known to be a daring and resourceful pilot, was the natural choice for such a long and dangerous mission to bomb RAF Sealand, an airfield in the far north-east of Wales. To fly across the English Channel in broad daylight, unescorted by fighters, was perilous enough but to then cross the Bristol Channel and fly the whole length of the English/Welsh border was almost a suicidal mission but, if anyone could successfully carry out such an order, it was Wiesemann.

With plenty of time on their hands prior to take-off, the three radio operators of the *Kette* mulled over the revised battle orders and carefully studied the new flight plan and target maps. The dangers of a round trip of almost 745 miles with a flight duration of 4–5 hours were obvious to all, but it was the ebullient Erich Frielinghaus, down to fly with 'Peter' Oeckenpoehler in 1G + DS (*Dora*), who was the first to realise the difficulty they now faced but he made light of the risks. Danger? What danger! OK, they may need some luck but this was an exciting assignment. This was not the time to be pessimistic.

Gietz, as reticent as ever, didn't need the dangers to be pointed out but he was comforted by the fact that the aircrews were mostly experienced old hands with a great deal of flying time to their credit and were good comrades. They would all do their duty and, should the bullets start to fly, they would not let him down. Attacking at twilight they might just catch the airfield defences unawares and, under cover of darkness, the return leg should be safe enough but as he clipped on his parachute he couldn't shift that sinking feeling in the pit of his stomach as he boarded 1G + CS ('Caesar'), even though it was to be flown by his friend and veteran pilot Fw. Oskar Dubral.

All of the airmen in the *Kette* were single and, except for Wieseman who had just celebrated his twenty-eighth birthday, were all aged between twenty and twenty-six. The quietly spoken Kochy kept his black thoughts to himself but mused that at least they wouldn't leave any grieving widows behind. His parents at home in the small village of Beierstedt would be heartbroken he was sure, but

The three Radio Operators of the *Kette*. Left to right: Walter Gietz, Erich Frielinghaus and Heinz Kochy. (Photograph: W. Gietz)

all such morbid thoughts were pushed to the back of his mind as their aircraft 1G + FS (*Friedrich*) lifted into the air. He had had a bad premonition about this mission even though he would be flying with Wiesemann, a gifted pilot with whom he had flown many times before in combat. They had come through some difficult situations in the past but this mission was longer and far more dangerous then anything they had ever attempted and, despite the bravado displayed by Frielinghaus, they would need more than a little luck to get through this one.

As the *Kette* taxied for take-off, Oeckenpoehler's plane lost a bomb that tumbled over and over before coming harmlessly to rest. Everyone breathed a sigh of relief. A lucky omen?

The three Heinkel's lifted into the air at 18.10 hours and, in a ragged formation, climbed steadily to 9,000ft before levelling off between two layers of cloud. Far above them was a thin layering of cirrostratus and below, at 4,500ft, a mass of heavy cumulus clouds that obscured the ground. Occasionally the clouds would open up and through a gap Kochy briefly caught sight of two islands with typical white breakers, which he took to be the Channel Islands. Soon they were out over the Channel and the nearer they got to the English coast the better the visibility became with the solid mountain of heavy cloud breaking up into smaller blocks of white tumbling fluff intermixed with larger lumps of rolling black cloaks of darkness.

The radio communication between the three Heinkels left much to be desired but, as the success of the mission could well rest on maintaining contact, they stayed in touch, either unaware or unconcerned that the RAF could latch on to

He111Ps of KG 27 at Rennes in the summer of 1940. In the foreground is 1G + DS and in the background, 1G + AA. (Photograph: H. Wappler)

their frequency. Keeping a sharp look out for any fighters they flew over Lyme Bay and approached Exeter when, against a white feathery sheet of cloud, Kochy saw two black dots closing fast. He calmly reported this to their pilot and Flt Leader Obltn. Wiesemann, who ordered the accompanying aircraft to open formation and take up battle stations.

For a brief moment Kochy held out a faint hope that the rapidly approaching aircraft could be friendly but, to be on the safe side, he fired a few cursory rounds in their direction to alert the *Kette* of the possible danger. But now events overtook them at a frightening pace as the chasing fighters climbed higher in the sky positioning to attack, leaving them in no doubt that they were the enemy. They were Hurricanes of 'B' Flight of 213 Squadron flying out of Exeter, made up of two aircraft from Green Section and two from Blue Section.

Over the intercom someone shouted out 'Enemy fighter behind!' and Frielinghaus, sitting facing the rear in 1G + DS, instantly realised that he was in the right position to have his head blown off. Fearfully scanning the skies he saw them. Two 'Spitfires' coming out of the clouds, closing fast and opening fire from long range on Dubral's Heinkel on the left of the formation. The three radio operators immediately returned fire and, as the fighters veered sharply away, they were sure that some of their shots were on target but the Spitfires had the edge. They attacked again and again with a salvo of bullets that tore holes in their tail plane, miraculously whizzing past either side of Frielinghaus.

Then through his earphones he heard 'Landing gear down, tanks and engine hit!', but he didn't recognise the voice. Frightened to death he hurriedly looked

Schreiber, Dubral, Knoblich and Gietz with Heinkel 111P (1G + CS) in the background. (Photograph: W. Geitz)

Fw. Oskar Dubral at the controls with Fw. Walter Schaum. (Photograph: W. Schaum)

Fw. Heinrich Rodder. (Photograph: H. Rodder)

around to check out the condition of the other machines. *Caesar* was done for, its undercarriage hanging half-down with black and white streams of petrol and oil pouring from the engines. But the rear gunner wasn't going down without a fight and flashes of tracer could still be seen snaking skywards in one last attempt to keep the fighters at bay.

Dubral must have pushed the controls all the way forward to try and maintain some sort of control because his plane was now almost standing on its nose. As it dropped out of the formation it would not be long before it would have to be abandoned but the rear gunner was still firing. In the lead Heinkel, Obltn. Wieseman sought to gain the protection of the clouds as a fighter sped forward to try and head him off but the fighter was not quick enough and 1G + FS, seemingly undamaged, was last seen disappearing into the murk.

To Oeckenpoehler, the clouds were tantalisingly just too far away and the fighters much too fast. He had to endure a running battle before he could shake off the Spitfires that were still glued to his tail. As one came in fast from behind he heard Frielinghaus cry out 'Turn away!', and he swung the plane sharply to the right.

The fighter skidded past, its bullets heading harmlessly into the void. On full power he headed for the safety of the clouds but two fighters were soon back on his tale. Only the rear machine-gun of Frielinghaus offered any protection as the Hurricanes attacked from behind and above. 'An impossible task', he thought. One machine-gun against eight was unfair. His head was bound to be blown off. Concentrating his sights on the nose of the nearest fighter he fired an entire magazine in its direction and it lurched and fell back. But his elation was short lived for the second fighter continued with the attack, blazing away at long range, cleverly using the rudder of the Heinkel as cover.

Frustratingly he couldn't get a clear shot. Then the drum was empty. With his right hand he yanked off the old drum, with the left he grabbed a full magazine from the flight mechanic and rammed it home. Within seconds he had recommenced firing but it was difficult and dangerous because the enemy was hiding behind the rudder. He aimed his shots either side of the rudder but the fighter was not deterred and closed in for the kill. With a loud cry Frielinghaus screamed at the pilot 'Skid' and the aircraft really did skid presenting him, at last, with a clear shot but the fighter unleasahed the first telling burst. Tremendous streaks of fire pour out from his gun-ports as he closed to within 90ft but he came in much too close and received a full seventy-five-round blast from the dorsal MG 15 that splattered the Hurricane, forcing him to turn away. Before he could renew the attack the Heinkel hit the edge of the clouds and almost immediately disappeared from view.

Such was the intensity of the air battle that Frielinghaus had managed to shut out the sounds coming through his earphones but now he heard something like 'Bale out!' Was that Dubral or Wieseman? Who gave the order? Is must be Dubral. He urgently tried to make radio contact with both aircraft but there was no answer. Had they been shot down?

Heinkel 111P of KG 27 after the crash-landing at Rennes. (Photograph: H. Kochy)

Fw. Walter Geitz and Fw. Walter Schaum celebrating a lucky return. (Photograph: W. Geitz)

Heinkel 111P (1G + CS) flying over the Zugspitze. (Photograph: H. Rodder)

His thoughts were suddenly interrupted by Franz, the flight mechanic, who called out 'Erich, look at our poor crate!' There were bullet holes in the wing, in the right engine and landing gear, and they would have to nurse it home.

Once before they had made it back in a badly shot-up plane, and with Oekenpohler at the controls believed they would do so again. Having successfully limped across the Channel they come in sight of their home airfield at Rennes but, as they prepared to land, disaster. The landing gear wouldn't come down. Peter told the flight mechanic to 'Try and jack it down' and, with the help of the navigator and beam-gunner, they wrestled with the manual controls to try and lower the undercarriage but to no avail. The landing gear remained stuck in place. Again and again they circled the airfield and fired off red distress flares.

The entire airfield was now well aware of their plight and watched the drama unfold. The betting was on a crash-landing and everyone hurriedly cleared a wide area around the landing strip.

'Make ready for a belly-landing' Peter told the crew. As he throttled back on the controls the plane hovered lower and lower until it appeared to stop in mid-air. Almost on the point of stalling it hit the ground with a powerful jerk, the propellers grinding with rage. As it crunched its way forward the belly crashed up into the fuselage and the interior of the plane filled with swirling dust and debris. It skidded along for a few feet only slightly careering off a straight line as it slowed to a stop.

As they scrambled out of the wreck the fire engine and ambulance were quickly on the scene. Within moments the plane was ringed by the curious as they inspected the damage and counted the bullet holes. But the really big question was what about Wiesemann and Dubral? They had not heard anything from either aircraft and feared the worse.

The four Hurricanes that had been closing fast on the *Kette*, coming in from above and behind, were almost the last serviceable aircraft that 213 Squadron could put into the air. During the previous three days they had suffered heavily at the hands of the Luftwaffe with five pilots failing to return from combat over the Channel. Another four Hurricanes had limped back to base so badly shot-up that the battle damage would take weeks to be repaired.

The loss of nine aircraft in such a short time, and the delay in the arrival of replacements and the shortage of spares, had so reduced the fighting strength of 213 Squadron that it was barely operational. Perhaps the squadron should have been temporarily withdrawn from front line duties but for the moment, as long as it could put fighters in the air, it was still in the war.

On patrol at 16,000ft above Seaton it was late in the day, past 19.30 hours, when Pilot Officer Harold Atkinson, flying as Green 2, spotted the three Heinkels, just below, flitting in and out of the rolling cloud heading north-west. They were about 6-8 miles off shore, out in the middle of Lyme Bay, and with a rush of adrenalin he cried out 'Tally-ho!' over the radio and opened the throttle to give chase at maximum speed. Green Leader desperately tried to keep up.

As they neared the English coast the crew of 1G + CS still chattered to one another over the intercom, unaware of the approaching danger. To their half-right and slightly ahead hovered 1G + FS, under the command of deputy Staffelkapitan Artur Wiesemann, and to the right cruising alongside was 1G + DS, flown by Oekenpohler. It was a loose formation but closed up tight to present a concentrated cone of fire should they be come under attack from one of the RAF's few remaining fighters.

Sitting in the revolving mount behind the sliding roof on top of the aircraft Walter Gietz, the wireless operator, had a completely clear view, only slightly hampered by the radio mast and the tail plane, and from this position he continuously scanned the sky to the rear. Suddenly away in the distance he saw two black dots which he assumed were German fighters that routinely carried out constant patrols as far as the English south coast.

At such a distance it was impossible to recognise the type of planes that were rapidly closing and, even though he was convinced they were in no danger, he nevertheless notified Dubral of the situation and brought his machine-gun to bear on the nearest dot as it grew ever larger. Then it happened. All hell broke loose. The wings of the fighter seemed to catch fire as the covers over the gun ports split open sending a salvo of bullets mixed with incendiaries hurtling in their direction. Gietz retaliated, instantly emptying a full ammunition drum at the fighter and shouted to the crew 'Enemy fighter!', but the warning was not needed as the first swathe of bullets crashed into the port wing. He also heard cries of agony from up front and feared that the pilot had been hit.

The first blast from Atkinson's guns had hit home, right on target, and smoke was seen to billow from the port engine with flames spreading out along the wing. To outmanoeuvre the Heinkel he broke upwards to stop the enemy from reaching the clouds and, closing down to a suicidal distance of only 450ft he again let rip a four-second burst that crashed into the Heinkel, bringing down the undercarriage. The whole of the aircraft was now hidden by smoke but he fired another four-second burst into the port engine that stopped and caught fire. With flames licking all along the wing four men were seen to bale out and, seeing that the aircraft was done for, he turned and chased after another Heinkel that was heading for the safety of the clouds.

But the other rear gunners kept firing and a final salvo of bullets shattered the cockpit of his Hurricane, sending up a shower of small Bakelite splinters that imbedded in his left forearm. The shards shredded his tunic, penetrating deeply into the flesh and causing a multitude of small painful wounds. The temperature gauge was now rising fast and, with blood oozing from the shattered arm, he abandoned the attack and headed back to base.

Gietz emptied drum after drum of MG 15 ammo at the attacking fighters, but they resolutely continued to attack, firing volley after volley into the tight-knit formation. As a hail of bullets crashed into his plane Gietz felt a sharp glancing blow in his left leg, followed by a sharp, burning pain. He had been hit by a splinter from a tracer bullet and the initial spurt of blood from the wound

Fw. Heinz Thiel and Ofw. Anton (Toni) Wiesmeier

dyed his leg a deep red. But before he had time to think, his attention was immediately diverted.

Below him he heard both Knoblich and Schrage cry out in panic as the bullets crashed into their plane. They were helpless, being unable to return fire against fighters that attacked from above and astern. Bullets splattered against the armour plate. The din was deafening and he thought he too was going to die when the fighters suddenly broke off the attack.

It was only a brief respite but it was a golden opportunity for the three wireless operators to adjust their defensive fire and concentrate on one fighter at a time. It was up to them to save the *Kette* as the other air gunners could only fire below, ahead or from the sides and, for the time being, they were out of the fight.

With every fifth shot being a tracer Geitz could clearly follow his line of fire and, as the attacking fighter closed to within 200ft, his shots were dead on target. He was sure he had knocked out a Hurricane but there was no let up in the ferocity of the attack and Dubral took the aircraft down in a steep dive to try and escape the fighters.

Glancing to one side Gietz caught a glimpse of 1G + DS just as it vanished into the thick cloud below. But would they too reach the safety of the clouds? Their 1G + CS was in serious trouble. It was shot full of holes and billowed a long trail of black smoke from the port engine that was pumping out jets of oil and petrol all along the wing. They were in deep trouble and then things got even worse as over the headphones he heard Dubral cry out 'A man to the front! A man to the front!'.

Neither Knoblich nor Schrage made a move to help. They were glued to their gun positions so Gietz clipped on his parachute and struggled forward through the narrow passage between the bomb bays towards the cockpit. There he was confronted with a horrific scene. The canopy was shot to pieces with the wind whistling through the gaping holes. The observer, Tony Wiesmeier, was drenched in blood and hunched in a crumpled heap with the silk spilling out from his chest parachute. Caustic smoke swirled around the cabin as the port engine had now ignited and flames were spreading ominously along the wing. It was high time to get out of that hell-hole but first he tried to save his wounded comrade and, bending over him, he released the clasp and stuffed the parachute back into its holder. He signalled to Toni that he would lay him down but, as he did so, his gaze fixed on Gietz. The imploring look in his eyes, seeking help, Gietz remembered the rest of his life.

Dubral indicated that they must bale out through the sliding roof above the pilot's seat. He had tried to slide it back but it was stuck fast and now all his strength was needed to keep the plane in the air. Just a moment's loss of attention could send them crashing into the sea. It was up to Gietz to free the escape hatch but despite all his efforts, it remained firmly in place. They had to try and escape through the small sliding window beside the right-hand seat but as Gietz stepped over Wiesmeier and yanked it open the plane slid sideways in a steep dive.

He pushed himself through the tiny opening and was immediately hit by the force of the slipstream but a parachute strap had caught inside and he was hanging perilously in mid-air. Dubral freed the strap, sending Gietz plunging into space. He missed the tail plane by a hair's breadth and opened the parachute.

Floating down his first thought was to get rid of his secret radio code and he tossed it away before he splashed into the sea and then saw the plane, with Toni Wiesmeier inside, crash into the sea.

The water was icy cold and Gietz quickly freed himself from the parachute that was becoming increasingly waterlogged and threatening to pull him under and blew up his *schwimmweste* thinking to swim ashore, which he hoped to reach within one or two hours. But after swimming for about an hour the coast seem no nearer and his strokes were becoming weaker and weaker as his body started to react to the cold. Then in the distance he sighted an Air Sea Rescue launch and he was hauled aboard.

Dubral had already been fished out of the sea and was huddled in the rear of the boat covered in a thick, grey blanket. Someone also threw a blanket over Gietz and handed them both a cup of rum as they were freezing after spending so long in the water. Gietz realised he still had his pistol in his side pocket and gave it to Flight Sergeant Burns as a souvenir.

The launch continued a sweeping search of Lyme Bay for the other two airmen who were seen to bale out, but their search was in vain. Heading back to Lyme Regis they were brought ashore at the Cobb where a large crowd had gathered. Amongst the crowd was Ronnie Baker who had legged it down to the harbour just in time to see two captives covered in blankets bundled into the back of an open army lorry that headed up Cobb Road towards the local police station.

They were kept in overnight and the following morning heard that Heinrich Schrage had been pulled out of the water by another boat, but had been so badly wounded that he died as he was brought ashore. Then they had an unexpected visitor; an airman with a bandaged arm. It was Pilot Officer Harold Atkinson who had shot them down. But the meeting was short lived as later in the day they were transported to London for interrogation. Like most Luftwaffe POWs they would subsequently spend the rest of the war behind wire in Canada. The body of Feldwebel Franz Knoblich was washed ashore at Puncknowle on the Dorset coast over two weeks later.

But what about Kochy? Almost in unison the rear gunners had opened up on the incoming fighters and Kochy, in 1G + FS, was sure that many of their tracers were on-target but that didn't stop the heavy return fire that rained down on them. The seventy-five-shot magazines were being used up in single bursts, and over the intercom he heard the repeated cries, 'Where are the fighters?' The shouts were coming from the flight engineer down in the bola and from the side gunner who had fired a few speculative shots into the sky hoping to frighten off any incoming attacker. But Kochy was fully occupied in trying to ward off the attackers, and spent cartridge cases from over five magazines were rattling around the aircraft before there was a slight lull in fighting.

And what happened to the left-hand machine? It had fallen way behind and its port engine was giving out clouds of thick black smoke. Glancing to the other side Kochy only saw the belly of the right-hand machine as it turned and dived fast away. Everything happened so quickly. Both *Kettenhund* had vanished and he continually tried to establish radio contact but, despite repeated signals, there was no answer.

They were now alone and out of the small protective bank of clouds, and if the two fighters came at them again with all sixteen guns firing it would soon be all over. Their plane had taken some hits but there was no material damage so Oberlt Wiesemann decided to press on with the attack.

Over the West Country the clouds were fairly scanty and they kept a sharp lookout for fighters expecting them to reappear at any moment. The Kochy had a shock. Right behind them, and coming up fast, he saw another He 111 being attacked by two fighters but it broke away, taking the fighters with it.

They were somewhere over the Bristol Channel when they finally reached the protective cloud cover and, with the knowledge that safety was just a few feet below, they skimmed over the tops of the clouds, darting in and out of the high crests. Without knowing it they had sailed straight through the defensive screen put up by the Spitfires of 92 Squadron and, as they headed further north, with still no sign of fighters, the tension subsided and they settled down for the remainder of the long flight.

Their ever-calm flight engineer, Walter Schaum, opened up his flask and as he passed around mugs of hot, strong coffee their confidence returned but Kochy

Fw. Heinrich Rodder. (Photograph: Rodder)

was continually haunted by visions of fighters hiding in the clouds. He would remain on high alert all the way to the target.

Over the intercom he sometimes managed to catch Wiesemann and Heinrich Rodder, the navigator/bomb-aimer, discussing their course and height as they continued to close on their target. They knew there were no RAF fighter squadrons this far north and the only opposition they were likely to encounter was from powerful AA guns surrounding the aerodrome. If Sealand had such weapons.

RAF Sealand had been the home of No.5 Flying Training School based at West Camp for over twenty years and, at South Camp, the other side of the London & North Eastern Railway line, was No.36 Maintenance Unit, a crating and packing depot. Also at Sealand was the expanding No.30 Maintenance Unit, with a complement of over 1,400 personnel, based at the newly built East Camp the other side of the dividing A550 Queensferry to Birkenhead Road. It was such a higgledy-piggledy site that it was difficult for the raider to pick out a main target but the hangers at South Camp seemed the obvious choice.

Being so far from the air battles taking place in the south of England, even though they had experienced an isolated night attack in the last week of June, no one at RAF Sealand thought the enemy would risk a daylight attack. Even after that night attack no AA guns had been brought in and the defence of the aerodrome was limited to a few machine-gun posts scattered around the perimeter. The aerodrome was practically defenceless.

Having got rid of its old bi-planes, the Flying School was now using Miles Masters for flight training although some Airspeed Oxfords were still being

Uffz Borgerding, Uffz Heinrich Schrage, Uffz. H. Rodder and Uffz. Kleinjohann with an unknown armourer (Photograph: H. Rodder)

used for twin-engine instruction. Some of the Masters had been converted to single-seaters equipped with six machine-guns and were intended to be used as back-up for the front-line fighters should the invasion become a reality. They were not intended to clear the skies of enemy daylight raiders and normally stood idle. They were certainly armed and could be used in an emergency but, caught on the hop, it was too late to get them into the air as the raider swept beneath the clouds.

Probably they were too busy dealing with the aftermath of accidents earlier in the day when two Miles Masters had collided in mid-air over Holt. One crashed to earth with the pilot, Sgt S.A. Goodwin, successfully baling out while the other, flown by Sgt T. Healey, limped back to base. But far more serious was the accident involving Miles Master N 7898 that dived into the ground, killing Sgts F. Collins and C. Smith. Dealing with these accidents took priority and the sound of an aircraft overhead went unheeded.

However, any daylight intruder could still be in for a shock because RAF Hawarden, some 3 miles south of Sealand, on the other side of the Dee, had three fully armed Spitfires ready for action. Although Hawarden was the home of No.7 Operational Training Unit, its instructors were all experienced pilots, some veterans of the Battle of France, and its commanding officer Wing Commander J.R. Hallings-Pott, realising the area was wide open to attack, had organised an *ad hoc* battle flight for local defence. And in the officers' beer tent there would always be at least three pilots awaiting any warning signal from the Observer Corps at Manchester.

After about two hours' flying time the crew of 1G+FS again resumed battle positions as they drew ever nearer to their destination. Wieseman took the aircraft down to beneath the clouds levelling off at 1,500ft; their easily recognisable target lay dead ahead. Rodder was elated with his navigational skills. In the cramped cockpit of the Heinkel 111P there was no place to lay out his maps and instruments, and they had to be spread out on his lap. To have exactly located RAF Sealand was a testament to his training. Now he would have to test his skill as a bomb-aimer.

To give him a better view of the target, Wieseman took them down even lower and Kochy could hear them calmly discussing the line of attack. Directly ahead they could see two hangars, one slightly larger than the other, buildings and barrack blocks and a large open square that was presumably the parade ground. Coming down to little more than 600ft they commenced their bombing run unhindered by any AA fire from the ground. As Wiesemann steadied the approach, Rodder waited for the hangars to come into focus but then, overcome with excitement, he released the bombs just a fraction too early.

Stan Holt Weston, a cub reporter with the *Birkenhead Advertiser*, had joined the local LDV at its inception and, in early July, they received cases of First World War Canadian .303 Lee-Enfield rifles packed in grease but without any bullets. Many hours were spent drilling and standing guard, with empty rifles, over a large wire compound erected in Arrow Park in Birkenhead to house French soldiers and sailors. Eventually the bullets arrived and, having learned which end of the rifle to point, they were ordered to carry out rifle practice at the firing range at Sealand.

It was a motley crew of young men nursing acne and old men with clicking dentures and stiffening joints that arrived at Sealand aerodrome at 20.00 hours, each equipped with a rifle and five rounds of ammunition. They had no kit or uniforms and, except for the LDV arm band, they could easily be taken for civilian visitors.

But all that drilling had not been in vain and, with safety catches on, they lined up smartly in ranks ready to march to the range when, from out of nowhere, a large plane flew above the road at no more than 200ft. The noise was deafening. There had been no air-raid warning but the German insignia on the fuselage and the tail was plain to see, and the arrival overhead of the Heinkel stopped them in their tracks. Wide-eyed and speechless they broke ranks and began running in all directions, like headless chickens.

Stan made it to a large doorway protected by sandbags up to knee level, and quickly slipping off the safety catch he worked the bolt to load his rifle. Lining up the raider in his sites he dispatched three bullets in its direction. It was so low he must have hit home.

On a mild summer's evening there was little to disrupt the thoughts of Eddie Ashworth, an instrument basher, as he leisurely strolled towards the bridge over the Queensferry–Birkenhead Road that separated No.5 Flying School from No.30 Maintenance Unit. He could hear the drone of approaching

Oberlt Artur Wiesemann. (Photograph: Wiesemann)

plane's engines but no air-raid warning had sounded and he didn't pay it too much attention.

As the noise increased he looked up and saw a twin-engine bomber coming in low over Shotton Steel Works and wondered if it was in trouble when suddenly the bomb doors opened and a stick of bombs tumbled out. He tried to run for his machine-gun pit on the bridge but it was far too late and as the bombs whistled down he dived to the ground.

For such a long-range mission their Heinkel 111P carried a reduced bomb load of only 1,150kg, made up of two SC 250kg thin-walled high-explosive bombs for maximum blast effect and the lighter Flambo 250, an oil-filled incendiary, one being fitted with a delayed-action fuse. It also carried four smaller SC 50kg blast bombs and four SD 50kg thick-walled fragmentation bombs. A total of only eleven explosive bombs, but they could cause plenty of serious damage against key targets. Rodder was sure they would.

The first bomb landed 15ft in front of the main guardroom causing damage to its façade and the main blockhouse. The next bomb fell between the Guard Room and the sergeants' mess, badly damaging an airman's barrack block and tearing up the concrete road leading to the mess and severing the main electricity cable. The third struck the south corner of the sergeants' mess, demolishing the sleeping quarters and causing chaos in the rooms below. The fourth fell in front of the sick quarters, blowing out the windows of the hospital and scaring its few occupants. Pilot Officer Robinson, sheltering behind some sandbags, was thrown into a trench by the blast but, although dazed, he was next seen on top

Heinkel 111P (1G + FS). (Photograph: Rodder)

of the Sergeants' mess, along with two other servicemen, striving to dig out the injured.

The fifth bomb, the 250kg incendiary, landed near the main entrance of the Sick Quarters and its doors were blackened by the blast but the fire that took hold was quickly brought under control. The sixth fell on the ramp of the bridge perilously close to Eddie Ashworth, and to within only a few feet of the Motor Transport Repair Squadron. The seventh cratered the sports field, and the eighth and ninth bombs landed in the adjacent fields, killing a horse. Bombs we also reported to have fallen near the western boundary and alongside the 'C type hangar.

The blast had lifted Eddie clean off the deck and showered him with earth and debris. Peering through the dust and smoke he could see that the bomb had fallen almost directly on the ramp of the bridge and, thinking that some of his fellow airman had been injured, he hurried to help.

But his assistance was really needed at the Sergeants' mess where airmen buried under the rubble were screaming for help. With their bare hands the servicemen lifted the bricks to get at the injured below and, slowly, most were brought out alive though many were maimed and bloodied. A senior NCO, Warrant Officer Edward Frank Edwards, who was drinking in the Sergeants' Mess was killed outright and six sergeants badly wounded with Sgt James Freeman the most seriously injured, being almost close to death but miraculously he survived. Seven aircraftsmen were also injured, some seriously, and many more were suffering from shock. All the casualties were men from No.30 Maintenance Unit. Later the top floor of the Sergeants' mess was demolished and the roof erected over the remaining single storey. It was never rebuilt to its original configuration.

As they made their pass over the airfield, Kochy noticed a column of men of about a platoon's strength wearing dark uniforms, which he took to be technical personnel, marching down a road that seemed to lead to their accommodation block. They needed shaking up, he reckoned, and he fired a couple of rounds in their direction and watched them run like rabbits. Not very sporting, but he knew but his nerves were on full alert and, when someone poked his head out of a doorway, he emptied the rest of the magazine at the buildings.

In the last second as they flew over the hangers, he caught sight of about twenty fighters standing in a row opposite the hangars on the other side of the airfield. They were a sitting target and, as they circled to inspect the bomb damage, he indicated their presence to Wiesemann and urged him to fly down the middle of the airfield so that they could bring all their machine-guns to bear on the lined-up fighters.

Wiesemann signalled that he liked the idea and, after circling the airfield, he brought the Heinkel down very low and each of the four machine-guns emptied a full drum at the targets sending a combined salvo of 300 rounds into the planes that lurched as the bullets struck home. Despite one in every five shots being a tracer, they did not burst into flames though some were so peppered with bullet holes that they would probably never fly again. But three Oxfords and eight Miles Masters were shredded by the firepower.

To Holt-Weston, still hiding in the doorway behind the sandbags, the Heinkel seemed much lower as it made its second pass. The machine-gun fire was running like the lash of a whip along the ground towards him, the concrete splintering under the impact of the bullets. But steeling himself he managed to fix the bomber in his sights and discharge his two remaining rounds of .303. This time he wasn't so sure his shots were on target. With the immediate crisis over the sergeant in charge of the LDV squad, a little chap with a waxed moustache and a splash of technicolour on his chest, who swaggered with his newly endowed authority, insisted on a head count but he was three men short. A search revealed them locked in the toilet, not too eager to emerge.

The last few eventful minutes had stained the nerves of Kochy almost to breaking point but, now that he had calmed down a little, he felt in all-conquering mood after that remarkably successful attack. The crew were busy congratulating themselves when over this babble of voices could be heard, loud and clear, Kochy's fatal words, 'Shouldn't we go back and shoot up that line of aircraft one more time?' Throwing caution to the wind Wiesemann brought the Heinkel about for one more attack. So began the fatal return flight to the airfield outside Chester.

Norman Whittle, a porter at Capenhurst Railway Station, was making his way to the signal box to report the number of wagons that could be accommodated next day to facilitate the building of the new Ordnance factory next to the station. He was about to enter the signal box when he heard a burst of machine-gun fire from the direction of Sealand Ranges. He had often heard the sound of gunfire from the ranges and thought nothing of it, but he was a bit puzzled as it was getting dark and he remarked to the signalman that it was rather late to be practicing at the Ranges. He then heard the sound of a plane when, from behind the trees, a bomber appeared with a swastika on its tail.

Pilot Officer Peter Ayerst. (Photograph: Ayerst)

After contacting control he rang the signal box at Hooton South to tell them that if they looked in the direction of Capenhurst they would see a German bomber approaching. 'To darn right,' was the reply. 'But hang on a minute it's turning and coming back towards you. Norman was convinced it must be making a second attempt to find and bomb the Ordnance factory but, as it came into view, he could see that it was now much lower and being attacked by Spitfires.

Over at RAF Hawarden the instructors had packed up flying for the day and Wing Commander John Hallings-Pott was having a drink in the officer's beer tent with Squadron Leader John McLean when they heard the sound of bombs exploding in the distance followed by the rat-tat-tat of machine-gun fire. It was clear that Sealand was under attack and Hallings-Pott and McLean sprinted towards the three Spitfires on standby, closely followed by Pilot Officer Peter Ayerst, a veteran of the Battle of France and still only nineteen.

Grabbing their parachutes they shouted at the ground crew to fire up the engines as they ran across the airfield. Leaping into the Spitfires they were quickly airborne in search of the audacious daylight raider but the conditions were in his favour as there was a blanket of low cloud and the light was fading fast. Gaining height to stop the raider hiding in the clouds they managed to pick him out in the gloom, but he gave the appearance of being lost as he came around for his third pass over the airfield. Lost or not they had no intention of showing him the way home.

One Spitfire dived right behind Kochy's tail giving him barely enough time to blurt out 'Fighter' before it opened fire. Someone below shouted out

'How many? Where?' but he had no time to reply. Instinctively he wheeled his MG 15 around on its ring mounting but he couldn't get in a telling shot. The Spitfire was just off the angle of his mounted gun, and shooting either side of the elevators meant he ran the risk of blowing holes in the tail plane. The fighter then let rip and a violent shudder went along the length of the plane. Bullets crashed into the fuselage sending metal splinters flying through the air and Kochy felt a sharp of stab of pain and a burning sensation above his left ankle. He had been hit.

Hallings-Pott and McLean were the first ones to attack and, coming in one behind the other, was the reason why Kochy believed they were being attacked by only one fighter. In fact they had been ambushed by *three* Spitfires. Peter Ayerst bringing up the rear could see that although the first attacks had riddled the aircraft and holed the tail plane it was not on fire and seemed intent in gaining height. The rear gunner was having a pop at him but his shots were way off target and, closing to within 600ft, Peter fired a continuous salvo at the Heinkel, raking it from end to end and knocking out one of the engines which started to smoke. He gave it a last quick burst before it was lost in the fading light. But he hadn't given up on the chase and, in the increasing gloom, he continued to search for his illusive prey.

To Rodder sitting beside the pilot the noise from behind was deafening like 'a giant pissing on a tin roof' as bullet after bullet struck home but, protected by the armour plating, the cockpit was untouched. He had heard someone cry out and feared the worst but he couldn't leave his post as the fighter might make a frontal attack. Was there more than one fighter? He had no idea. He hadn't seen any, and when the enemy momentarily stopped firing he still hadn't discharged a shot in return. With the next attack he somehow sustained a blow to the head and with the intercom cable attached to his flying helmet shot through, he lost all contact with the rest of the crew.

With its tail section in tatters and huge chunks missing from the engine cowling the plane was in a pitiful state, and as oil poured from the starboard motor Wiesemann shouted out to Rodder that the engine was on fire. Looking out of the window he surveyed the spluttering engine, not realising that Wieseman was looking out of the other window. Glancing at one another they realised the situation was hopeless. They would never make it home. Could they make it to Ireland?

Discarding the empty magazine, Kochy rapidly loaded a new drum into his MG 15 but the fighter had disappeared, gone like a puff of smoke. There was no sign of it in any direction but he was sure it had not gone away. He prayed that they would reach the safety of the clouds before it came at them again but he could tell by the way they were flying that something serious had happened. Had the death sentence been passed on their plane?

Wiesemann had already called Schaum, the flight mechanic, to come to the front to help with the controls. The port engine was so badly shot-up that the props had stopped and could not be reactivated. They were flying on one engine but with luck they could still make it to neutral Eire and, even if they had to ditch in the Irish Sea, there was still a chance in they would be picked up by an Irish

The burnt out shell of Heinkel 111P (1G + FS)

Gustav Ullman astride the bomb. (Photograph: Kochy)

Military and civilians alongside Heinkel 111P (1G + FS)

boat. Internment in the Free State was preferable to incarceration in an English POW Camp.

Over the intercom he heard someone cry out 'Into the clouds!', but from the pilot came a disheartening reply, 'I cannot get her to climb any higher!' The starboard engine was also sputtering and the loss of oil pressure and the rise in temperature showed it was losing oil. Schaum strived to pump the oil from the stationary engine to the one still running but this wasn't a success. Kochy feared they had little time left.

Then Wiesemann said, 'We must go down, I cannot hold her any longer!' Those few brief words shook them like a blow to the head. Still fearful that the fighter might return to finish them off, Kochy was determined to get in the first shot but he couldn't quite position his MG at the expected angle of attack. The machine was now sinking fast and, at this low height, it was no longer possible to bale out as the parachutes might not fully deploy. Suddenly the fighter made an appearance and making a climbing turn it parked itself about 150ft above their port wing.

It had caught Kochy by surprise but as it sat there watching them, without firing a shot, it exposed its entire belly. With hardly a moments hesitation Kochy swung the gun mount almost half-way around and fired a full drum at the fighter's exposed underside. At such a short range he couldn't miss and the fighter must have taken some hits as it again disappeared from view. It did not return.

Three times Kochy sent now out an SOS 'From 1 GFS forced-landing on target' but later, in a POW camp, he learned that it wasn't picked up. As it crossed over the fairway of Curzon Golf course the plane had now sunk so low that it flew under some high-tension wires as it headed for the large field Wiesemann had picked out for a forced-landing. The engine was shut down and Kochy heard the order 'Ignition off! In the cockpit Rodder involuntarily shut his eyes as it crashed through a 10ft hedge and braced himself for a belly landing as a farmhouse loomed up in the distance. Hitting the ground it clattered and banged as it slid across the field, coming to rest amid a shower of earth and dust, pulling up just short of the farmhouse under a canopy of trees.

The bottom 'bath' tub had been sheared off in the first short bounce, disgorging a combination flying suit stuffed with blankets and all sorts of odds and ends that had been discarded by the flight mechanic. It gave the impression of a dead body and the reason for carrying such a lifelike dummy would later be the subject of intense questioning during the subsequent interrogations. The intelligence officers were unwilling to accept that it was only used for storage.

Fearful of the impact, Kochy had lifted himself high in the revolving turret but the plane had slid so smoothly to a halt that he was ashamed that he had felt so scared. Kochy got out of the rear turret taking with him an incendiary device to set their faithful 'F' aflame. Wiesemann's last order was 'Destroy the aircraft. It mustn't fall into enemy hands.'

Glancing back at the damage, Kochy realised how lucky he was to be still alive. The sliding roof over the rear turret was completely shattered, the radio mast bent over and the rudder shot full of holes. There were holes all over the fuselage but no one was seriously hurt, although their gunner Gustav Ullman was bleeding from a leg wound. Kochy hadn't examined his own wound but it wasn't giving him any problems so he concentrated on trying to prime the incendiary but he must have been doing something wrong as it failed to ignite.

Wendy Anderton and her cousin Cathy Jones - both aged eleven – were playing in the garden of Border House Farm in Bumpers Lane when they heard the sound of gunfire and saw aeroplanes flying in over Blacon Woods. As the sound of the engines grew ever louder one of the aircraft was seen to be in trouble with smoke billowing from one engine. It was coming down and heading in their direction, and Wendy ran into the farmhouse to tell her parents but they were busy listening to a programme on the wireless and quietly ignored her. She ran back in again but was still not believed and, as she ran back out again, she could see that it was about to crash and in desperation she ran in screaming 'It's coming down!' and they finally came out to see what all the fuss was about.

In amazement they watched the stricken bomber fly under some electricity power lines, plough through a hedge and slide across the field stopping just 90ft short of the farmhouse. It was only when they saw the swastika on the tail did they realise it was an enemy bomber and that the men who scrambled out were Germans.

The aircraft had slithered to a stop barely 30ft from the Wales-England border and Wendy's father John, who was a corporal in the Home Guard, sent her back into the house for the rabbit gun and first-aid box. He loaded the single-barrelled shot gun and together with his brother-in-law Llewellyn Jones advanced rather nervously towards the aircraft as the crew scrambled out. If the crew were armed they were in a perilous position, but after a couple of shouts of 'Hands Up! Hands up!' they were relieved to see them slowly raise their arms and surrender.

Schaum who had been hidden from view now appeared with his hands held high. In those brief moments he was out of sight, he was able to prime his incendiary device and toss it into the petrol tank. They waited for the device to explode with a bang but there was only a quiet splutter as it went off and set the aircraft on fire. It was soon ablaze from end to end and they were sure there was nothing of importance that could be recovered by the enemy. But a paper did survive the blaze that gave the code letters for Sealand, Filton, Cardiff and Yeovil, which was thought to relate to a reconnaissance mission – the cover story used by Wiesemann and Rodder during their interrogations.

It was stalemate as the farmers and the Germans stood their ground, neither side knowing how to proceed. Even with their hands above their heads the Germans were a formidable group and the one with an Iron Cross round his neck, who they took to be the pilot, stared at them defiantly. The impasse was broken by the arrival of the police closely followed by the Military, the Fire Brigade, the Home Guard, Air Raid Wardens and the Ambulance Service. The meadow was filling up with all sorts of vehicles and the public were not far behind.

A determined-looking soldier aimed his rifle at them shouting 'Hands up – rufen', so they hoisted them higher showing their wristwatches which quickly changed owners along with their parachute knives. An army officer soon took charge and, with a wave of his hand, he signalled them to follow him. As they were led into the farmhouse dressed in full flying gear, fur-lined boots and leather helmets they made a lasting impression on the young girls who had been told to remain outside, but it didn't take them long to sneak back in and join Mrs Jones who was in the kitchen making tea. They could see that the captives were now sitting in the armchairs in the living rooms and heard someone ask if any were wounded.

Ullman had been shot in the upper thigh and, as part of the bullet could be seen sticking out the flesh and the flow of blood had reduced to barely a trickle, he tried to extract it using the farmer's pliers but the pain was too great and he quickly gave up. He needed hospital treatment.

Rodder had slightly injured a finger and Kochy now had time to examine his own injury, and could see there was a hole in the side of his flying boot where a bullet had passed through and caused a burn blister the size of a 10p piece. As he took the boot off the spent bullet fell to the floor that he would have dearly liked to have kept as a memento, but the officer bagged it as a souvenir. What really irked was the loss of his wristwatch. But at Christmas in 1941 he was able to rectify this theft when, under a personal directive from Goering, an extra allowance was given to Luftwaffe POWs in Canada. From the 'Eaton Catalogue' he chose a wristwatch that gave him excellent service for the rest of his life.

Kochy was surprised at the friendliness of his captors. The soldiers gave them cigarettes, the farmer's wife brought them tea and the farmer, very pleased with himself, made a great show as he bandaged Rodder's hand. The Germans didn't feel like prisoners; it felt as if they had only dropped in for a visit as they were able to talk freely amongst themselves. They quickly agreed that any statements to the military were only to be made by the pilot and the observer, and that the three lower rankers were to keep silent, maintaining their ignorance of all operational procedures.

Wiesemann then rummaged through his briefcase, which had not yet been confiscated and, hoping he hadn't been seen, he surreptitiously passed a paper to Schaum that contained a list of everyone in the the *Ketten* and the 8th Staffel air crews. Schaum stuffed it down the side of the armchair cushion but he must have been seen because the document was produced during Kochy's interrogation, when he was also questioned about his role in the machine-gunning of the men at Sealand, which of course he denied. Also produced was a note giving details of the destruction of Dubral's aircraft and the probable fate of the third *Kettenhund*. With the loss of all three Heinkels, Kochy realised that the core of 8th Staffel had been destroyed in just one day, but he tried not to react to this news and continued to act dumb anxious not to give away any sensitive information.

Back in that farmhouse, though, there was an almost a party atmosphere with Kochy and Rodder, who could both speak some English, the centre of attention. Wendy's curiosity now got the better of her and she spoke to Kochy and offered him some of her sweet ration, Rowntree's fruit pastilles, and in return he gave her some chocolate. This brief encounter that would be re-enacted almost fifty years later when the crew made an emotive return visit to RAF Sealand.

It was not too long before the meeting was abruptly broken up and the prisoners were led out of the farmhouse to the awaiting vehicles. The night sky was lit up by the flames and sparks from their burning aircraft and, at that moment there was a crack as a bullet went off and Kochy couldn't help thinking that it was the death rattle of a living creature. A wave of sadness swept over him as he remembered how their brave 1G + FS had always brought them safely back from flights over France and England.

At first light the following morning the three Spitfire pilots arrived to examine their kill, and the guards posted around the aircraft turned a blind eye when they retrieved a propeller boss that would eventually grace the entrance to the Officer's Mess at Hawarden. And they were not the only souvenir hunters on the prowl as the locals swarmed all around the plane picking up pieces and having their photographs taken with the guards that had been posted to keep them at bay. Later in the year these 'collectors' would feel the wrath of the local magistrates when they were fined eight shillings plus costs for removing enemy flying equipment that could be of use to military intelligence.

Ullman was helped into an ambulance and taken to the hospital at RAF Sealand, while Kochy and Schaum were taken away to spend an uncomfortable couple of days and nights in the small jailhouse at the old police station in the town hall. Rodder and Wiesemann were shipped off together but they soon parted company. Rodder spent only one night in a detention cell at Chester Castle before being sent by train to London where, at Euston Station, he received a bar of chocolate from an ATS girl. Puzzled by all the good treatment he was receiving he didn't immediately realise that this was all part of the softening up process prior to being interrogated at Cockfosters. But after only four days of questioning he was sent to a POW Camp at Oldham where he met up with his Kochy, Schaum and Ullman. Dubral and Geitz were also there having only been briefly interrogated. Still confident of Germany's ultimate victory, there was no talk of escape.

In January 1941 they were shipped to Canada aboard the *Duchess of York*, landing at Halifax in Nova Scotia before being transported by train to camp Angler on the shores of Lake Superior. It was long journey that gave them plenty of time to think, but it was impossible for them to image that the war would drag on for exactly another five years from the day they were shot down.

Wieseman had also spent his first night of captivity in a cell at Chester Castle but, as an Oberleutant and acting Staffelkapitan, he came in for a rather more subtle course of treatment at Cockfosters. However, he too was soon released and sent to Grizedale Hall, a grim POW camp for officers in the Lake District near Coniston Water. There he would play football with Obltn. Franz von Werra and be party to his escape and four days of freedom. And, by a strange coincidence, he was in the same railway carriage as von Werra when he jumped from the train as it rattled its way across Canada. Crossing to neutral America he got back to Germany to later become famous as 'the one that got away'.

George Foxley of
Chatcull Farm.
(Photograph: Kochy)

Taking up residence in the officer's POW camp at Bowmanville near Lake Ontario, he was later joined by his reliable navigator Heinrich Rodder who had just received his promotion to leutnant via the Red Cross. Unfortunately he arrived just in time to partake in the infamous 'Battle of Bowmanville' during which he felt the full force of a fire hose. He didn't get involved in any more incidents after that and immersed himself in theatrical productions and leisure activities, though he was always uplifted by any escape attempts. He was also provided with books to enable him to keep up with his medical studies that he hoped to pursue on his return home.

When the war ended he was transferred to Wainwright near Edmonton and, just over a year later in July 1946, he again crossed the Atlantic staying briefly at Sheffield before arriving at a POW camp in Abergavenny. From here, via Leicester, he boarded a ship at Hull and arrived back in Germany in July 1947. He had been in captivity for seven long years. He finally qualified as a doctor in 1953 and became a family practitioner in Troisdorf in 1957.

Kochy was released from captivity some six months earlier on 23 December 1946, by which time the border fence and the towers between East and West Germany had been erected. It was so close to his village that he could only drive west out of his home. It was not until the fall of the Berlin Wall in November 1989 and the reunion of Germany a year later that matters improved.

Gietz was to travel a more round about way home because in September 1945 he was selected with about 100 other comrades at the POW camp at Lethbridge to be repatriated to Germany and be part of the new police force. But, after arriving back in Southampton and a further debriefing in London, he was instead sent

Reunion at Troisdorf, August 1990. Kochy, Schaum, Ullman, Ayerst, Wiesemann and the back of Rodder

Peter Ayerst, the author, Gus Ullman and Walter Schaum, 1990

Uffz Gustav Ullman, air gunner in He111P
(1G + FS). (Photograph: Ullman)

to work on farms near the POW camp at Market Drayton. He then boarded ship
at Hull bound for Cuxhaven but found that he could not return home as East
Pomerania had become part of Poland and his parents had been forced to flee to
Kiel, where he also now lived. In January 1947 he was taken on as a clerk with the
British Military Government in Kiel and remained in the post when a few years
later it came back under German control.

Everyone was back home by 1947 except for a few hardliners, the so called
'bad boys', and they were released in dribs and drabs throughout 1948. When
Wiesemann arrived back in Germany in March 1948 there was a reunion with
Rodder, Schaum and Kochy at his home in Hagen. Missing from the party was
Ullman but they had no idea of his whereabouts for over forty years.

Peter Ayerst was awarded the DFC in November 1944 in recognition of his fine
record of operational flying and devotion to duty during the Battle of France, the
Battle of Britain, operations in the Western Desert and low level sweeps over occupied
Europe, and as a result he was initially allowed to attach the small silver-gilt 'Battle of
Britain Clasp' to the ribbon of his 1939–45 Star. However, permission to wear the
clasp was revoked in 1948 following a review of his medals, presumably because he
had not served with a recognised fighter squadron during the Battle of Britain, even
though he had flown defensive patrols and shot down an enemy bomber.

This anomaly should have been resolved in 1960 when the 20th Anniversary
of the Battle of Britain prompted the RAF to revise the list of operational
units that took part in the battle between 10 July 1940 and 31 October 1940

but, again, those pilots who flew operational sorties with the 'Battle Flight' of No.7 Operational Training Unit, under the command and control of Fighter Command, were either overlooked or not considered worthy of the Clasp. And it was this definition of a designated fighter unit that was the stumbling block, for as long as you flew the statutory operational sortie with one of the chosen fighter units you were entitled to wear the clasp. Just one operational sortie was enough.

After briefly questioning his inability to display the Clasp he let the matter lie for many years, but the year before he retired as a wing commander in 1973 he took the matter up again with the RAF. Despite protracted correspondence, even involving the RAF Board, he was again refused permission to wear the Battle of Britain Clasp. Not being officially classed as one of 'The Few' was a great personal disappointment.

Kochy remained in loose contact with most of the crew over the years and, on 19 June 1983, some thirty-five years after their last meeting, a reunion was held near Dortmund that Walter Gietz and Walter Kleinjohann also attended. These meetings were then held annually, usually on 14 August but, when they visited an air show at Norvenlich in 1984 to commemorate the 50th anniversary of the founding of their Geschwader 'Boelke' – KG 27 – they were the only ones of the old guard in attendance. They were celebrities for a day.

Oscar Dubral died in January 1983 and never made it to any of the reunions, but he was the only one to have a continuing link with aviation. After the war he started work at Frankfurt Airport and later began building a career with Lufthansa. From 1959–69 he was their UK and Ireland representative working out of London and then back at their Bonn office before he retired. He was always remembered at the reunions.

By 1986 I was attending these reunions and, at the 1987 reunion at the home of Dr Heinrich Rodder, a plan was hatched to make a return journey to Chester the following spring to visit all those haunts they had briefly visited in August 1940. Flying into Manchester airport the visit went way above expectations because they were given dinner in the Officers' mess at RAF Sealand and met, for the first time, Wing Commander Peter Ayerst, their protagonist all those years ago. Within minutes they were firm friends and this friendship lasted for many years, with Peter becoming a welcome guest at the home of Dr Rodder.

But the story was not yet finished as there was still the matter of the missing Gustav Ullman, and when I asked Kochy in 1988 he said they still couldn't track him down and was astounded to hear that I had a 1977 address for him. This had been inadvertently given to me by the German authorities before the Data Protection Act came into force. Picking up the phone he somehow obtained Ullman's new telephone number and, within minutes, he was deep in conversation with his old friend.

With the attendance of Ullman the 1989 reunion was the first time since they were shot down that the complete crew had been reunited, and with Peter Ayerst also present they were filmed for a TV drama documentary entitled *We Only Came For Tea*. The reunion was a resounding success and, during the long discussions into the night over a few beers, the talk invariably centred on the political rumblings in Hungary and Russia but the 'Fall of the Wall' was not thought to be an imminent prospect. Erich Honecker, the autocratic leader of East Germany, was an old hard-line communist who wouldn't readily give up the reins of power. But before the year was out the Wall had been breached and Honecker placed under house arrest.

The 50th Anniversary of the Battle of Britain in 1990 was the last time the complete crew and Peter Ayerst would come together at the home of Heinrich Rodder. The party beside the pool started at the precise time that they took off on 14 August 1940, but it went on well into the night, way past the time they were shot down. They toasted their 50th Second Birthday and the reunification of Germany. With the end of communism in the countries behind the 'Iron Curtain' the poisonous aftermath of the Second World War was finally purged and, after forty-five years, Koch could at last drive east out of his home.

Luftwaffe Combat Losses
14 August 1940

2/Erpo Gr 210 Messerschmitt Bf 110D (S9 + MK)
Hit by AA fire and broke up in the air during a low-level attack on Manston and crashed on the airfield at 12.10 hours.

Uffz. Hans Steding	Pilot	Killed
Gefr Ewald Schank	Radio Operator	POW (wounded)

2/Erpo Gr 210 Messerschmitt Bf 110D (S9 + NK)
Dived straight into the ground at Manston at 12.10 hours after being hit by AA fire.

Lt Heinrich Brinkman	Pilot	Killed
Uffz. Richard Mayer	Radio Operator	Killed

6/J G3 Messerschmitt Bf 109E
Failed to return from a combat mission over southern England, probably crashed into the Channel.

Ofw. Erich Labusga	Pilot	Missing (presumed killed)

8/JG 3 Messerschmitt Bf 109E
Shot down into the Channel during combat with fighters off the Dover/Folkestone coast.

Uffz. Karl Flebbe	Pilot	Body recovered from the sea and originally buried at Calais.

1/JG 26 Messerschmitt Bf 109E-1 (4827)
Shot down by Pilot Officer Rupert F. Smythe of 32 Squadron during combat over Dover and crashed at Coldred at 12.45 hours. The pilot baled out.

Uffz. Gerhard Kemen	Pilot	POW (wounded)

4/JG 52 Messerschmitt Bf 109E
Failed to return from a fighter sweep over Ramsgate. Fate unknown.

Ofw. Gunter Ruttinger	Pilot	Missing (presumed killed)

4/JG 52 Messerschmitt Bf 109E
Shot down during a combat sortie over Ramsgate and crashed into the sea.

Ofw. Heinz Weiss	Pilot	Body washed ashore at Joss Bay and buried at Margate.

5/JG 52 Messerschmitt Bf 109E

Shot down by Spitfires during a chase and crashed into the Channel off Ramsgate.

Ofw. Hans Potthast	Pilot	Missing (presumed killed)

8/KG 27 Heinkel He 111P (1G + CS)

Shot down into the sea at Lyme Bay, off Charmouth, by the Hurricanes of 213 Squadron at 19.40 hours. Only four of the crew managed to bale out.

Feldw. Oskar Dubral	Pilot	POW
Feldw. Walter Gietz	Radio Operator	POW
Feldw. Franz Knoblich	Flight Mechanic	Killed
Uffz. Heinrich Schrage	Gunner	Killed
Feldw. Anton Wiesmeier	Navigator	Missing (presumed killed)

8/KG 27 Heinkel He 111P (1G + DS)

Badly shot by the Hurricanes of 213 Squadron over the Channel and crash-landed back at Rennes; aircraft subsequently written off.

Uffz. Eric-Friedrich Frelinghaus	Radio Operator
Uffz. Franz Losecke	Flight Mechanic
Fw. Johann Oeckenpoehler	Pilot
Fw. Erich Schrieber	Navigator
Gefr Zwelter	Gunner

8/KG 27 Heinkel He 111P (1G + FS}

Damaged over the Channel in combat with the Hurricanes of 213 Squadron and shot down while attacking RAF Sealand, in North Wales, by the Spitfires of the battle flight of No.7 OTU. Force landed at Border House Farm, near Chester at 21.00 hours.

Uffz. Heinz Kochy	Radio Operator	POW
Fw. Heinrich Rodder	Navigator	POW
Uffz. Walter Schaum	Flight Mechanic	POW
Uffz. Gustav Ullman	Gunner	POW (slightly wounded)
Obltn. Artur Wiesemann	Pilot	POW

9/KG 27 Heinkel He 111P (1G + NT)

Shot down by Spitfires of 92 Squadron, Pembrey, and crash-landed at Warren Farm, Charterhouse, near Cheddar at 18.00 hours. The crew scrambled out unhurt.

Uffz. Adolf Blumenthal	Radio Operator	POW
Fw. Nicholas Jug	Flight Mechanic	POW
Gefr Kurt Kuptsch	Gunner	POW
Obltn. Ernst Ohlenschlager	Pilot	POW
Uffz. Kurt Sulzbach	Navigator	POW

9/KG 27 Heinkel He 111P (1G + OT)

Shot down by Spitfires of 92 Squadron, Pembrey. It crashed and disintegrated at Cann's Farm, Puriton at 18.03 hours. All the crew baled to safety.

Uffz. Edo Flick	Radio Operator	POW (badly injured)
Uffz. Josef Krenn	Flight Mechanic	POW
Ogefr Hans Ramstetter	Navigator	POW
Gefr Gerhard Rother	Gunner	POW
Lt Otto Uhland	Pilot	POW

9/KG 27 Heinkel He 111P (1G + FT}

Shot down by Spitfires of 92 Squadron, Pembrey, and plunged into Sully Bay, near Barry at 17.52 hours.

Uffz. Hans Dolata	Radio Operator	Killed (buried Weston-super-Mare)
Fw. Ernst Haumann	Navigator	Missing (presumed killed)
Hptmn Josef Riedl	Pilot	Missing (presumed killed)
Uffz. Adelhard Witt	Flight Mechanic	Missing (presumed killed)
Gefr Emil Wolf	Gunner	Missing (presumed killed)

Stab Staffel KG 55 Heinkel He 111P (G1 + AA)

Shot down by Flying Officer John Dundas of 609 Squadron and Sgt Mike Boddington of 234 Squadron. Crashed and broke in half at the Royal Naval Armaments Depot at Dean Hill, near East Dean, at 18.30 hours.

Obstltn. Bruno Brossle	Pilot	Killed
Oberst i.G. Walter Frank	Gunner	Killed
Fw. Heinz Grimstein	Radio Operator	POW (severely wounded)
Oberst Alois Stoekl	Navigator	Killed
Fw. Jonny Thiel	Flight Mechanic	POW (severely wounded)

2/ KGr 100 Heinkel He 111H (6N + HK)

Damaged by AA fire at 04.30 hours during a sortie to the Midlands. The crew were ordered to bale out but only Uffz. Freidrich Dorner jumped before the aircraft righted itself and returned safely to base.

Uffz. Freidrich Dorner	Radio Operator	POW

1/LG 1 Junkers Ju 88A-1 (L1 + - H)

Shot down by Sgt Alan Feary at 17.05 hours following an attack on Middle Wallop. Crashed and disintegrated at Turf Hill, North Charford.

Obltn. Wilhelm Heinrici	Pilot	Killed
Gefr Heinz Stark	Radio Operator	Killed
Gefr Freidrich Ahrens	Mechanic/Gunner	Killed
Gefr Eugen Sauer	Gunner	POW (severely wounded)

2/LG 1 Junkers Ju 88A-1

Shot down into the Channel south of Portland at 17.00 hours by fighters of 43 Squadron.

Uffz. Reinhardt Lehman	Gunner	Missing (presumed killed)
Gefr Karl Neff		Radio Operator Killed (washed ashore France)
Uffz. Heinz Poppe	Mechanic/Gunner	Missing (presumed killed)
Lt Werner Stahl	Pilot	Missing (presumed killed)

10/LG 1 Junkers Ju 87B

Shot down by into the Channel at 12.15 hours by fighters during combat over Folkestone.

Obltn. Kurt Gramling	Pilot	Missing (presumed killed)
Uffz. Frans Scwatzki	Radio Operator	Missing (presumed killed)

10/LG 1 Junkers Ju 87B

Damaged in combat with fighters over Folkestone at 12.15 hours and crash-landed back at base.

August Muller	Radio Operator	Wounded

RAF Casualties as a Result of Enemy Action on 14 August 1940

Pilot	Squadron	Fate	Battle
AC2 Maurice S. ALLCOCK	39 MU	Injured	Air attack, Colerne, 17.50 hours
Cpl Frank H. APPLEBY	609 Sqn	Injured	Air attack, Middle Wallop, 17.15 hours
AC2 Vernon C. ARNOLD	9 SFTS	Injured	Air attack, Hullavington, 18.51 hours
LAC Alfred D. ATKINSON	39 MU	Injured	Air attack, Colerne, 17.50 hours
Sgt George ATKINSON	151 Sqn	Shock	Shot down into the sea, 12.10 hours
P/O H.D. ATKINSON	213 Sqn	Wounded	Over Lyme Bay, 19.40 hours
AC2 Douglas L. BATES	39 MU	Injured	Air attack, Colerne, 17.50 hours
Sgt Alfred N. CAMPION	10 Group	Killed	Crashed into sea off Lympne
AC1 Alfred W. CLARKE	Andover HQ	Killed	Air attack, 18.45 hours
P/O Peter COLLARD	615 Sqn	Killed	Shot down in combat off Dover
AC1 Basil G. COOK	30 MU	Injured	Air attack, Sealand, 21.05 hours
W/O Edward F. EDWARDS	30 MU	Killed	Air attack, Sealand, 21.05 hours
Sgt James FREEMAN	30 MU	Injured	Air attack, Sealand, 21.05 hours
Sgt Bernard G. GARDNER	610 Sqn	Wounded	Off Dungeness, 12.30 hours
Cpl William J. GOODSELL	9 SFTS	Injured	Air attack, Hullavington, 18.51 hours
P/O Henry M. GOODWIN	609 Sqn	Killed	Shot down over the south coast

LAC Leslie G.H. GOULD	30 MU	Injured	Air attack, Sealand, 21.05 hours
AC2 Richard GREEN	30 MU	Injured	Air attack Sealand, 21.05, hours
AC2 Richard HALLAMS	30 MU	Injured	Air attack, Sealand, 21.05 hours
AC2 Percival W. HOBSON	9 SFTS	Injured	Air attack, Hullavington, 18.51 hours
AC1 Bertram F.M. HOLT	9 SFTS	Killed	Air attack, Hullavington, 18.51 hours
LAC Morley G. HUNKIN	9 SFTS	Killed	Air attack, Hullavington, 18.51 hours
AC2 John A. JONES	39 MU	Injured	Air attack, Colerne, 17.50 hours
AC2 Ivor H. KING	9 SFTS	Killed	Air attack, Hullavington, 18.51 hours
AC1 Jonas LONG	30 MU	Injured	Air attack, Sealand, 21.05 hours
AC2 Haydn MINES	9 SFTS	Injured	Air attack, Hullavington, 18.51 hours
AC2 Victor W. MITCHELL	9 SFTS	Injured	Air attack, Hullavington, 18.51 hours
P/O C.R. MONGOMERY	615 Sqn	Killed	Shot down over the Channel
Sgt H.F. MONTGOMERY	43 Sqn	Killed	Crashed into the sea, 18.05 hours
LAC Charles N.A. NASH	9 SFTS	Injured	Air attack, Hullavington, 18.51 hours
Cpl Thomas NORCOTT	39 MU	Injured	Air attack, Colerne, 17.50 hours
P/O Clifford B. NORTH	39 MU	Injured	Air attack, Colerne, 17.50 hours
P/O Ernest I. PARSONS	10 Group	Killed	Crashed into sea off Lympne
AC2 Charles E. PHILLIPS	30 MU	Injured	Air attack, Sealand, 21.05 hours
AC1 Glyndwr J. PRIOR	9 SFTS	Killed	Air attack, Hullavington, 18.51 hours
F/Lt Arthur W. RIDLER	9 SFTS	Injured	Air attack, Hullavington, 18.51 hours
AC2 Cyril RODGERS	39 MU	Injured	Air attack, Colerne, 17.50 hours
AC2 Fred SHARROCKS	39 MU	Killed	Air attack, Colerne, 17.50 hours
Cpl Robert W. SMITH	609 Sqn	Killed	Air attack, Middle Wallop, 17.15 hours
LAC Harry THORLEY	609 Sqn	Killed	Air attack, Middle Wallop, 17.15 hours
LAC Bernard WALTON	39 MU	Killed	Air attack, Colerne, 17.50 hours
AC1 John J. WESTHEAD	30 MU	Injured	Air attack, Sealand, 21.05 hours
LAC Kenneth WILSON	609 Sqn	Killed	Air attack, Middle Wallop, 17.15 hours

Bibliography

Beedle, James, *43 Squadron* (Beaumont Aviation, 1985)

Bishop, Edward, *Their Finest Hour* (Macdonald & Co., 1968)

Collier, Basil, *Defence of the United Kingdom* (HMSO, 1957)

Collier, Richard, *Eagle Day* (J.M. Dent & Sons, 1980)

Deighton, Len, *Fighter* (Jonathan Cape, 1977)

Dierich, Wolfgang, *Kampfsgeschwader 55 'Grief'* (Motorbuch Vertag, 1975)

Forrester, Larry, *Fly for Your Life* (Frederick Muller, 1958)

Hough & Richards, *The Battle of Britain* (Hodder & Stoughton, 1989)

Irving, David, *Hitler's War* (Hodder & Stoughton, 1977)

Mason, Frances, *Battle over Britain* (McWhirter Twins, 1969)

McKee, Alexander, *Strike from the Sky* (Souvenier Press, 1960)

Ramsey, Winston, *The Battle of Britain – Then & Now* (After the Battle, 1980)

Tasco, John, *Bombsights over Britain* (JAC Publication, 1990)

Wakefield, Ken, *The First Pathfinders* (William Kimber, 1981)

Wood & Dempster, *The Narrow Margin* (Arrow Books, 1969)

Wynn, Ken, *Men of the Battle of Britain* (Gliddon Books, 1989)

Ziegler, Frank, *Under the White Rose* (Macdonald & Co., 1971)

Equivalent Ranks

Luftwaffe	RAF
Generalmajor (Gen. Maj)	Air Commodore
Oberst (Oberst)	Group Captain
Oberstleutnant (Obstltn.)	Wing Commander
Major (Maj.)	Squadron Leader
Hauptmann (Hptmn)	Flight Lieutenant
Oberleutnant (Obltn.)	Flying Officer
Leutnant (Lt)	Pilot Officer
Stabsfeldwebel (St Fw.)	Warrant Officer
Oberfeldwebel (Ofw.)	Flight Sergeant
Feldwebel (Fw.)	Sergeant
Unteroffizier (Uffz.)	Corporal
Obergefreiter (Ogefr)	Leading Aircraftman (LAC)
Gefreiter (Gefr)	Aircraftman First Class (AC1)
Flieger (Fl.)	Aircraftman Second Class (AC2)